12/8

BJÖRN BORG
AND THE
SUPER-SWEDES

Stefan Edberg, Mats Wilander, and the Golden Era of Tennis

MATS HOLM AND ULF ROOSVALD
Translated by Cecilia Palmcrantz

Skyhorse Publishing

Skyhorse Publishing books may be purchased in bulk at special discounts for sales promotion, corporate gifts, fund-raising, or educational purposes. Special editions can also be created to specifications. For details, contact the Special Sales Department, Skyhorse Publishing, 307 West 36th Street, 11th Floor, New York, NY 10018 or info@skyhorsepublishing.com.

Skyhorse® and Skyhorse Publishing® are registered trademarks of Skyhorse Publishing, Inc.®, a Delaware corporation.

Visit our website at www.skyhorsepublishing.com.

10 9 8 7 6 5 4 3 2 1

Library of Congress Cataloging-in-Publication Data is available on file.

Interior photos by Associated Press

Cover design by Tom Lau
Cover photo credit Associated Press

ISBN: 978-1-5107-3363-3
Ebook ISBN: 978-1-5107-3364-0

Printed in the United States of America

The authors would like to thank . . .
A warm thank-you to Björn Borg, Mats Wilander, and
Stefan Edberg for sharing their time and memories so generously.
Thank you also to all the other people we interviewed, especially
Percy Rosberg, Kjell Johansson, John-Anders Sjögren, and
Carl-Axel Hageskog, without whose help the writing of this book
would have been so much more difficult.

CONTENTS

A NEW GANG IN TOWN   1
"If you saw this whole circus from the outside, you'd be furious."

FROM ROYAL PASTIME TO THE PEOPLE'S SPORT   22
"He's the world's only undefeated tennis player. 'Just don't beat the king' was what other players were told as they set out to play him."

AROUND THE GLOBE IN TENNIS SHORTS   45
"I wasn't surprised that I lost, but that the best players were so good, they played at a level I barely knew existed."

CARRYING SWEDEN ON HIS SHOULDERS   67
"Labbe always talked about how bad things were in Sweden. The taxes, the mentality, how Swedes can't do anything and don't understand anything."

A ONE-MAN TEAM IN A COLLECTIVE TIME   86
"My thing was to do something on my own. I think that's what motivates every athlete in an individual sport."

DESIRE, WINS, AND WIMBLEDON   98
"Nastase was the favorite; me being there was more of a shocker. I know Nastase looked at it that way, too."

FAST FEET VERSUS GOOD HANDS   120
"Is Björn trying to psych me out or get me to relax? Or . . .
is he just a nice guy?"

THE TEENS WHO COPIED BORG   147
"Do you have some kind of laboratory for tennis machines
in Sweden? Machines you put small heads on?"

GOOD GUYS ALWAYS WIN   173
"I had a hell of a time against Stefan. I was annoyed because
I was older and should win, and he was so damn good."

A LONE WOLF WITH HIS OWN TACTICS   186
"Stefan had such a beautiful backhand volley, it cut like a
knife. I noticed it and said to him: 'Stop playing your
two-handed backhand.'"

WHEN SMÅLAND RULED THE WORLD   206
"How can a guy who's always been a classic baseline player
change his game so radically?"

A CRACK IN THE FACADE   220
"There was no way I was going to play that match. I lived in
America and could just escape there."

ARTIST IN A HAIRSHIRT   235
"Your body language is so bad. It affects your game. You won't
win any matches if you look like that out on the court."

A SALT-AND-PEPPER GANG IN TOWN   248
"Ah . . . these Swedes . . . they always beat me, I hate them."

ACHIEVEMENTS   263
ATP RANKINGS 1973–1996   265
BIBLIOGRAPHY   270

A NEW GANG IN TOWN

"If you saw this whole circus from the outside, you'd be furious."
—BJÖRN BORG

"We want to decriminalize cancer," said the promoter, a thin-haired mustached man wearing a pepita-checkered jacket. "The sick shouldn't have to feel worthless and alienated from society."

Björn Borg sat—or, rather, slouched—on a chair next to the promoter. He seemed ready to fall asleep. A third man on the podium, a film producer, told everyone that he'd make sure the money was there. The revenues would come from a sold-out Scandinavium arena, where the 19-year-old Swedish tennis phenom would play the Australian legend, Rod Laver, in a PR event. The pepita-checkered-jacket-wearing man said he planned to sell the TV rights to both the USA and Australia.

He explained: "Fifty percent of the proceeds will go to people suffering from cancer, and, as promoter and risk-taker, I'll keep 50 percent. McCormack, Björn's agent, has approved of the arrangement."

Björn Borg nodded and began receiving questions from the journalists on whether exhibition matches like these were good for the sport: "There shouldn't be too many of them, because then all the money ends up in just a few players' pockets. But this one, between me and Laver at the Scandinavium, has every chance to be something special."

One of the reporters turned to the promoter:

"Have the negotiations for TV rights been completed? Have revenues been secured?"

The promoter lit a cigarette: "Not quite."

On this gray Göteborg morning, in the press room at the Scandinavium arena, hubris was up against skepticism. The man wearing the pepita-checkered jacket was known for having no qualms about exploiting cancer sufferers at various events. Over the last few years, such events had included galas with old has-been boxers like Bosse Högberg and Lennart Risberg. As for the film producer, his latest effort had been a film aiming to revive the career of a now-extinct star, Anita Lindblom. But a match between Borg and Laver had all the makings to be a success.

A reporter from the local newspaper *Göteborgs-Posten* grimaced and wrote: "Nobody knows how large the profits will be, so the cancer patients' association must wait before they know if they can add to their funds. Meanwhile, of course, the winner of the tennis match needn't worry. Regardless, he'll happily put 500,000 kronor in his pocket. From the pockets of the rich . . . No player is worth that much."

It was late fall of 1975. The Social Democratic Party was well into its 44th continuous year in power. The year, designated International Women's Year by the United Nations, had seen Olof Palme's government continue and accelerate its reform policy. Free abortion for women up to the 12th week of pregnancy. Parental leave for both mothers and fathers. Shared custody for divorcing mothers and fathers. A law on workers' participation in decisions in the workplace. Sweden's economy also appeared to be going strong. The OECD praised the country, and the parties on the labor market had signed a record-breaking agreement granting 30 percent wage increases over two years. Late in the summer, an initiative from the Swedish trade union orga-nization *Landsorganisationen* proposed that unions be guaranteed a share majority in all companies with more than 100 employees. The concept was called wage-earning funds.

The center-right opposition parties had been knocked down ideologically. "Social reforms without socialism" was the catchphrase of the Liberal Party. The Center Party, which was the largest of the center-right block parties, focused its election strategy on the dismantling of nuclear power plants.

Everyone appeared to be a social democrat. Except Björn Borg. Not that anyone believed him to suffer from any political passions. But he did choose his own path. Earlier in the year, when he'd left Sweden for Monaco, he hadn't been shy about his reasons: "To avoid seeing my money end up in the state treasure chest, 90 percent is too much." Björn had bought a condo in Monte Carlo, and another for his parents right next to it.

Now Björn, sunburned from a Kenya safari he'd taken with Lennart Bergelin, Sweden's Davis Cup captain, and his girlfriend, Helena Anliot, remained in the press room after the promoter and the producer had left the premises. They needed to make sure that an ad with Björn's image and the text "THIS YEAR'S CHRISTMAS GIFT—a challenger match at the Scandinavium, 1/2 million kronor to the winner. Buy your tickets today!" was submitted to *Göteborgs-Posten*.

For Björn, the meeting with the press in Göteborg was only an afterthought. The real reason he was in Sweden was to participate in the two most important competitions ever held on Swedish ground—both were to be held in Stockholm in the next two weeks. First, the Masters tournament, the season finale for all of the best professional players. Then, the Davis Cup final, Sweden's first ever, against Czechoslovakia.

Björn lingered and chatted with the journalists about his vacation: "It was one of the most wonderful vacations I've ever taken. It's the nicest country I've been to, ever. Those nights out in the bush—we slept in tents and heard all the strange sounds up close, really close out there in the night somewhere. It was nice to feel really small for once."

The latter statement provided an unexpected glimpse into the 19-year-old star's inner life.

But the journalists couldn't resist: "How do you feel about your fitness coming up on next week?"

"Not that great. I played with a couple of Kenyans down there, but they weren't that good," said Björn.

"If you win the Masters, you could end up number one in the world this year. How do you feel about that?"

"I don't think about it. The ranking isn't part of my job."

The tennis pros had visited Sweden before, but never to play a tournament of this magnitude. A question was asked about the importance of the Masters, and Borg laid it out like a patient scout leader: "Wimbledon is the biggest, then comes the U.S. Open at Forest Hills and the French Open, followed by the Masters and the WCT Tournament of Champions. Those are the biggest tournaments we have in tennis."

BJÖRN BORG AND THE SUPER-SWEDES

"We" in tennis—that was Björn and his contemporaries. If Björn had been met with bitterness when he left the country citing its taxes, then the Masters tournament was the perfect payback. Stockholm had been chosen to host this supertournament, and it was, of course, because of Borg's successes and the Swedish people's fanatic tennis interest. Audience statistics from the Swedish public service radio, Swedish Radio's, broadcasts of the previous year's Masters tournament in Melbourne had reached the headquarters of the tennis bigwigs in New York, and the statistics showed that half of Sweden's population had stayed up through the night to listen to Borg's long matches. Tennis was the pop sport of the times. To have Sweden host the Masters tournament was the best way to ride the wave. More than 100 tennis journalists from around the world had made hotel reservations in Sweden's capital.

Around twenty men wearing overalls worked all of Monday night to resurface the courts in the Kungliga Tennis Hall in Stockholm. The new surface, which had been flown in from the USA, had a slow bounce. It was forest green within the white lines and red outside the lines. On Tuesday morning, as the windows in the building's vaulted ceilings filtered the winter sun, the tennis arena sparkled in its new, gorgeous advent colors.

The first player to arrive, at 1 p.m., was Guillermo Vilas, the Argentinian who topped the year's Grand Prix charts. He took off his sheepskin fur coat, hung it on one of the courtside chairs, and pulled out a bag of sand from his duffel. The sand was collected from one of the ocean beaches in Mar del Plata, and Vilas always carried a filled bag with him whenever he traveled abroad.

Before entering the court, Vilas stretched for a few minutes, his muscles curving around his thighs like thick snakes. After that, he hit for a while with his coach and sparring partner, Ion Tiriac. He then walked off the court, returned the bag with the sand to his duffel, took his fur coat and his rackets under his arm, and walked over to the restaurant. There, he ordered a steak, fries, and a Coke, while again hanging the fur coat across the back of his chair. He said to Tiriac: "If I lose it in this climate, it'd be a disaster."

Soon, more players started to drop in. Arthur Ashe, the reigning Wimbledon champion, arrived wearing a black bear fur coat he'd just bought at the Stockholm department store Nordiska Kompaniet, which attracted the attention of two ladies on their way to the tennis courts. Manuel Orantes, the Spaniard who'd won at Forest Hills earlier in the fall, stepped out of his car wearing a waist-length jacket, and Ilie Nastase, the

Romanian player who'd won the Masters tournament three out of the last four years, arrived in a green tracksuit carrying his rackets under his arm. Nastase and Ashe were joined on the center court by Adriano Panatta, who was fresh off his win at the Stockholm Open. When Panatta commented to Ashe that the ladies outside had given his fur coat a good look, Ashe smiled and responded:

"Have you ever seen a well-dressed Swede?"

The three players then hit back and forth for an easy workout.

After Vilas had finished his lunch, Borg showed up, went to change, and returned wearing a pair of yellow shorts and a white t-shirt. He accompanied Vilas to the far side court, where they each took a baseline. Vilas whipped his topspin groundstrokes inside the lines. Borg's feet danced.

As the tennis pros were stepping out of their limousines, six boys and three girls rose from their desks at the Sätraskolan Secondary School in the southwest part of Stockholm, their chairs scraping against the floor. They grabbed their tennis rackets, threw their bags over their shoulders, and left their Swedish language class. Half an hour later, they were standing on the three indoor courts at the Mälarhöjden sports fields. Their gym teacher yelled out the three golden rules of tennis: "Watch the ball! Move your feet! And for goodness' sake—turn your side to the net when you hit the ball!"

Tennis as an elective was new this semester, and the class filled up quickly. Those who weren't able to get a spot had to settle for the badminton class in the school's gymnasium, where another teacher taught the long and short serves. The students listened; however, when it came to stroke technique, they already knew how they'd play, and no teacher in the world could change their mind. After all, Borg had taught them it was fine to ignore well-meaning advice and just do what felt best. Thus, the students in the badminton class let the shuttlecocks sink toward the floor, bent their knees low, turned their side to the net, fixed their eyes on the ball, and whipped back two-handed backhands with heavy topspin.

Sätra was a young suburb. It mirrored the Swedish welfare society, where the social classes lived in close proximity to one another but were still easily separated. The school sat in the middle. Everyone went there. The daughter of the leader of the Liberal Party, Ola Ullsten, came from the community of townhomes, as did the sons of the president of the journalists' association. From the high-rises came the boys who sat in the city center sniffing glue and the girls who hung out at the youth center. Rolle Stoltz, the legendary ice hockey player, greeted them all when he walked home with his bag of groceries from *Konsum*.

But hockey and soccer were no longer the kids' favorite sports. At the remodeled Sätra sports field, the eight brand-new tennis courts were always completely booked. To meet demand, the leisure committee decided to convert the hockey rinks to tennis courts in the summertime.

Most of all, the new passion could be seen in spontaneous settings, in courtyards between high-rises, and between the townhomes' garages and parking lots. Cars were parked in the garages, and parking lots turned into tennis courts, measured out stride by stride, the lines painted with chalk. When a hard-hit forehand sailed past an opponent and with a bang made a dent in the metal on someone's brand new Saab 99, things quieted down for a little while. Promises were made to take it easier. Possessions were not all that mattered in the world.

In the summer of 1975, in one of the communities, the year's second local tournament was already in full swing. It started with the round of 16, and practically everyone participated, regardless of age. A wife who worked as a secretary at the motor vehicle inspection facility beat the appeals court judge in the first round, only to meet her fate in the next round, losing to a long-haired fifteen-year-old. The newly divorced recreational instructor lost to the property manager, and a thirteen-year-old reached the finals but had no chance against a neatly bearded, very consistent and coordinated architect.

One of the many tennis-crazy kids in Sätra was Mats Törnwall, who in 1975 was a ninth-grader at the Sätra High School. Today, he works as a stock broker at a bank near Stureplan in Stockholm. In 1975, he knew one thing for sure: that he'd never work at a bank like his dad and that he'd become a sports journalist, or even better, a tennis player.

"We were inspired by Björn Borg's garage wall, and there were a lot of pedestrian tunnels in Sätra. My friend and I used to go there and hit against the wall, every other shot until one of us missed. That made it 15–0, and then we continued on to game, set, and match," says Törnwall.

Björn Borg, or *björnborg*, which was the common pronunciation—without a pause between his first and last names—had changed Sweden. When Ingemar Stenmark skied, the entire country came to a complete halt for a few minutes. The national hockey and soccer teams could create moments of euphoria. But Borg penetrated deeper layers, more existential and complex. He wasn't beloved—he seemed too different for that—but he was admired. People marveled at what he was accomplishing on his own and couldn't stop thinking about him. And the game he played was so much fun, yet so difficult.

Elective classes were a novelty and a brainchild of Olof Palme, then-minister for education, a few years earlier. They were part of a new national curriculum in which the most important changes were no grades in lower and middle secondary school; no grades in order and conduct; and no Christianity teachings, which were replaced by studies of all the major religions. Palme believed that the winds of change required a school system characterized by enlightenment, equality, and content before form. The purpose of the elective classes was to promote students' individual development.

Even before the school reform was fully implemented, this theory had been tested by Björn Borg, who'd left school to follow his own, uncompromising, individual path. All interests were just as important for individual development, and seeing the tennis idols who this week appeared in extra color inserts in the newspapers was more important than ongoing school group projects on the Vietnam War.

Mats Törnwall and one of his classmates took the subway from Sätra to Gärdet. The doors to the Kungliga Tennis Hall were open.

"We skipped school. I still have my autograph notebook and all the autographs are there, except for Borg's. It wasn't that we didn't see him or couldn't have gotten it, we could have. But he was in a semifeud with the Swedish press back then, and I remember thinking it'd be nice to leave him alone," Törnwall recounts.

Borg and Vilas practiced all out; the tempo was furious. Borg chased after a short drop shot and had moved up to the net when his thigh got in the way of a hard-hit forehand passing shot from Vilas. The Swede fell to the floor. Vilas looked at him, but Björn was still down. Vilas walked up to the net, and Borg lifted an arm. Vilas smiled and lay down on his side of the net; the two tennis stars took a break, breathing hard on their backs.

Nearly 40 years later, Borg still remembers everyone's expectations before the Masters tournament, his own and the Swedish people's. He's still sweating a little after an intense workout at Janne Lundqvist's tennis hall in Stockholm. Björn plays here a few times a week to stay in shape. He looks good. His silvery-gray hair is slicked back and damp after his shower. The tennis hall, whose walls are covered with images of him, breathes tennis history.

"It was always important for me to perform at home, at the Stockholm Open and in Båstad. And then the Masters came here with the eight best players in the world, and I had qualified. I remember that I played tennis at an extremely high level in several matches," Borg explains.

"I practiced hard with Vilas the days before the tournament. Superhard workouts. I think I was the first player, along with Vilas, who began to train a lot. He could stay out on the court and play maybe even longer than me, but I ran more than he did, trail running on hilly courses, interval training, things like that. We were the first players who really applied ourselves and started training professionally. Then others followed. I might have been the most extreme, but when they saw what Vilas and I could endure, everyone understood this is what you had to do."

Borg and Vilas hailed from opposite corners of the world and had become good friends. Aside from their workout discipline, they also had in common similar long curls, identical headbands that held those curls in place, and a similar style of play—heavy ground strokes and tireless grinding from the baseline. To an outsider, though, they still seemed to have more dissimilarities than similarities. Vilas was four years older and was portrayed as a man with different ideals than Borg.

Before the Masters tournament, the morning newspaper *Dagens Nyheter* published a long article describing Vilas: "For Vilas, the friendships with other players and the joy of playing the game that matters most are more important than money," wrote the reporter, Kurt Lorén. Vilas grew up in an upper-class Argentine family but was a self-declared communist. He wore Che Guevara t-shirts, read serious books, and had already published a book himself, a mixture of poetry and essays, which, according to Vilas, was about "humans, love, and loneliness." The evening newspaper *Expressen* reviewed the book on its culture pages, and *Dagens Nyheter* reported that the book had received positive reviews in South America. However, the great Argentine writer Jorge Luis Borges dismissed the book as a pectoral: "Vilas writes poetry similar to how I play tennis." The evening daily *Aftonbladet* described Vilas as "the world's best-paid poet."

"Do you have Björn's killer instinct?" asked *Dagens Nyheter*.

"Killer instinct is just a word," answered Vilas. "When you're out on the court, you don't think about killing."

"You read and write a lot?"

"Yes, but it's not true that I prefer Dostoyevsky above all others. I'd like to take the opportunity to refute that here. My favorite is Khalil Gibran. Currently, I'm reading *El Vagabundo* by him, but his best book is *The Prophet*. Don't miss it!"

After the practice, Borg, too, was asked about his reading habits. A reporter wanted to know if he still read comic books. "The truth is," said Björn, "I haven't read a single comic book in a year. My image might need a little updating after all."

The reporter asked why Björn had stopped reading comic books. "Why?" said Borg and laughed. "Well, probably for the same reason all other kids stop reading them. They don't give me anything anymore."

Borg said he might go back to school the day he stopped playing tennis. Sometimes, he said, he'd tried to read textbooks between practices and tournaments. "It just doesn't work, I have no energy for it. I guess tennis takes too much energy. I can't do it."

Björn was everyone's idol at the Kungliga Tennis Hall, but despite the young phenom's successes, some tennis purists criticized his style of play. Borg hits like a lumberjack, read one front-page headline in *Dagens Nyheter* after one of the summer's Davis Cup matches. Don't play like Borg urged a headline in *Expressen* a few days before the start of the Masters tournament.

Because tennis was also a matter of style. Comparing Borg to Arthur Ashe, the Swede seemed boorish as he moved between the points. Was it a matter of character? Ashe was from Richmond, Virginia, the son of a cotton picker. He'd been raised in a world where, because of the color of his skin, he was chased away from the tennis courts and forced to sit in the back of the bus. Arthur Ashe was quiet, just like Borg, but his aura was not the same. Rather than stubbornness, he radiated stature and purity, which gained in gravity from his position on civil rights issues. No newspaper failed to mention that Ashe had flown to Stockholm from Soweto, where he'd just opened a tennis center for black children. His colleagues called him "Mr. Cool." He had a brilliant season behind him, which had brought him close to his dream of finishing a tennis season as the world's number one.

"Four of us are playing for that," said Vilas. "Arthur Ashe, Manuel Orantes, Björn Borg, and myself. If one of us wins the Masters, he is likely to be ranked number one in 1975."

On Saturday, Ashe, Nastase, and Panatta practiced on the center court. Nastase horsed around, pulled down his pants to his knees, and wobbled as he tried to run down his practice partners' shots. Ashe laughed. Nastase brought out a tape recorder and proceeded to do push-ups to the rhythm of David Bowie's "Young Americans" and The Eagles' "One of These Nights." Ashe served up an ace.

"Arthur, your nerves won't hold up against me in the match tomorrow. You don't have a chance," yelled Nastase.

According to Mats Törnwall, "The player I remember most from the Masters is Nastase. We watched him practice, he put on a show and joked around. He broke his rackets and then he walked up to us and gave us the broken racket. He could speak so many languages, we admired him almost as much as we admired Borg."

That evening, Nastase was the center of attention in the cocktail bar at the Grand Hotel. "I'm going to drive Ashe crazy tomorrow. I'm going to give him all the old tricks and some of my new ones."

Ashe came down to the bar.

"Hey Negroni," yelled Nastase. "I'll make you sweat tomorrow."

The evening at the Grand Hotel was boisterous. The air was filled with gamesmanship. Tennis stars came and went, and other guests followed the spectacle with wide-open eyes and ears. All the Masters participants stayed at the Grand, which is located opposite the Royal Palace. Everyone except Björn Borg. The newspapers reported that he was staying at a private address, or a "secret location."

"It was kept secret from most people, but I stayed with a man we called Engblom the Barber, a property owner and tennis player who owned a large property two stations away from Äppelviken, where I stayed in an apartment that week. To stay at the Grand with the other players was out of the question; I needed peace and quiet. Helena Anliot stayed there, too," says Björn.

"Fascist pig," shouted someone in the crowd to Manuel Orantes early in the tournament's opening match between the timid Spaniard and Adriano Panatta. Franco had been dead for a week, but the hatred against the Spanish dictatorship ran deep. Just two months earlier, Olof Palme had called Franco and the Spanish government "bloody murderers." No matter, Orantes beat Panatta. Björn, wearing yellow shorts and a yellow shirt, crushed Raúl Ramírez. He impressed like never before.

The evening session began with Vilas beating Harold Solomon, an American small in stature. It ended with Ashe playing Nastase in a match that was to set the tone for the entire week. The Swedish people learned once and for all that the professional tennis circus, which Borg had made so popular and which was the reason so many had started to play tennis, was in fact something very un-Swedish.

The start of the match offered brilliant tennis. In the first set Ashe, elegant in a shirt with a horizontally striped pattern and light-blue shorts, was blown off the court by Nastase, who was wearing all white. In the second set, Ashe cleaned up his serve and took the lead, 5–2. This caused Nastase to lose his temper. The Romanian did what he usually did, and just like he'd promised: he resorted to his special methods for making opponents lose their rhythm. He questioned calls, threw his racket, delayed the game, and chatted up the chair umpire and the crowd. It worked. Ashe lost his equilibrium, started to miss drop shots, and placed easy volleys outside of the lines. Eventually, Nastase had a break point to go ahead, 6–5, but Ashe managed to escape, held his serve, and immediately followed it up by breaking Nastase's serve in the next game to win the set. Nastase spat on a TV camera and smacked a ball into the wall right next to a linesman.

In the third set, Ashe was ahead by a score of 4–1 and 40–15 in Nastase's service game. The Romanian seemed to have psyched himself out. What happened next happened around ten o'clock at night, when the Swedish television, which had broadcast live all afternoon, had scheduled a replay of highlights from Borg's match. Instead, the cameras kept rolling live, and all of Sweden could see Nastase hit a serve and Ashe catch the ball in his hand. The American signaled that he hadn't been ready to return Nastase's serve. Nastase lost it. The umpire asked him to serve again. Nastase walked up to the umpire, asked what was going on, he'd already served, he'd played, he hadn't seen a signal from Ashe before he hit his serve. A good serve had been wasted. "Please play," said the Swedish umpire. Nastase continued his rant, first at the umpire, then at the crowd. Ashe waited. Nastase threw up his hands. "Please play," repeated the umpire. Nastase got ready at the service line. He pointed with a ball in his hand toward his opponent and yelled: "Are you ready, Mr. Ashe?"

Someone laughed. Others hushed.

Nastase gestured again, seeking some form of confirmation from Ashe that he'd heard the question, then lowered his racket, let the racket rest at his side, and gave Ashe a long stare. The seconds passed.

"Are you ready, Mr. Ashe?" repeated Nastase while holding up two fingers in the air, a clear sign since the rules state that the serving player has two serves. Another look at Ashe, the umpire, the crowd.

"15–40," called the umpire, "two balls." Nastase turned toward the umpire in an exaggerated, submissive manner, bowed his head, and answered: "Yes, ma'am!"

The crowd was so caught up in what was happening that it no longer knew how to interpret the situation. Laughs were heard, but the silence surrounding the laughs revealed a feverish atmosphere. This was unknown territory, a reminder that the Masters tournament was not at all the same thing as the quaint Stockholm Open week. This was for real, this was ruthless.

Nastase waited for the buzz to subside and began his service motion, bounced the ball, and bent down low and with rhythm between each bounce, exaggerating his motions. People squirmed on the wooden benches. The Romanian had a natural comic talent; it was difficult not to laugh.

"Nastase, please serve," said the umpire at the exact moment the Romanian had, in fact, tossed the ball up in the air.

The Romanian interrupted his service motion, walked up to the umpire, and started his yapping shenanigans once again. In the midst of all this, Ashe left his position behind the baseline and walked assertively across the court. He'd had enough. He quickly gathered his things and began walking toward the locker room. The referee—a man from West Germany named Klosterkempfer—hurried out on center court and tried to get a word with Ashe. But the American wasn't going to negotiate. He left the court.

And with that, he was disqualified.

Nastase, now suddenly the winner, also walked off the court, very slowly at first. Then he turned his back to the chair umpire and walked backwards to his chair, picked up his rackets, and walked up and sat down in the stands, in the midst of the crowd, where he gulped down a soda. The match was over. The crowd remained seated in what seemed like a state of shock, as if it were waiting for a sequel, a reconciliation, a negotiated resolution Swedish style.

And there was one. Speaking into his microphone, the Swedish chair umpire explained that he'd been ready to disqualify Nastase for unsportsmanlike conduct right before Ashe left the court. He just hadn't had a chance to announce his decision. Therefore, a new result was declared. Both players had been disqualified.

The press room was jam-packed with journalists. Ashe and Nastase sat at a table, staring at each other. Klosterkempfer placed himself in the middle.

"The umpire's decision is correct," said Nastase. "I have no complaints, everyone knows it's always my fault."

He got up from his chair to stand by the wall.

"When I left the court," said Ashe, "Nastase had broken almost every rule there is without being disqualified, even if I had pleaded with the umpire."

Nastase screamed: "Pleaded with the umpire? The only thing you should do on the court is play, or do you need President Ford to rule on everything that happens on the tennis court, too?"

Ashe said nothing.

"Who are you, really?" yelled Nastase.

Ashe still said nothing.

"Who the hell do you think you are?" shouted Nastase. "You should try to just play tennis."

"It's impossible to talk to *that ass*," said Ashe. "Even if it's meaningless, I'm going to file a complaint with the Players' Association at its meeting this week. And I'm going to have to argue with myself, since I am its president."

Ashe and Nastase were both part of Borg's circle of friends, and everything that had to do with Björn was becoming increasingly fascinating. The first thing Swedes discussed the following day—at every workplace around the country, across every coffee table, in every schoolyard—was Sunday's scandalous match. It was front page news in all the newspapers. The inner workings of the pro circus had been exposed, and what it showed was something different from the Fjällräven jackets and Stenmark hats everyone was wearing these days.

The morning newspaper *Svenska Dagbladet* wrote about Nastase's violation of the spirit of the sport: "What's at stake here is the idea of the game. This view shouldn't be obscured by a stack of dollars. And the fact that Nastase is the most successful Masters player of all time shouldn't do that, either. Clownish behavior and direct sabotage have no place in a tournament that, when you translate the English word, means 'The Championship of Champions.' If Nastase misbehaves one more time, he should be immediately expelled—and at the same time, the Swedish organizers should also decline any and all future visits."

Dagens Nyheter's Bobby Byström thought it was a shame that the umpire had let Ashe make the decision the umpire himself should have made: take a stand against Nastase's behavior: "At any rate, we as spectators, we thank Ashe. What we want to see and pay a hefty price for, is Nastase the player, not the clown. As such and in that case, he is grossly overpaid." *Expressen* articulated an ultimatum in a bold front-page headline: STOP ACTING LIKE A CLOWN, NASTASE—OR STOP PLAYING TENNIS. The newspaper had also sent one of its reporters, Maria Schottenius, to Nastase's hotel room. From there, she reported that Nastase hadn't been able to get used to the fact that he was no longer the best player. This tormented him, and his nerves were the culprit.

While the newspapers were busy analyzing, the players took the opportunity to sort out their differences on their own. That Monday morning in the Grand Hotel's breakfast room, Ashe sat picking though his food, staring out across the gray waters of Stockholm. He was feeling disappointed, empty, irritable, and bitter. After all, he was the president of the professional tennis players' association and the players' face externally in negotiations with organizers and sponsors. Now he'd lost his famous equilibrium and damaged the sport's reputation. He promised himself to never speak with Nastase again.

"Hey, Negroni . . ."

There was only one person who'd use that epithet; the same man who constantly greeted South African tennis pros with "Hey, Racist" and Germans with "Hey, Nazi." Nastase was hiding behind a large bouquet of red, yellow, and white flowers, which he handed to Ashe. Then he gave his antagonist from the day before a kiss on each cheek. All Ashe could do was laugh; he wasn't good at holding grudges. About an hour later, the tournament organizers announced that Ashe had been given the victory. And thus, the match was given its third final result. Nastase sulked yet again, hopped into a car that took him to the Kungliga Tennis Hall, and sat down in the stands to watch Vilas defeat Ramírez. At one time, the play was stopped so that a man with a heart condition could be removed from the stands to receive care. Nastase sighed: "This is my fault, too. Everything is my fault."

WHY DO WE BULLY NASTASE? read the headline of an article written by the author P O Enquist on *Expressen*'s culture page the following day. "For goodness sake. Of course, we shouldn't weep crocodile tears over tennis millionaires who travel around the world like crazy rats and cash in while doing it," Enquist began and went on to criticize the stiff rules of tennis, which stemmed from "English lords and pale-nosed sons of the Eton nobility."

The Eastern European Nastase, on the other hand, was a genuine and precious proletarian who could care less about manners and obedience. "The only human," wrote Enquist, "in tennis's wax cabinet of mask holders."

Enquist's interpretation reflected the Swedish people's feelings. Nastase was popular and admired by many. Women found him handsome, tennis connoisseurs enjoyed his hand-eye coordination, and the kids laughed at his antics.

Aftonbladet's readers called in and offered their opinions on Sunday's events at the Kungliga Tennis Hall. The next day, their reactions filled two full pages. "Nastase resembled Torbjörn Fälldin, a turncoat," opined one reader. "It's the money's fault," said someone else. Another reader reasoned: "Just imagine if a factory worker had done what Ashe did. He'd be sacked immediately."

The Kungliga Tennis Hall sold out every night. Nastase defeated Orantes. Torbjörn Fälldin, Olof Palme, King Carl Gustaf, and the Formula 1 race car driver Ronnie Peterson attracted the photographers' attention between games, when people stretched their legs and got up to buy pilsner and ice cream. When the spectators had reclaimed their seats, Björn beat Solomon and advanced to the semifinals. In a radio interview, Björn said that if he continued to play this well, he could win the Masters, and maybe become the world's number one player. Meanwhile, Nastase was sitting in yet another packed press room, where he answered questions after his win against Orantes.

"Weren't you mentally tired after the Ashe match?"

"Not just mentally, but physically, too, thanks to a wonderful night of lovemaking with my wife, Dominique. So yes, I was tired, but I still felt pretty good, as you can probably imagine . . ."

Nastase went on to defeat Adriano Panatta, in a match where he got the crowd up on its feet after the Romanian ran down a lob and, with his back to the net, hit an overhead smash that left his opponent no chance to return it. It was an artistic stroke nobody had seen before, and a stroke nobody else could've pulled off. The next day, after Ashe defeated Orantes, the Romanian advanced to the semis. The American was quick to point out that by winning, he'd done Nastase a favor. "I've just given him the $40,000 opportunity. If I meet him in the final, I won't be walking off again. Things are completely back to normal now."

The semifinals: Borg–Ashe, Vilas–Nastase.

Neither the TV companies nor the organizers could have dreamed up a better season finale.

The international tennis journalists held Ashe and Vilas as the favorites to win. Ashe had A-plus statistics against Borg. Vilas had looked very confident through the group rounds. And in the first match on Saturday afternoon, in front of a sold-out arena and three million Swedes who followed the match via radio or television, it was indeed Ashe who set the pace. The American clearly played better than Borg in the first two sets, but Borg managed to steal the first, mostly because Ashe hadn't yet fine-tuned his attacks. After Ashe had won the second set, Borg seemed stunned. He wasn't able to get to Ashe's serve. Borg hung his head. Everything suggested he was going to lose the match.

Percy Rosberg, Borg's coach before Björn moved to Monaco, was in the radio booth acting as sidekick to the match commentator, Tommy Engstrand:

"I remember it well. A ball boy came up to the radio booth. Björn had asked him to come and get me. Ashe was serving well, he was a serve-and-volley player. And Borg could never pass him, so Ashe won his games easily. I had a small key for a solution. Björn's mistake in the first two sets was that he wasn't positioned right to the ball. He acted like an obedient student in a tennis school during the first two sets, set his feet early. . . . It's true that you should hit with your feet firmly set, but Björn looked like a buried tulip bulb. He needed to move his feet much closer at the moment of impact. It's classic. As a tennis player, some days you feel more like a statue, your feet don't listen. So, I took a seat on the stairs beside the court, because coaching wasn't allowed. Lennart Bergelin, who was Björn's real coach, was sitting on the other side. But I sat down pretty close to Björn's chair and said to the ball boy: "Tell Björn to move his feet as much as possible before he hits the ball, so he can get to the serve."

Borg received the message in that changeover and immediately proceeded to break Ashe's serve. Rosberg remained seated where he was. The referee, Klosterkempfer, noticed the rule violation and approached Rosberg, whose actions risked Borg's disqualification. Rosberg denied having said anything.

In the next day's newspapers, he said: "I said nothing. I just sat there silent like a wall."

Nearly 40 years later, he laughs sheepishly at the memory:

"I knew the German guy who was head of the tournament. He explained that Björn could be disqualified for taking advice from someone in the stands, and he again asked what I'd told Björn. I answered that I just said to the guy sitting next to me that Björn should move his feet, and if I happened to say it a bit loudly so that Björn happened to hear it, then so be it."

Björn Borg also remembers the situation well:

"Nobody else was sitting next to Percy. That's what was so funny, that space was empty. They must have thought Percy had started to lose it, sitting there talking to himself. . . . But what he said was good, it helped me."

Björn turned things around and beat Ashe, 3–1. In the final sets, he played his best tennis all week. Meanwhile, Nastase surprisingly crushed Vilas, 3–0, in the other semifinal.

At the press conference before the final, Borg had high expectations: "I have high hopes of winning the final."

But Björn wasn't at all as calm as he tried to appear. Percy Rosberg's coaching from the stairs in the stands had helped Björn get the win, but it had also shaken a sensitive relationship.

Percy Rosberg remembers:

"Ashe didn't say anything about it. He and I knew each other pretty well personally. We'd met in Båstad, and he was fond of my babysitter. He'd seen me sit there on the stairs, so he knew I had coached, but he probably thought he should've beaten Björn anyway. It was worse with Bergelin. He was really angry afterward. He thought he was the one that should be coaching Björn, not I. But Björn had asked me to come and I gave him a tip that helped him turn the match around, so there wasn't much Bergelin could say."

The problem was that the coaches' conflict affected the prodigy. Lennart Bergelin was furious that Borg had received advice from Rosberg, and he let Borg know it. But Percy Rosberg was the man who'd discovered Borg and then taught, coached, and shaped him into the player who now, at the age of 19, had a chance to become the world's number one.

Lennart Bergelin, on the other hand, had grown into a sort of extra father figure for Björn. He was the one who traveled with Björn around the world, booked the hotel rooms and flights, arranged for hitting partners, and administered massages. He also made sure to keep journalists, fans, and not least girls at arm's length from Björn. Their relationship was indeed so close that when Björn went on a safari vacation with his girlfriend, Helena, Bergelin tagged along.

Now these two men, the adults Borg trusted the most in life aside from his parents, were feuding openly. And Björn found himself stuck in the middle.

After the semifinals, when Swedish TV reviewed its Sunday programming schedule, it planned for a long tennis final. Thus, it decided to scratch a season opener in bandy, as well as a ski race. Tennis was what everyone wanted to see.

But it became a quick affair. Nastase won by 6–2, 6–2, 6–1. The match was over in 65 minutes.

Björn Borg is still disappointed to this day.

"I had played extremely well against Ashe in the semifinal. But the final was bad. In fact, I think it was the worst of all my finals in any big tournament, and against Nastase of all people. I played terribly."

Borg had developed a need to not let anything outside of tennis disturb him before his matches. The bickering distracted him, and against a Nastase who was in a great playing mood, he had no chance.

"The head of the tournament made me sit all the way up on top in the stands," says Rosberg. "'You'll sit up there, you hear!'" he said. "I wasn't even able to make eye contact with Björn. And he played so crappy in that match. But it wasn't his feet that weren't working. His head was tired after all the arguing about the coaching during his match with Ashe."

The conflict between Rosberg and Bergelin wasn't known by the press or the general public. The foreign journalists noted that Nastase had demolished Borg in a way that revealed the shortcomings in the Swede's game, and which also showcased the classic tennis artistry that existed behind Nastase's clown mask. "Because above all it was an elegant massacre, an outstanding visual image, the lovely, curled backhand strokes from Nastase, and the ball dropping precisely in the corners," wrote *Sports Illustrated*.

After the match, Nastase said that his two last matches were the beginning of a new era in his career. "This is the second time that I concentrate in—how old am I, 29?—in 29 years. The first time was yesterday, I realize now. That's good for my game."

Reporters from the Swedish evening newspapers joined Nastase and his wife for dinner in Stockholm's Old Town and reported the full menu: shrimp cocktail, smoked salmon, filet mignon, ice cream, and Irish coffee. Dominique, Ilie, and a few persistent reporters then followed up dinner by a visit to the dance club Alexandra.

Aftonbladet delivered heavy criticism of Björn the day after the final. A front-page headline mentioned Borg's money. The article said that Björn had made a million as early as 1973 and that he doubled that amount in both 1974 and 1975, in prize money alone. Borg was called a "Tax Swiss" in Bengt Therner's text, in which the reporter pointed out that Borg was a Swedish citizen but didn't pay one krona in taxes. He only paid taxes in Monaco, 35 kronor per year. His finances were managed by an American, Mark McCormack, who'd now made an offer on an exclusive mansion in central Sweden on Borg's behalf. The newspaper asked readers to call in and share their thoughts.

The next day, the letters to the editor's page filled an entire spread in the newspaper. "Something's wrong with our society, not with Borg," wrote a metal worker from Hjo. A machinist from Nynäshamn argued that Borg had "started from nothing." Those opinions aside, the rest of the published letters were critical in nature. Carpenters, office clerks, construction workers, a warehouse worker, a taxi driver in Farsta, a cook in Göteborg, a philosopher in Gävle. . . . They all agreed: it was terrible, ungracious, horrible to earn such huge sums. At the same time, the Swedish people didn't seem prepared to put into practice their theoretical criticism of Borg. When the tickets to Borg's exhibition match against Laver at the Scandinavium arena were released, there were long lines, and the 12,000 tickets sold out in the blink of an eye.

Björn felt obliged to address the criticism. He met with a reporter from *Aftonbladet* at a hotel in Uppsala. "I understand if people are angry that I make so much money," he said. "It really is almost shameful how much money can be made in tennis today. If you saw this whole circus from the outside, you'd be furious. But at the same time, of course, I'm thankful for myself that this is how it is. That the prize money is so great. That you can secure your future in a rather short period of time by playing tennis. And maybe the money has done something to me—although I don't know exactly what. Money is great to have. Money provides a sort of freedom. But money isn't everything. I don't really care about clothes. I dress just like I did before. Jeans and a shirt, clothes I like. But when and if I see something I really like, I never bother to ask how much it is. That's when it's good to have plenty of money. That's the freedom money provides."

Borg said that his personality had changed, as well. "For the better: I have an easier time containing my emotions now. There were many times when I was younger, back home in Södertälje, when my mom and dad had to sneak away from the outside courts, blushing and embarrassed. I was a monster on the court—I cursed and threw my racket every time I lost a point. I thank my mom and dad for putting a stop to that. But oh, how they had to nag, threaten, and lecture me. For the worse: I have become messier. I have a hard time keeping things neat around me. My car is a terrible mess, old chewing gum wrappers and other trash is piling up everywhere. Maybe it's because nowadays I have to spend so much time keeping my body and equipment in shape, so there's no time for all the rest. I remember when I was little and we'd go visit my grandfather in the hospital. I don't really remember a lot, other than that it was unpleasant and that I was sad he was there. And that scares me still, that everything is so fragile, illnesses, and I don't mean sports injuries—I know they're coming and I'm ready for it. But that you might not be able to walk, or move. Yeah, that you might suddenly just not wake up one day.

The reason Borg was staying at the hotel in Uppsala was that the Davis Cup team had assembled there. Borg, Ove Bengtson, Kjell Johansson, Birger Andersson, and the team captain, Lennart Bergelin, had already begun fine-tuning for the final against Czechoslovakia that would start the day after the Masters tournament. For the first time, Sweden had the chance to bring home the oldest team competition in sports.

But the fact that Borg had been so outplayed in the Masters final was a concern. How was his fitness? If he couldn't handle the stress of playing the biggest singles final ever on Swedish soil, how was he going to handle a Davis Cup final? The leaders of the Swedish Tennis Association played an unexpected card. When Lennart Bergelin stepped out to lead the first practice sessions, he had a new colleague by his side: Ilie Nastase.

FROM ROYAL PASTIME TO THE PEOPLE'S SPORT

"He's the world's only undefeated tennis player. 'Just don't beat the king' was what other players were told as they set out to play him."
—PERCY ROSBERG

The name of Sweden's first tennis player was Gustaf. He was the crown prince, and, in the summer of 1879, he turned 21 and spent four months in England. This was the last stop on his grand tour, the journey undertaken by all young members of royal families for educational purposes and to find a marriage partner at one of the foreign royal courts (the line of succession to the throne must be secured). Gustaf had traveled abroad the previous year, too, when he'd visited the Danish royal court. He'd also made stops in Constantinople, Rome, and Paris but hadn't been successful in reeling in a catch.

In England, he was introduced to princess Beatrice as a suitable partner. Such a marriage would have been both advantageous and appropriate for the Swedish royal family, but it was not to be. Gustaf wasn't interested. His mind was stuck on something else, a new game. He'd seen young men in white clothing move smoothly around rectangular courts on well-groomed lawns. They held rackets in their hands and played a game called lawn tennis. Gustaf became more than interested. He fell in love.

When he returned home, he taught the game to his friends, and tennis became a popular sport in the upper society. Gustaf had two of the country's first tennis courts built, a grass court at the royal palace in Tullgarn and an unassuming clay court at Skeppsholmen in Stockholm, where many naval officers came to play. People who walked by thought it looked silly; adults running around while hitting a small ball back and forth to each other. But the crown prince made sure to have the rule book of the game translated into Swedish, and the game grew in popularity. The crown prince belonged to a growing group of people who believed that tennis was the best thing that life had to offer. They were behind the construction of a tennis pavilion at Djurgården in Stockholm, an exclusive and modern facility featuring hot water showers. Gustaf competed under the alias Mr. G. and founded his own club, Kronprinsens Lawn Tennis Klubb. When he was crowned king, Gustaf had it renamed Kungliga Lawn Tennisklubben, KLTK.

As a newly appointed monarch by the name of Gustaf V, his political power was more restricted. At the end of the First World War and with parliamentary democracy about to break through, the European royal families' glory days were over. Tennis could have met the same fate. It could have followed other gentlemanly pleasures such as horse polo and fox hunting into the periphery of society and lived out its days as an obsolete cultural phenomenon.

There were signs in Sweden that pointed in that direction. In 1920, one of them could be seen by all in newspaper images: a melancholy monarch trudging around in the ashes and remains of the burned-down royal tennis pavilion.

But out in the world, things were going in a different direction. The French woman Suzanne Lenglen, a commoner, won Wimbledon in 1919. With her, the game was brought into the Jazz Age and the era of the Lost Generation. Lenglen cursed, drank, smoked, and was often escorted to the court by one of her numerous lovers. At this time, the British suffragettes fought successfully for women's equality, and Lenglen managed to reach further than that in her field: tennis became a sport where the biggest name was a woman. The masses lined up for a chance to see her play. Wimbledon had to build a new arena. On the court, the French woman moved as gracefully as a ballerina. She ignored the fashion of the times, which stipulated that ladies played in corsets. Airy, shorter dresses became her trademark and the fashion for women in large parts of the world. Hemingway wrote about her in *The Sun Also Rises*. Suzanne Lenglen was obsessed with winning, and between 1919 and 1926, she remained practically undefeated. More than anyone else, she transformed tennis into a competitive spectator's sport. Lenglen became one of the world's most famous athletes during the 1920s, when the balance between celebrities was changing: royalty now found themselves in the shadows of artists, scientists, and sports personalities. Following behind in Lenglen's surging waves, new male tennis profiles also started to step forward. One such new phenom was Bill Tilden, the gay actor and playwright who transformed tennis into a physical power sport and every match into a spectacle. Others included the French tennis musketeers Henri Cochet, René Lacoste, Jean Borotra, and Jacques Brugnon.

The politically conservative Gustaf V followed the development of international tennis with fascination. Swedish tennis was still a game for the high society; the upper class played to bask in the glory of royalty. In the Davis Cup, the bankers Marcus Wallenberg and Sune Malmström represented the Swedish national team. They noted their notorious losses in neat columns.

Gustaf V wanted to meet Lenglen and play a game of tennis with her. This was arranged for, and, as a bonus, the king became close friends with her fellow countrymen, the successful French tennis musketeers.

In January of 1926, news reached King Gustaf V that a new American tennis star, Helen Wills, had disembarked from a transatlantic ocean liner in Le Havre, France. Was she thinking of challenging Suzanne Lenglen, "La Divine"? Lenglen had reached the age of 26 and had racked up victories in Wimbledon and Paris, but she hadn't bothered to travel to America to play. She also hadn't bothered to defend her Olympics title in 1924. Instead, that title went to Wills, then only 18 years old, who since then had gone on to win the American Championships three times. This was what everyone had been waiting for, a match between the reigning tennis queen and the young American.

Thanks to Suzanne Lenglen, the French people had regained much of its wounded pride from the First World War, and they viewed the tennis challenge like a global duel in a wider cultural sense. Americans, wrote the daily newspaper *Paris-Midi*, were "degenerate and rotten, physically, intellectually, and morally. They are an insult to our ears, eyes, and nostrils."

But when 12 reporters met with Helen Wills in Le Havre, all such rhetoric was silenced. The young American woman made a deep impression. Before boarding the train to the Riviera, she explained that she'd come to France not primarily to play tennis, but to paint.

But she was going to play tennis, too, and it wasn't difficult to guess with whom.

TIME magazine kept a journal of Wills's travels in France, without interviewing her. Each day, as she got closer to Cannes, the journalists became even more convinced they knew what she was thinking about in her train car.

When King Gustaf V found out that Lenglen and Wills had been entered into the same tournament and most likely would meet in the final in Cannes on February 16, he had his bags packed, changed into his alias, Mr. G., and boarded the train to the Riviera.

The match was going to be played on a pink-colored clay court and was described as a showdown between French elegance and American simplicity. Charlie Chaplin described Helen Wills on a tennis court as the most beautiful sight a human eye could see, seasoned with "a healthy dose of sex appeal."

Suzanne, for her part, was not a classic beauty. Her teeth pointed in all directions, and her nose was crooked. However, her sex appeal was described as magnetic, and her eyes were irresistible.

"We're after the dough. It's only a matter of money," said the American organizer Bernie Hicks, who'd sold the rights to report from the match for 100,000 dollars and raked in 4,000 dollars from a ball manufacturer for the right to deliver the balls for the match. However, both Wills and Lenglen demanded that the match be open for anyone who wanted to film and show it. And that's how it came to be. Nevertheless, there was money to be made for so many, among them an English woman who came across a thick stack of 50-franc tickets, which she sold for 1,000 francs apiece.

Mr. G. met both Helen and Suzanne. Before retreating to her room, the American had a meal of clear soup, filet mignon, green beans, boiled fresh potatoes, and ice cream and cake. In her autobiography, she writes that she slept like a rock, despite being tortured by the orchestra on the terrace below, which played the season's hit song, "Valencia," over and over.

The match was scheduled to start at lunchtime, but the 7,000 spectators started to fill up the stands early in the morning. Freeloaders climbed up in trees and on fences and roofs. The journalists squeezed in with their large typewriters on their laps. The Spanish novelist Vicente Blasco Ibáñez had been paid 40,000 francs from a South American newspaper to report from the event. He'd never seen a tennis match before but assured his client: "I understand psychology."

Lenglen came out on the court wearing a fur coat and a scarf wrapped around her head; Wills wore a white cap. The spectators cheered loudly for their favorite Suzanne and pushed and shoved so hard that they almost knocked down one of the grandstands. Lenglen walked up to them and told them to behave themselves. Meanwhile, French gendarmes climbed the eucalyptus trees to hunt for freeloaders. They managed to nab some of them by the waistband of their underwear. But the freeloaders kept on climbing. The policemen were forced to follow, one hand desperately hanging on to the climbers' boxers, so as not to lose their balance and fall.

Mr. G. had never experienced anything like it, but he liked it.

Lenglen drank water before the match, Wills nothing. Both players began nervously. Lenglen, who was famous for her risk taking, stayed back. Wills, famous for her ball touch, misfired. But Lenglen soon warmed up as she found her rhythm with her varied and angled style of play. She often mixed short and deep shots to her opponent's weaker backhand. Wills had to do a lot of running. Lenglen won the first set.

In the second set, Wills began finding her target with her heavy-hit shots. After one long point, she hit a topspin backhand down the line that landed behind Lenglen's back, completely wrong-footing her. Wills went up, 4–1. Lenglen, whose fitness wasn't her strong point, gasped for air, pounded her heart with her fist, and walked back to her seat, where she downed a glass of cognac on the rocks. Then she walked back out on the court, fought her way back into the match, and went on to win it, 6–3, 8–6.

Mr. G., who'd been watching the match seated next to an expatriate Russian duke and an Indian raja and his wife, was spellbound. The quality of the play, the festivities—this was something a Swedish tennis audience must have the chance to experience!

Suzanne Lenglen was presented with roses and champagne. Helen Wills was led off the court by a supporter, Frederic Moody, who praised her game. Mr. G. sought out both Lenglen and Wills and extended to each player a standing invitation to come to Sweden to play an exhibition match. Wills said she was sure there'd be an opportunity for such a visit.

The next day, the *London Times* summed up the match: "It seemed as if the Earth was about to stop rotating, as if all the international excitement would end in an appeal to the League of Nations. Anything could happen, including a war between the USA and France. But now the match is over, and the universe can go on as if nothing happened."

After her victory in Cannes, Lenglen went on to win the French Championships. That summer, she signed a pro contract and boarded an ocean liner to America. There, she played in sold-out arenas everywhere. She was the first woman who'd chosen to become a professional.

She received questions about it and responded: "I haven't made a penny on my tennis, my life's calling. I'm 27 years old, not rich, so should I start a new career and leave behind the one in which people call me a genius? Should I smile at the prospect of a life in poverty and continue to make millions for someone else?" Amateurism was fake, thought Lenglen: "Only the rich can compete under these absurd and antiquated amateur rules, and the fact is that only rich people compete. Is that fair? Does it develop the sport? Does it make tennis more popular? Or does it prevent an enormous amount of dormant tennis talent in young men and women's bodies to come out, bodies whose owners aren't found in the nobility register?"

Helen Wills eventually replaced Lenglen at the tennis throne. She further developed tennis into a concentration sport. A few years later, she fulfilled her promise to Gustaf V and traveled to Stockholm, now as a five-time Wimbledon champion.

Helen Wills Moody, who was now married to the supporter who'd escorted her off the court in Cannes, stepped off the transcontinental train at Stockholm's central station on November 24, 1932. The platform was crowded with people who'd come to get a glimpse of her. "Like a Californian fruit of the most precious kind, with her beautiful skin and her Greek profile," scribbled a reporter. The American couple then disappeared into a cab that drove them to the Grand Hotel, where they were met by more reporters. On her way to the elevator, Wills Moody stopped and answered some questions. She informed the reporters she'd come to show them that "a lady can play tennis just as well as the most skillful of gentlemen." She also said that she hadn't played against Mr. G., but that she'd met him.

"What is it about tennis that you like so much?"

"I love the sport. To play, and to paint and write, those are the only remedies for my melancholy."

Then Wills Moody disappeared up to her room, but she soon reappeared wearing a black hat. A car was there to pick her up to go sightseeing. Mr. Moody, a banker by profession, was only interested in shipyards, ports, and maritime museums, but his wife had other plans. "I don't want to see only the palaces, I want to see how the people live," she said. The driver stopped at an address on Norr Mälarstrand, where he showed the tennis queen his own functionalism-style apartment, where his wife served coffee and their newborn baby offered smiles. Back in the car, Wills asked how the country had been affected by the riots in Ådalen the year before and the Kreuger crash the same year. The driver gave her a brief report, explaining that a new government with entirely new policies had come to power. The cab then passed by Stockholm's steam kitchen and the numerous homeless who hung around there, people who'd sold their coats and vests and pawnshop receipts and were now trying to stay warm between their nightly wanderings back and forth across the city, waiting for the five o'clock ringing of the church bells. That's when the newspaper ladies began scurrying through the doorways and the steam kitchen would open and serve hot coffee once again.

In response, Wills talked about the newly elected President Roosevelt. She remarked that politics seemed to be the same here and there.

The Moodys had lunch at the restaurant *Den Gyldene Freden,* and at five o'clock that afternoon, the reporters found "beautiful Helen" in the B hall at the tennis stadium. They noted that nothing as posh had ever been seen on a tennis court before. *Dagens Nyheter*'s sports columnist, the alias Mr. Jones, wrote: "I've just seen Mrs. Wills Moody practice. She is remarkable. She hits the ball harder than most any man." Wills Moody, wearing a knee-length white skirt, then hit with Mr. G., after which the 74-year-old monarch and the tennis queen retired to the stadium's tea room.

According to reports in the newspaper columns the next day, that evening Wills Moody had charmed the banker and Davis Cup player Marcus Wallenberg at his villa at Parkudden. There, she also announced a surprise: "I haven't come here to play against women. I want to play against men."

The organizers squirmed but had to let the intended opponent, Mrs. E. Aquillon, know that her match with Wills Moody had been canceled.

Instead, they called on two elite male Swedish players, John "Jonte" Söderström and Sune Malmström.

At the tennis stadium the following day, "the fairer sex was most plentiful." "This could be perceived," wrote one reporter, "if not through your eyes, which tended to be focused on the beautiful Helen, but by the abundant soprano laughter and rambunctious staccato applause. But rightly, the men should have supported their man, Jonte Söderström, who bravely dared to get in the game with the Earth's balling queen." Wills Moody pummeled her thundering forehand shots past the Swede and won the first set easily. However, in the second set, she graciously let Söderström win "many amusing points," *Dagens Nyheter* reported.

Helen Wills Moody's visit to Stockholm and her surprising frolicking with the domestic male elite had exposed the fact that Swedish tennis was stuck in its role as a royal pastime. Gustaf V took note of this and changed the direction of his tennis support. He started an international elite indoor tournament, Kungens Kanna (the King's Cup), and made sure that his club, KLTK, which was inaccessible for the general public, receive a new, modern indoor facility on Lidingövägen: the Kungliga Tennis Hall.

These measures were an attempt to open the door to new ideas, to let some light into the sport. However, in the end, Gustaf was stuck in his role. To truly free the sport from its label would require him to stop playing, something the King refused to do. He continued to play until he was almost 90 years old.

Also, every summer, Mr. G. boarded the royal blue train car to Båstad, where he attended the tennis week. The newspapers solemnly reported about this constant presence of royalty. The press had a lingering desire to make everything associated with the royal court more fantastic than it was, not least the quality of the King's tennis game. The mandatory praise of "Mr. G.'s exquisite lobs" and his "excellent understanding of the game" heaped ridicule on tennis and continued to stifle the sport's development.

The best players were always expected to make themselves available when the King called. The most successful of the Swedish tennis players during the '30s, and the first-ever of international class, Kalle Schröder, had won indoor championships in Germany, France, and England. Between his trips abroad, he was often called to the King's summer residence in Särö to act as doubles partner to Mr. G. On one such occasion, Schröder hit his partner in the back with a serve, causing Mr. G. to tumble forward and lose his dentures. The monarch bent down to pick them up, while Schröder bounced the ball at the baseline. When Mr. G. had picked up his dentures, he didn't seem to know what to do with them. "Put them in your pocket, your Majesty," yelled Schröder.

Lennart Bergelin had learned tennis in his hometown, Alingsås. There, he used to hit against the kitchen wall with rackets he'd borrowed from his father, to the ubiquitous background noise of rattling pots and crushed plates. In the summer of 1938, Bergelin traveled with his father the 30 miles to Särö to play a doubles match against the King and his partner, Consul General Nils Åhlund. Mr. G. and Åhlund came out victorious.

But soon, the King would have more important things on his plate. Nazi Germany was becoming an increasing threat to the European peace, and the King would get involved as one of the lead actors in a diplomatic tennis conflict that even threatened to jeopardize Sweden's safety.

In the spring of 1939, one of Mr. G.'s doubles partners, the Davis Cup player Curt Östberg, urged the king to grant the German tennis star Gottfried von Cramm protected status in Sweden. Along with Fred Perry and Don Budge, the baron von Cramm was the best tennis player of the '30s, a two-time winner at Roland Garros and a three-time Wimbledon finalist. But above all, he'd become the most respected name in the sport, beloved in Germany and admired in the rest of the world. One reason was his appearance; von Cramm, with his dark blond slicked-back hair and clean features, was considered more gorgeous than the movie stars of his time. Moreover, he played more elegantly than anyone had ever done before, and he was tennis' biggest gentleman. The Nazis realized that, if they could persuade von Cramm to join the party, it would be a PR triumph like no other. After one of the finals at Wimbledon, Joachim von Ribbentrop, who was then the German ambassador to London and would later become the country's foreign minister, approached von Cramm and offered him membership in the party. Von Cramm rejected the offer and called Hitler a buffoon. Shortly thereafter, the speaker of the German parliament, Hermann Göring, called von Cramm to inform him that he'd settled all of von Cramm's property loans in Jewish banks.

"Now you're completely free," said Göring.

"That's even more reason not to join your party," responded von Cramm.

Von Cramm came from a well-to-do aristocratic family. He loathed the Nazis. In that respect, he resembled the Swedish king, who was friendly with Germany but despised Hitler. As early as the spring of 1933, Gustaf V had cut short his tennis vacation at the Riviera and traveled to Berlin to scold the German dictator for his Jewish policies. Gustaf V invited the German leaders to lunch at the Swedish delegation, where he explained to Hitler that the way the Nazis treated the Jews was sure to become a black mark on Germany's reputation. A Swedish minister named Wirsén eavesdropped behind the door and reported that he could hear Hitler raise his voice and bang his fists on the table. To emphasize his position in the matter, Gustaf V paired up with a German Jewish player in the tennis match that followed the luncheon. The player, Daniel Prenn, was the world's No. 6 at the time. The opposing doubles team was headed by von Cramm.

Prenn was later suspended from German tennis because of his Jewish ancestry and went into exile. The consequence for the sport was a weaker German Davis Cup team, but Hitler's *Anschluss* policy compensated for the damage through the annexation of Austria. In 1937, Germany again had a competitive team. Specifically, Germany had von Cramm, who'd played brilliant tennis for several years. In 1937, Germany, under the Nazi swastika flag, was on the threshold of finally bringing home the Davis Cup, the most prestigious tennis title at the time. One serious obstacle remained: the United States. The match was going to be played on grass at Wimbledon in July.

By now, the Nazis' interest in the baron von Cramm as a PR figure had made a 180-degree turn. Von Cramm socialized with Jews, he was married to a Jewish woman, and he'd come to the realization that he was bisexual. As early as 1933, he'd entered into a relationship with a male Jewish actor in Berlin. In the eyes of Hitler, von Cramm had become symbolic of the "Jewish-inspired, decadent lifestyle" that the Nazis sought to extinguish. Von Cramm understood that his days were numbered. Only as long as he continued to win on the world's biggest tennis stages could he count on the Nazis to hold off arresting him.

During his doubles matches with Mr. G., Curt Östberg had not only presented his opinion to the Swedish king, he'd also realized that Gustaf V liked the tennis baron and was trying to arrange for a resolution. During a practice session with von Cramm, Östberg even told him: "If things get too hot in Germany, you can always come to us." But for Gustaf V, this wasn't an easy decision. He knew that the Nazis assumed that neutral Sweden, with its German-friendly royal family, wouldn't dare or want to challenge Germany's politics. Perhaps extending political asylum to the world-famous superstar and anti-Nazi von Cramm would be seen as a provocation?

Gustaf V didn't go to Wimbledon to watch the match between Germany and the USA, but he was able to follow it via on-site reporters. Leading the American team was Don Budge, the son of a truck driver from Oakland. The redhead Budge was a legend in the making. He'd just won Wimbledon, and the following year he would become the first player to complete a Grand Slam. Budge saw von Cramm as his biggest role model and best friend, but he'd crushed the German in the Wimbledon final two weeks earlier.

During the Davis Cup match, English royalty enjoyed nice conversations with Nazi ministers. On the court, both von Cramm and Budge won their first matches easily. Then, each country won one match. The two stars were to face off in the decisive fifth match, and everyone knew what was at stake. The players walked toward the court, both wearing cream-colored flannel pants; von Cramm also wore a red-and-white blazer. Queen Mary sat in the royal box, surrounded by 15,000 spectators. Not far from her sat Joachim von Ribbentrop.

As the players approached the court, a young locker room attendant came running and announced that von Cramm had a phone call. The official escorting the players muttered that there was no time for that, the Queen was waiting for the match to start. But the baron smiled and said that maybe it was important. Budge later said he overheard von Cramm say: *"Ja, mein Führer."*

What did Hitler say?

Von Cramm was pale as a ghost as he stepped out on the court, and he started the match furiously, as if playing for his life. His style of play was the most elegant ever seen, exactly according to the instruction manual. In particular, his serve was very difficult to handle. Von Cramm won the first and second set. Budge later wrote: "I played as well as ever, but the fewer mistakes I made, the fewer he made, too."

Budge's best stroke was his fierce backhand, which helped the American win the third and fourth sets; however, in the fifth, he found himself trailing. Bill Tilden, who now served as Germany's Davis Cup coach, formed a circle with his thumb and index finger and pointed to von Ribbentrop in the stands, signaling that the victory was complete. Then Budge began stepping into the court and taking von Cramm's serves early on the rise. Budge hit a couple of amazing backhands, and long games followed. Ahead 7–6, Budge hit a diving return off a difficult shot from von Cramm; the ball somehow went over the net. Budge had won the match.

The German baron walked up to the net and congratulated Budge with a sunny smile as he said in perfect English: "Don, this was absolutely the greatest match I've ever played, and I'm so happy it was against you, whom I like so much. Congratulations!"

So, von Cramm had lost. He realized that now he was forced to stay abroad. That summer and fall, he played tennis across America, from New York to Los Angeles. From Los Angeles, he boarded a ship to Australia, where he played tennis and continued to express his disdain for Hitler. Nevertheless, in the spring of 1938, he returned to Germany and was immediately arrested at his family home in Bodenburg. He admitted to his relationship with Prenn but said it had gone no further than masturbation. He was incarcerated in a prison in Berlin. The Nazi newspapers covered neither the trial nor the verdict; however, the *New York Times* published the news, which quickly spread across the world. His mother went to visit him in prison, and von Cramm said he was going to commit suicide. Don Budge organized a campaign to free von Cramm. Helen Wills and 29 others signed the petition, which was sent to Hitler. Gustaf V pleaded with the dictator to treat the baron well.

Finally, in the spring of 1939, von Cramm was released and traveled to Stockholm. With Sweden as his base, he was planning to play at Wimbledon, but the organizers said he wasn't welcome, referring to the fact that he had a conviction for homosexuality. Von Cramm was still in Sweden at the outbreak of the war, but he returned to Germany in 1940 and was immediately drafted as a private soldier. In the summer of 1941, the Nazi regime realized it could easily dispose of one of its most famous critics by having von Cramm serve in the military campaign against the Soviet Union, as a machine gunner on the front line.

A short time after the campaign, Gustaf V wrote a letter to Hitler in which he praised the German dictator for his war successes and wished him luck in the fight against "the Bolshevik plague." The Swedish government prohibited the king from mailing the letter, but Gustaf V was defiant and did so anyway.

The king's willful political act irritated people, but few interpreted it as Nazi sympathies. In retrospect, the wording has been interpreted as an expression of concern over the advances by the Soviet Union in the Baltic countries and Finland. In his autobiography, Swedish politician Tage Erlander writes that he didn't appreciate, but could understand, the king's role in a decision that was made at this time to allow the German divisions to pass through Sweden to reach Norway and Finland.

In the winter of 1942, von Cramm was outside Moscow. He was suffering from severe frostbite and was sent to a hospital in Warsaw. From there, he was released under unclear circumstances, according to historians, because the Nazis suspected he was conspiring with the enemy. Von Cramm arrived in Sweden the following year, as a guest of the King. A short time after von Cramm's arrival, the syndicalist newspaper *Arbetaren* raised a question that spread in articles across the world in a time of feverish speculations on who worked as a mole and for whom: Had the Germans in fact allowed von Cramm to escape? Was his status as an anti-Nazi refugee noble or rather a part of a deeper rooted and larger political game, directed by the German-friendly Swedish king and anti-Nazi aristocrats in Germany, with the aim of reducing hatred against Germany at the end phase of the war? Was von Cramm only a pawn in a game?

The baron traveled back and forth between Sweden and his mansion in Bodenburg, where he conspired with underground resistance groups on plans to assassinate Hitler. He moved in the fringes of a group that carried out a failed attack on the Führer in 1944. In Bodenburg, he once saved an American pilot who'd been shot down nearby.

"Why are you helping me?" asked the pilot.

"Because I once played tennis with Don Budge."

"Ah," said the pilot. "Then you must be Gottfried von Cramm!"

In terms of the development of tennis in Sweden, three matches—the Lenglen-Willis match in Cannes in 1926, Wills Moody's exhibition match in Stockholm in 1932, and the German-American final at Wimbledon in 1937—reflect Gustaf V's role as a matchmaker between the isolated Sweden and the sport's new international elite players. Although for the Swedish elite players at the time, these relations were not of much help. Rather, the effects would come retroactively, when the young Swedish players who'd become interested in tennis and needed to venture out to gain international experience after the war could take advantage of Mr. G.'s network.

The very best Swedes were still called on to play matches with the king. In 1946, Bergelin was clearly the best of the Swedish players, while the king at 88 years old was frighteningly skinny. Now these two men were standing yet again on the same tennis court, this time at the Kungliga Tennis Hall in Stockholm, and this time on the same side of the net. On the other side were the Davis Cup player Torsten Örnberg and an attorney named Grönfors, who had a good serve. Bergelin suddenly and unexpectedly hit a ball that happened to strike Mr. G. in a sensitive spot, or like Bergelin would later put it when he relayed the story, "the family jewels." The king's pantlegs started to shake, and his body crumbled. Bergelin rushed forward and was able to catch his doubles partner in his arms just in time. The king's face was white as a sheet. The royal court physician came running, furious. Bergelin thought: *The King will die and I'll get the blame.*

But the king caught his breath, stood up, and asked: "Have you ever been hit on the cock by a ball?"

"Yes, Your Majesty," said Bergelin.

Those who are looking for firsthand recollections from this era and simultaneously seek the deepest roots to the '70s and '80s Swedish golden era in tennis will end up in the SALK hall in the Stockholm neighborhood of Alvik. Here, we find Percy Rosberg standing on one of the courts. He was born on one of the days when Helen Wills Moody visited Stockholm to brighten the life of the rich. Percy is 85 years old today. He's the man who convinced Björn Borg to keep his two-handed backhand and Stefan Edberg to abandon his, and he's still the person whose help everyone covets. In 2013, when Joachim "Pim-Pim" Johansson was making a comeback and surprisingly won a few matches at the Stockholm Open, it was with Percy he'd worked up his game plan. And when Björn Borg trains at Janne Lundqvist's tennis hall a few kilometers from the SALK hall, Percy goes there to watch.

Now a tanned girl strides up to Percy from the courts. She's unhappy with her serve.

"I have a hard time placing it," she says.

"But your motion is totally fine," says Percy. "You let your elbow rest down low. So many players lift their arm way up above their shoulders when they're just getting ready, but no fool would throw a ball like that, how would you generate any power?"

"But I didn't hit it well."

"It might be because your ball toss is wrong. There are five spots where you can hit it, and if you get that wrong, then you won't get the maximal effect of your motion, you'll have to bend backwards and that's unnatural. That's what you are doing wrong, and it's easy to change. But the service motion was really fine, like a damn butterfly lifting off from a flower."

Percy grew up with a father who was a mason and a mother who had a chronic skeletal disease. One of their other children had died. Percy was their eleventh, and he had to fight for space with eight brothers and a sister in a small house in the Stockholm suburb Norra Ängby. In Södra Ängby at this time, a major construction project was in its beginning phases; beautiful villas were being built for the most prominent people of the new welfare state. Every morning, the mason master Herman Rosberg rode his bicycle to Södra Ängby to build fireplaces, to see to it that his family had food on the table every day. But there were no signs that Percy would become a tennis player, let alone a tennis coach for players ranked number one in the world and successful business bigwigs.

"My mom and dad didn't even throw a beach ball to each other," says Percy. "Tennis was the rich man's sport."

Percy would follow his older brother to the clay courts about a hundred meters from their home. He was going to watch when the older kids played, but his brother's partner never showed up, and Percy got the chance to jump in and hit some balls with his brother.

"That lit my fire. I liked tennis because it was an individual sport, you're left to your own devices. I quickly decided to try to start playing in a club."

There weren't that many clubs around yet, but SALK, *Stockholms Allmänna Tennisklubb*, which had been founded as an antipode to KLTK, had built a tennis hall in Alvik.

"In August, SALK held tryouts for tennis juniors. I was 13 when I tried out—today, nobody that old would ever be accepted. Nowadays you're supposed to start at six or seven. But I was accepted to the club and got to practice just like players do today, three or four players on a court with one coach."

Percy Rosberg quickly became skilled, but he was too young to play against Gustaf V. However, his close friend Curt Östberg was not.

"There was a line of people who wanted to partner with 'V-Gurra,'" says Percy. "He is the world's only undefeated tennis player. 'Just don't beat the king' was what other players were told as they set out to play him."

Percy describes Gustaf V as a "damn shuffler." As for his own game, Percy's was smooth and technical, and he became the Swedish junior champion.

"Then you got to go and play at Wimbledon and Roland Garros. Everyone who won the Swedish championships in their age group was allowed to go there. I began playing internationally. When you returned home between tournaments, you had to work and save up for the travel and accommodations. I worked everywhere. As a mail carrier at the post office in Traneberg. This was great, because I could practice in the afternoon, as soon as I got off work. Then I worked at Slazenger, I mailed stuff from there, from their warehouse at Skeppsbron. For a while I delivered tea, too, and I worked at SAS at the Bromma airport. It's not like today, when kids expect the parents to pay."

"I traveled alone, by train and bus. Sometimes I was joined by the Danish champion. This was in postwar Europe. Germany lay in complete shambles from the bombs. There was no talk of prize money. You won things, like a toaster, a tennis racket, or a nice tennis bag. I had a hell of a lot of toasters."

In the SALK hall, sometime in 1949, Percy was introduced to Gottfried von Cramm.

"Curt Östberg brought us together. The Führer down there didn't like von Cramm, and von Cramm had continued to come to Sweden after the war. 'V-Gurra' liked him, von Cramm had such a great spirit and attitude. And if anyone played tennis according to the rulebook, it was von Cramm. He offered me to stay with him at his estate in Bodenburg, when I traveled in Europe. It was incredibly nice. I have a framed picture of the estate in my garage at home. I became friends with von Cramm.

"Me and Bertil Blomqvist, a tennis friend from SALK, we went down there shortly after my first meeting with von Cramm. We stayed with him ten or fourteen days. He probably looked at us as damn good sparring partners. His game was beautiful, he had a great eye for tennis. His ground strokes were flat, clean, and straight. But I'd be exaggerating if I said he developed me when it came to my strokes. That's not really how we practiced. He let us practice serves, especially first serves. He put handkerchiefs in different corners of the service box, and we're supposed to hit them with hard first serves, not spin second serves. We stayed on the upper floor of his mansion, which had a moat around it, I believe. There were two women in the house, who cleaned, cooked, and took care of his clothes. I noticed that he liked me a lot, and I guess he looked at my body. He became fond of me, but it didn't bother me. Sometimes I noticed that he watched me more than the ball, out of the corner of his eyes, so I became close to him. But he was very nice, and generous. When I traveled around Europe, I didn't have a lot of money, but he made sure that I could stay for free at places he arranged."

When Rosberg began competing in the elite division, he was often accompanied by Torsten Johansson, who was the No. 2 player in Sweden at the time. Johansson had a big, nice Volvo, in which the two tennis players and Johansson's wife, Lise, traveled to tournaments all over Europe. Many tournaments were played on the French Riviera—in Cannes, Nice, Menton, Bourgette—where distances were short between the various towns.

But the best player in Sweden at the time was still Lennart Bergelin, who was seven years older than Percy. Bergelin traveled to Germany, Monte Carlo, Milan, and Wiesbaden in the first car he ever owned, a Horch, later in a burgundy Lancia, and finally in a black Ford convertible. He was often joined by young players like Sven Davidson, Staffan Stockenberg, and Bengt Axelsson. Bergelin reached the international elite level. He was a new tennis type, not at all slick and styled. His pants were ill-fitting, his shirt resembled a shapeless undershirt, and his demeanor resembled Huckleberry Finn's. He was like a thundercloud on the court. It was not unusual for umpires to have to flip a coin to decide who'd call Bergelin's matches. Nobody wanted to risk being the target of his bad temper. Maybe his popularity stemmed from this, or maybe it was his commitment to the sport. There existed, wrote the magazine *Tennistidningen*, "a strange contrast between [Bergelin's] volatile temper and the slow soft rhythm in his work with the ball."

When he won the French Championhips doubles title together with the Czech Jaroslav Drobny in 1948, Lennart Bergelin became Sweden's first Grand Slam winner. That same year, he advanced to the Wimbledon quarterfinals and, in 1950, he received *Svenska Dagbladet*'s award *Bragdguldet*, thanks to his win over the Australian top player, Frank Sedgman, in a rainy Davis Cup match on grass, in which Bergelin played the decisive set barefoot. After he lost the Swedish Championships finals to Sven Davidson in Skrea Strand in 1955, Bergelin refused to shower and sat down in his car and drove straight home to Stockholm promising to never again touch a tennis racket. He was by far Sweden's most popular tennis player. But playing tennis on an amateur level was not for those who weren't from privileged circumstances, which Suzanne Lenglen had already noted three decades earlier. Bergelin's background was humble but stable. For him, what was important was how he was going to support himself and tackle life after his tennis career. He was 30 years old and had received offers to turn pro but had rejected them all. He simply believed it was time for him to do something else. He had a family to support and began selling scooters.

The discussions about whether tennis players should be allowed to earn money from their sport had become more prevalent within Swedish tennis in the '50s. Sven Davidson, who with his win over Bergelin in 1955 took over the spot as the country's best player, didn't think that the sport should be professionalized. Davidson suspected that the sport would suffer if the amateur rules were abolished. He argued that all the volunteer umpires, coaches, and groundskeepers wouldn't find the same joy in tennis if the players were paid.

Davidson reached the French Championships final three straight years. He lost the first, and in his second, in 1956, the Australian Lew Hoad waited. Hoad had won the doubles title on Saturday, gone out and partied that night, and come home drunk as a skunk around six in the morning. Meanwhile, Davidson had prepared in his usual manner, with nine hours of sleep and a combined breakfast/lunch consisting of a large piece of well-done meat with lots of veggies and a potato or two, all washed down with a Ramlösa and topped off with a fruit salad. The Swede then took a nice walk before he went back to bed to read a little, think about the match, and rest. Before his match, he took his usual shower, stretched, carefully changed into his tennis clothes, and stepped out onto the court. In his bag, he carried a jug of tea with sugar and a bottle of fresh water.

As for Hoad, he gulped down a few liters of water, took a taxi to the tennis stadium, and proceeded to demolish Davidson in three straight sets.

Hoad and his countryman, Ken Rosewall, were superior in the world of tennis. In 1957, the two Australians turned professional and went on to completely dominate the American pro tour, along with Pancho Gonzalez. It was clear that the pros were several classes better than the amateurs at Wimbledon and Forest Hills.

Thus, in 1957, the road was open for Sven Davidson, who at the French Championships brought home Sweden's first title in a Grand Slam tournament. The following year, Davidson and Ulf Schmidt won the Wimbledon doubles final.

"We had to stay at the Swedish Embassy the second week, because we hadn't made any hotel reservations. We never thought we'd advance that far," says Ulf Schmidt 55 years later.

Percy Rosberg established himself as the fourth-best player in Sweden.

"There were no ranking points at the time, but I was the fourth man on the Davis Cup team. The three above me were Sven Davidson, Ulf Schmidt, and Janne Lundqvist. I often beat them in practice and was sometimes selected to play, but I always said: 'No, my mind is too weak, I don't have their winner instinct, I get too nervous.' But I was good at doubles, had good feet and a good volley, so I jumped in sometimes when we'd already won the match."

Percy's active career ended in 1958.

"I received money under the table and lost my amateur status. I was 25 years old and not allowed to play anymore. But I'd traipsed around and played for so long and it all cost money, so I was almost just relieved when I was forced to stop playing. It was fine, I received an offer to be head coach at SALK instead."

In the early '60s, tennis was still a minor sport in Sweden, despite the successes. The popular fitness movement was contributing to making the Swedish people exercise. Sports fields and facilities, where people could play soccer, run, ski, ice skate, play bandy, and swim, were popping up everywhere.

The reputation of tennis as a rich man's sport proved difficult to wash off. And it was indeed an expensive sport: rackets, balls, shoes, clothes, court fees, club member fees, and traveling all had to be paid for. During the '50s, the number of club players increased from 22,000 to over 25,000. In 1950, there were 345 tennis clubs in Sweden, and ten years later, there were 440.

There had been an increase, but compared to all other gains during these record years, tennis had in fact lost in terms of luminosity.

Sports researchers commonly talk about patterns of factors that are necessary for a sport in a certain country to reach lasting success in international competitions. They mention factors such as tradition, availability, access to educated instructors and coaches, sports idols as role models, access to sponsors and financial support, media attention, and initiatives on the state and local levels.

In Sweden in the early '60s, it was really only the tradition factor that was fulfilled. Of Davidson, Bergelin, and Kalle Schröder, none had achieved idol status. Bergelin and Ulf Schmidt could have become sport heroes, but it wasn't until 1962 that a true Swedish tennis hero appeared. He was extremely gifted and talented with the ball, as well as uniquely charismatic, and when the Swedish television broadcast a tennis match live for the first time, things started to fall into place.

Jan-Erik Lundqvist's breakthrough was expected, as he was considered the greatest talent Swedish tennis had ever produced.

"We lived near a tennis court; that's why I started playing, I was seven or eight," he says 51 years later. "I started to hit against walls. From that moment on, I played about two hours a day and kept in shape with outdoor activities, rope jumping, and all kinds of ball sports. But I was just nuts about tennis."

Jan-Erik became "Janne" with the Swedish people when, in front of a million TV viewers, he won both his singles matches and was one half of the doubles team in Sweden's Davis Cup match against Italy, the best team in Europe. The doubles match became extremely exciting and went to a decisive fifth set. The Italians, Nicola Pietrangeli and Orlando Sirola, were an experienced doubles team that had won 33 straight Davis Cup doubles matches. Nobody expected the Swedish pair, Janne Lundqvist and Uffe Schmidt, to have a chance to win. The Italians were a step ahead in the final stages of the match, as the audience was torn between hope and despair. On several occasions, Italy was only two points away from victory, and the match seemed a lost cause. But the Swedes somehow managed to escape from trouble and win the final set, 9–7. The entire tennis stadium in Båstad exploded in joy. On their couches in front of the TV, the general public learned for the first time the complex rules and scorekeeping of tennis. And more than anything, they found out how exciting and rich a tennis match could be. The sport began its transformation from royal pastime to the people's sport.

With his open personality and a game that was light and playful, almost magical, Janne was perfect for television. Soon, he was ranked as one of the Top 10 players in the world, and he won some 42 international tournaments. But in Sweden, the Davis Cup was the biggest and most important event. That's where heroes were made.

Sweden advanced deep in the tournament in 1963 and 1964. Both years, the team lost in the final rounds after being evenly matched with the very best teams in the world. It was all televised. The newspapers published tennis stories on their front pages. Janne Lundqvist had become an intelligent, well-spoken, and recognizable role model, who led Swedish tennis into something sports researchers call the success spiral. The idol made the sport known. Young kids started to play. Municipalities began building more courts, but it was still not enough. In Lund, tennis players slept in tents outside the local tennis court several nights for the chance to snap up season passes when they were released. In many towns, the tennis season was extended by enclosing outdoor courts with inflated tents. Private companies became interested in sponsorships. The clubs could afford to employ more and better-trained coaches. At the end of the '60s, the number of clubs had doubled, as had the clubs' total memberships. Moreover, in the spirit of the Swedish popular movement, the clubs were open for all. This created a situation that was unique in the world of tennis in the '60s and '70s. Almost all of Sweden's youth who wanted to try the sport of tennis had a chance to do so at the local tennis club, which usually also offered some form of organized tennis training. In less than ten years, Sweden created a huge recruitment base, unique in the world of tennis.

In the years that followed Janne's and Uffe's Davis Cup victories, one tennis program after another was launched. How could tennis become part of the school system? Become a sport that could be introduced during regular gym classes? Sketches were drawn up showing how school gymnasiums could be expanded to make room for tennis. At the Norra Latin high school in Stockholm, a gym teacher built special ball walls that could be hung from the lattice ladders, and modern ball machines were installed. Hundreds of students at Norra Latin were able to learn the fundamentals of tennis during gym class. Those who showed an interest received extra instruction and training from Curt Östberg and Percy Rosberg.

The sport's popularity in numbers seemed secure, but how could it produce a new top player after Janne Lundqvist, who'd retired from regular competitive tennis in the mid-'60s?

"Back then, it was considered irresponsible to invest in sports," says Janne Lundqvist. "'So how will you finance that?' was always the question. My mom and dad couldn't afford it. I got a job in marketing at Facit, and then I came up with this idea of running a tennis facility. You had to support yourself, and you couldn't do that by playing tennis alone."

In 1965, the grocery store clerk Rune Borg won a table tennis tournament in Södertälje, and the prize he received was a tennis racket. He gave the racket to his nine-year-old son, Björn, who, once he had his racket, immediately ran over to the Södertälje tennis club. But even in a distinct blue-collar town like Södertälje, the tennis club was completely booked. After having watched Janne and Uffe play in the Davis Cup, everyone wanted to play tennis. Instead, Björn would hit against the garage door in the rental complex, hour after hour.

"When I was standing there hitting the ball against the garage door, I dreamed of two things: to play the Davis Cup and Wimbledon. The main draw at Wimbledon. That was it . . . to have the chance to compete against the best. The garage door was my opponent and I could stay there forever, it was my thing. I was Sweden, the garage wall was the USA," says Borg.

The rules at the garage were just as simple as the tennis game that Björn developed. If he could keep the ball in play for more than ten shots, then he won the point, and Sweden won. If he missed, the point went to the USA.

"My hero back then was Rod Laver. I played him a lot of times in my dreams, in the Wimbledon finals and things like that. But when I played the Davis Cup against the wall, I was always Janne."

Eventually, a spot opened up in the club's junior program. Every morning at seven o'clock, Björn would stand outside the fence waiting for the courts to open. Only when it became dark outside did his parents come to get him.

"The biggest thing was when Janne and Uffe came to the Södertälje Tennis Club up in the park and I was a ball boy. I had seen them on TV, but then they came to Södertälje of all places, and it was a great experience to get to see them play. I guess I said hello and asked for autographs, and I got to meet them. That was huge for me. That was the beginning, and I had an incredible amount of interest. I wanted to become a tennis player, simple as that."

Björn also played hockey. He played center for Södertälje SK, which at that time was one of the best clubs in the country. But tennis was more fun.

"Tennis is lonely. I always liked that. It was something you did by yourself, something individual. I was proud of what I did on my own, because it was just me accomplishing something."

The tennis association assigned Percy Rosberg the task to travel around the country to the tennis clubs to see if there might be any talents out there. He says:

"Back then, there was something called Davis Cup schools. Every year twelve juniors, district players, came to Båstad. They were the best from each district, handpicked. I'd already seen many of them on my travels around the country. On one such trip, I came to Södertälje. The guys were good there. One of them was Leif Johansson, who was really good, Joachim "Pim-Pim" Johansson's dad. But the club was small, and to fill up the group with twelve players, we had to pick up a small kid. And I hit with them all, but this little runt, he was just eleven, he was so annoying, he hit everything back. He never missed a bloody shot, he had the attitude that if I hit a ball, he was going to hit it back, he wasn't going to miss."

As Borg recounts, "One of the older kids was sick, so I got the chance to hit a few balls with Percy for half an hour. He's Sweden's best technique coach of all time. He saw my forehand, which was unique, I hit it with a western grip and a loose wrist, a result of my dad's ping-pong influences. But Percy saw me and understood that this kid is pretty good, despite his strange strokes. There were many who were better, but he saw something. We made a connection then, and Percy told my parents and Södertälje Tennis Club that this kid should probably come over and play for SALK."

AROUND THE GLOBE IN TENNIS SHORTS

"I wasn't surprised that I lost, but that the best players were so good, they played at a level I barely knew existed."
—BJÖRN BORG

Every day when the bells rang at school, the boy left his friends and trotted over to the train station. The commuter train was always waiting. The trip to Stockholm's Central Station took a little over an hour, and from there he followed the stream of people to the subway. When the subway train emerged from the tunnel into the daylight, they were on the Traneberg Bridge, from which he could see out over the city. But more than anything, as the train rolled into the Alvik station, he saw the SALK tennis hall's rounded roof on the other side of the street. He grabbed his large bag and exited the train.

Björn always arrived to practice with plenty of time to spare. He was already there, 45 minutes before the scheduled practice time. He taped his fingers, fiddled with his rackets, and prepared mentally. When Percy arrived, they started to hit—the thirty-five-year-old coach with his classical game and Björn with his odd forehand grip and a backhand that brought to mind a slapshot in hockey more than a tennis stroke.

"Is this how you want to play?"

"Yes, I like to play like this," said Björn.

"It's a stroke that seems a bit odd."

"I know, but it feels good to me."

If the backhand was odd, the forehand was an extreme, a deviation, a ping-pong loop that looked like an ambush on the ball. Björn lifted his racket high above his shoulder before bringing it back in a circular motion and striking the ball. Percy had seen Rod Laver play with a lot of topspin. People at the SALK hall talked about Laver's topspin forehand as the biggest change the game had seen since the '40s, when Jack Kramer came up with "The Big Game," which was a hard serve followed by a quick attack at the net. The Big Game was still considered the best way to win tennis matches, despite Laver's great success.

All this eleven-year-old did was hit his strokes with topspin. He created a huge rotation on the ball, which sailed high over the net and gave Björn a great margin for error.

"Snow will stick to the ball up there," yelled Percy as he hit a low shot back.

After rallying with Percy for a while, Björn played with the other kids, who were three years older or more. Many of them were inspired by Janne Lundqvist's game, aggressive and with an early ball strike. Unexpected attacks to the net followed by slices, drop shots, and angled volley shots that landed on Björn's side of the net. Every now and then a lob was thrown in when the little guy dared come up to the net. Björn had no chance against the older kids; he got beat badly, time after time.

Björn's dad, Rune, used to show up toward the end of practice, straight from work. He'd drive his car up to Stockholm. Most of the time, he hung out in the lobby. Sometimes he sat in the bleachers.

On Fridays, there was cardio training. Attendance and exercises were marked with an X on a board. Björn was the only one with a check mark in every box. By the time Rune and Björn returned home to the apartment in Södertälje, it was after ten o'clock, and Björn crawled into bed.

Other gifted kids from modest backgrounds had been offered the opportunity to try out for SALK. Rolf Norberg, later a Davis Cup player and Swedish doubles champion, was living with his grandparents in a cramped apartment on the south side of Stockholm. His dad had walked out when he was little, and his mom wasn't able to raise him on her own. Rolf had discovered the joy of tennis on the courts near his home, and after he won a few youth tournaments, SALK invited him for a tryout.

"I'd never gone that far on the subway and I knew I couldn't do it on my own," says Norberg. "But luckily, at the time for my tryout I had a tennis buddy I could go with. He played first. I was still waiting for my turn, but when my buddy was done, he didn't feel like waiting around. I had no choice, I had to leave with him and missed my chance to try out. I didn't play tennis for a year. The next fall, I was accepted. Sometimes I wonder what had happened if I'd have started a year earlier, but of course that's something I'll never know."

Björn enjoyed the long train rides:

"My classmates probably didn't know what I was doing. They knew I played tennis but not much more. This new life, me taking the train from Södertälje to Alvik every day and my parents picking me up in the car after work, they had no clue about those things. I did go to school, and I saw everyone there, but my heart was in tennis. I just wanted to get better as a tennis player. Nobody needed to nag me, or say, 'you should go out and play tennis.' When I was sitting there on the train, I was doing exactly what I wanted to do. I saw my friends when I played hockey. But I had less and less time for that after I started playing with SALK."

The group The 5th Dimension, in the musical "Hair," sang of the start of the "age of Aquarius." The music spread around world from a stage Off-Broadway in 1967 and 1968. The musical tells the story of a bohemian "tribe" in New York City that resisted authorities, fought against the Vietnam war draft, and let their hair grow long. The antiauthoritarian wave set down roots in Sweden, too. It was no longer a given that you had to subject yourself to institutions like family, church, military, and school. Sexual morality was being dissolved, and you no longer needed to address another person formally. In the age of Aquarius, a modern and headstrong tennis instructor like Percy Rosberg could balance his pupils' needs with his own ideas of how the classical strokes should be taught. Occasionally, people from the Swedish Tennis Association would stop by. They spoke with Percy and asked him to teach Björn to hit his backhand one-handed.

"Are you sure this is how you want to play?" he asked Björn again.

"It feels good to me."

Percy saw what the kid's game was about. Regardless of the look of his backhand, Björn could use it to place the ball exactly where he wanted it to go. And wasn't that the objective of the game? And he hit the ball so damn hard, too. Percy noted the look in Björn's eyes. The kid seemed obsessed with getting the ball back over the net, he had a will to fight, to run, to hit like Percy had never seen before. *Grinder-tennis*, thought Percy. *Not much style to it, but things happen.*

On Saturdays, SALK had junior hour, and Rune would give Björn a ride there. The hour was between 4 and 5 p.m. Between 3 and 4, the court was reserved for the banker Mats Hasselqvist, chairman of the Davis Cup committee, and his tennis buddies, among them Hans-Åke Sturén. They knew they could play an extra 15 minutes, since the juniors always arrived 15 minutes late. But this spring, a long-haired kid suddenly started arriving 15 minutes early and sat himself down and waited next to the court. As soon as the bell rang, the kid walked in and began practicing his serves.

"Who's that kid?" asked Sturén.

"He trains here every evening now," said Hasselqvist. "His dad usually sits in the lobby sleeping."

The tennis hall was its own universe. People connected through forehands and backhands. Sweaty bodies in white shorts looked for rhythm in their ball toss. Only on rare occasions was the silence broken by a controlled expletive, or a "good play" when someone hit a successful passing shot. The only thing on people's minds was the game.

But this spring, it was difficult for Hasselqvist to completely shut out the rest of the world. In the city, demonstrations in support of the people of Vietnam seemed to be carried out constantly. Activists stood with collection boxes for Viet Cong outside every government-operated liquor store. Aside from Vietnam, there were also the campaigns against South Africa's and Rhodesia's apartheid regimes. In Rhodesia, Prime Minister Ian Smith had ordered the hanging of three black political opponents. Rhodesia was a country, like South Africa, where racism had been written into the constitution, exactly like in Hitler's Germany 30 years earlier. Rhodesia was the subject of an international trade embargo. It was banned by the Olympic Committee and had received a "no thanks" response to its request to participate in the Olympic Games in Mexico City later that year. Shortly thereafter, Hasselqvist had announced that Sweden welcomed Rhodesia to Sweden to play a Davis Cup match. That was the result of the draw. Hasselqvist argued that sports were sports. If you had entered into a competition, you participated, regardless of the opponent. Otherwise, you risked disqualification from participating the following year. And that was out of the question.

But Hasselqvist didn't need think hard to know there would be protests. The tennis association decided to move the match from the Kungliga Tennis Hall in the politically charged Stockholm to the quiet seaside resort town of Båstad, where the season wasn't yet in full swing.

As soon as the move was announced, people began applying for permits to protest against the match. The police held off giving out demonstration permits. A group of students from Uppsala—future lawyers, political and social scientists, young men and women, Swedish-born and African—were near graduation but still decided to buy a bus and drive down to the tennis metropolis. Most came from well-established families and considered themselves civil idealists and anarchists. They were educated and well-read. When the news of the tennis match in Båstad reached them, they could relate it to a thought expressed by Swedish writer Ivar Lo-Johansson in one of his books from the '30s: that sport, despite its many great characteristics, was harmful to humans and society, that top-level elite sports had mangled its own ideals. Elite sports seemed to hold a dangerous belief that it could disregard all other moral aspects except for fair play, that it didn't need to assume a moral responsibility. The middle-class students from Uppsala planned on converging with students from Lund and a local priest outside the arena. They knew that youth sections from the Liberal Party and the Social Democratic Party were also going to demonstrate.

Meanwhile, another trip to Båstad was also being organized in Stockholm, at the Café Marx on Kungsgatan 84. The café served as an information central for all large demonstrations in Stockholm. During the last few years, the conference room, called the Lenin Hall, had seen Vietnam activists, Black Panthers, draft dodgers, urban environmental activists, Trotskyists, independent theater companies, Chinese ambassadors, and immigrant Finnish Stalinists plan in detail demonstrations and prepare thousands of slogans and banners. The most important banner hung on the wall above the conference table, proud and red: "CRUSH CAPITALISM." The gathering to discuss Båstad was led by well-known members of the FNL movement. After a long discussion, they decided to go to Båstad; alas, not to demonstrate, but to actually stop the match. Someone had learned that a tennis court could be destroyed by throwing a mixture of eggs and cooking oil on the rust-colored clay.

Meanwhile, the mood in the Uppsala students' bus was upbeat and jovial. One of the young men stood up and provided continuous status updates.

BJÖRN BORG AND THE SUPER-SWEDES

The bus made a stop in Jönköping, where the young men and women had lunch at the governor's residence. It was the home of the parents of one of the students; however, the father, the governor himself, was not present as his wife fed the students. A few hours later, the students settled in at one of Sweden's most exclusive summer residences. It was located in the coastal area Hovs Hallar and was owned by the father of one of the other students. A few years earlier, the house had been rented to Ingmar Bergman and his film team during the filming of *The Seventh Seal*.

The Swedish Davis Cup team practiced on the tennis stadium's side courts. Ove Bengtson and Hans Nerell were going to play singles. They seemed less bothered by the political battle than by the sports writers' mocking articles about how useless they were and the darkness in which Swedish tennis existed, now that Lundqvist had retired. Bengtson recalls:

"We were complete unknowns. Nobody cared about us. The anger was directed towards the association, which said that sports and politics don't belong together. We practiced. And when match day came, we expected to play."

Two hours before the tennis match was scheduled to begin, the protesters gathered in a parking lot in Båstad. At the urging of the police, they lined up three to a row before they started marching. "Stop the match! Stop the match!" echoed between the small homes with their manicured bushes. When the demonstrators reached the side street in front of the north entrance to the tennis stadium, they stopped and looked around as if they'd lost their direction. Was this all there was going to be? Someone began shaking the gates, which slipped open. Four policemen appeared from the inside. Many more came rushing to close the gates. The protesters stayed where they were. The policemen brought out their batons and started using them. A woman rushed forward and yelled something that made the people in the back sit down. Soon, everyone was sitting. Someone yelled that this was civil disobedience in the style of Martin Luther King. The police tried to close the gate. A woman got stuck, another screamed. Two guys climbed up on a wall and tried to hit the policemen with the eggs they had planned to use for destroying the tennis court. "Wait with the eggs!" someone yelled. "We'll need them later."

The journalists showed up just as the police began spraying water on the protesters. A guy from Lund ran out on the court and cut the hose. The police connected a new one. Teargas was sprayed from police cars. The protesters were soaked now, and their fighting spirit was wavering. Some fled with burning eyes. Some fifty of them stayed and sat down, coughing. The gate was closed, but the protesters came back. The police showered the young adults with the fire hose, while they tried to protect themselves with their placards. The groups from Skåne, Uppsala, and Stockholm had bonded now. They chanted:

"Do you smell the stench, from the Enskilda bank?"

"Hasselqvist is a racist!"

The latter made the priest from Båstad leave the protest. "I leave because I know that Hasselqvist is not a racist," he said. Soon, the marchers began jumping to the battle cry "Get warmed up, comrades!" They sang the left-wing anthem "The Internationale." A mob of people protesting the demonstrations and wanting the match to go on made a move from behind. The chaos was difficult to oversee now. Just after 2:30 p.m., Hasselqvist stepped out on a balcony and said there would be no match. The protesters celebrated. Hasselqvist had already sent the players on their way to Stockholm in a plane, from where they'd continue on to France. However, nobody outside of tennis circles knew this. Not even the sports press. "Comrades, we have triumphed! We have triumphed here and now!" shouted a protester.

Hasselqvist watched the protesters from the balcony with a look that revealed the contempt he had for them. From his point of view, the decision to have the match moved to another location was as easy as the original decision to welcome Rhodesia to Sweden. The Swedish Tennis Association had entered the Davis Cup competition, and fair play required it to participate. A boycott would have meant the disqualification of Sweden.

A few days later, newspaper readers were met by the news that Sweden had defeated Rhodesia in France, 4–1. Nobody found this news to be cause for celebration—a pitiful national team in tennis had, as expected, defeated an even more pitiful opponent who represented a hated racist regime.

The rage on the nation's sports pages and in letters to the editors was directed at the protesters, who were called "mob" and "slobs." But the tone eventually changed, as the protesters had the spirit of the times on their side. A few months later, when the Americans John Carlos and Tommie Smith raised their gloved left fists in protest of how blacks were treated in the

United States, the action evoked respect and admiration around the world. Sports and politics did go together. After Båstad in 1968, all elite athletes in Sweden knew that their actions were also measured by a moral yardstick.

Of course, the eleven-year-old kid, soon to be twelve, who was busy hitting high looping shots in the SALK hall had no clue about all this. Or that he himself would face the same moral scrutiny seven years later. Björn's thoughts revolved around the ball that must go over the net. That's how he viewed himself and what he did; he was just a young kid who chased after tennis balls with a racket in his hand. And he wanted to become the best he could be at doing just that.

He continued to lose to the older juniors, who still thought he was something special. He took the workouts as seriously as the matches. The others would take breaks and laugh and joke around. To Björn, every practice point was just as important. Back and forth, far behind the baseline, he didn't stop running until the other player had outmaneuvered him. "It's exhausting just to watch you. You move really well, but your timing is off," said Percy.

At the time, Björn had no expectations that his tennis was going to make him rich. He played because he enjoyed it. Tennis was an amateur sport. There were professionals, too, but they played in their own leagues in the USA that few people cared about. In the classic tournaments, only amateurs were allowed to play.

But just like society was changing during these years, tennis was also undergoing a revolution. In the Western world in general, socialist winds of change were blowing—but in tennis, it was all about the money.

The same week the riots happened in Båstad, a tournament open to both professionals and amateurs was played in Bournemouth, England. A few weeks later, the French Open was played with both pro and amateur participants. In Wimbledon that summer, Rod Laver returned after a five-year suspension, during which he'd played professional tennis. With his magical topspin forehand, he beat all his opponents on the center court. Björn watched it all on TV—the freckled Australian with his poker face, his way of controlling his emotions and never getting rattled over a missed shot or a questionable call, made a deep impression on the Swede. That's how Björn wanted to be, that's how you should act on the court.

Millions of TV viewers started to watch the open tennis showcasing all the pro players. Sponsors smelled money. Tennis entered a new era. Skilled amateur players, including men who came from less privileged circumstances, suddenly had another alternative aside from quitting tennis to get a real job. It was the money that broadened the sport of tennis and provided the equality effect that Suzanne Lenglen had called for decades earlier.

Ove Bengtson was Sweden's best tennis player, and he was about to turn twenty-five.

"When I was growing up, tennis was for the upper class. We lived in Danderyd, a family of academics. My dad, Torsten Bengtson, was a member of the parliament, representing the Center Party. He was the first deputy speaker in the early '70s. Naturally, we'd play at the Kungliga Tennis Hall, the 'nice club,' when I was little. I was accepted there when I was eight or nine years old. The Kungliga became my home."

Ove was talented and made the junior national team, along with several other kids of academics from the Kungliga tennis hall: Martin Carlstein, Hasse Nerell, and Bo Holmström. Studying, practicing tennis, and traveling to junior tournaments in Europe and the United States was what life was like. You went to college to have a profession when the happy tennis and school years were over. Ove studied at the Swedish School of Sport and Health Sciences (GIH) to become a physical education teacher.

"In 1969, my friends had started to work as doctors, economists, or engineers. Playing tennis wasn't a job. But when tennis opened up for prize money, I tried it for a year. My wife, Lotta, and I traveled around the world and had a great time. I played as much as I could, Wimbledon, the U.S. Open. . . . Our measuring stick was that I had to make at least as much money as I would've made as a gym teacher."

Ove broke even, but without making big money. He played in indoor tournaments in the United States, where you had to sign a contract for two months.

"We often stayed with families, rarely in nice hotels. Sometimes you got $2,000–$3,000 for playing in the Caribbean, the food was free, and there was an allowance. We traveled, lived a good life, and held off on things like having babies. We thought, *we'll do that later.* . . . But then we ended up never having any kids. But I still receive a pension from the players' association, ATP, $274 a month."

In the summer of 1969, the Swedish junior championships were played in Västerås. The promising eighteen-year-old Kjell Johansson defeated the likewise promising seventeen-year-old Birger Andersson in the finals. Kjell, a farmboy from Dalsjöfors outside Borås, grew up 200 meters from a tennis court.

"When I was little, I sometimes went there and watched my dad play," Kjell explained. "My dad knew the bank manager, so there was a little bit of a class perspective. He played, and I hit against a wall next to the court. I had good hands, and I was good at ping-pong, too.

After his victory at the Swedish Junior Championships, Kjell advanced to the semifinals in the open Swedish Championships. In the seaside resort town of Malen just east of Båstad, the thirteen-year-old Björn Borg had signed up in all singles and doubles divisions up to the fourteen-years age group. He advanced to the finals in most of them and won five divisions, including for thirteen- and fourteen-year-olds. One day, he played for eleven hours. His mother, Margareta, took a breather in a break between matches and said: "It's a good thing Björn isn't playing in the ladies' doubles, because then we wouldn't have time to have lunch."

After having been beaten for over a year by practically all the older juniors in SALK, Björn was beginning to rack up wins against them. After his victories in Båstad, those who followed the game closely started to talk about Björn as promising and a hope for the future of Swedish tennis. He was given the chance to travel abroad to play junior tournaments in Europe.

"This was only because I'd played so much with better players, two or three years older. When you play against better players, you'll improve much more than if you play only with those who are worse or on the same level. Those first years in SALK were critical for me. That's why things happened so fast for me later. And receiving instruction from Percy was just as important. I really had some huge advantages. In two years, my tennis improved incredibly. During the winters, I played two hours every day. In the summers, all day. When I wasn't in Båstad, I played on the clay courts up by the park back home in Södertälje. My mom would come and get me there late at night. Then come fall, things started up with SALK again."

Björn decided to give up hockey, and Percy and Björn's practices became more advanced. Björn's movement pattern needed improvement. Running around to always hit his forehand made him vulnerable. Percy began talking to Björn as if he were already on his way to the top level in the world. "Good players like Laver and Gimeno will aim for the sideline on your open forehand side when you're far out on the other side protecting your backhand. You won't get there in time."

It was all about calibrating Björn's footwork, finding a system for his movements.

"Think about how you move on a dance floor," said Percy.

Björn nodded.

"I'm going to hit an easy floater to you," said Percy, and Björn positioned his right leg correctly. The next shot was more difficult. Percy yelled at Björn to position his leg in the same way, so he could learn exactly how he needed to get to the ball in different areas of the court. It was a form of speed training, finding a movement pattern. There was only one way to learn—by grinding. Hour after hour.

Suddenly, there was an abundance of young and promising tennis players from a variety of backgrounds. Ted Gärdestad was the type of player who could beat Björn. And Björn's neighbor in Södertälje, Leif Johansson, who was three years older, was still considered the town's greatest tennis hope. Leif's and Björn's parents knew one another. Margareta's mood would turn sour when Leif's mother stopped by with newspaper clippings about one of Leif's victories. Björn thought Leif was a snob.

But most of the promising and slightly older players couldn't afford to fully commit to their sport, or didn't dare to. Education was the road to a secure future. Kjell Johansson celebrated his victory in the 1969 Swedish Junior Championships by meeting his future wife. He remembers it, of course:

"I met Else-Marie the evening after the match. We decided to move in together very quickly. And suddenly, a certain laziness came over me, and my appetite for tennis decreased. I almost didn't give a damn about committing for several years. I said: 'I'd be happy to carry around spare parts at Volvo in Västerås and make 1,500 kronor a month, as long as I can be home with Else-Marie.' I received 400 kronor a month from the Västerås Tennis Club. The rent for the apartment was 236 kronor, I had 50 kronor left for food and 75 kronor a week for other expenses. I managed . . ."

That's where things were. The gifted Gärdestad began to show an interest in music. What's to say Björn wouldn't fall victim to a similar distraction?

With his haircut, he'd fit in just as well at a Vietnam war protest or in a pop group.

Tennis still had a dedicated audience, but that stemmed from the fact that every summer Janne Lundqvist was convinced to make a comeback. And he never could resist the temptation. The Swedish Tennis Association arranged its own annual tournament in Båstad, the Champions Cup, which consisted of four selected players. In 1970, Lundqvist would measure his strength against Ove Bengtson, soon-to-be-retired Manuel Santana, and Wilhelm Bungert, a timid businessman from Düsseldorf who'd played in the Davis Cup for Germany. The Champions Cup was held on a weekend in front of a large TV audience. It was a nice event, but it had one small and one large problem. The fact that it was only a make-believe competition was perhaps not a big deal. More of a concern was that the dependency on Janne Lundqvist was a reminder of the vacuum in which Swedish tennis existed with respect to high-caliber international players. In the long term, it wouldn't be possible to maintain the general public's tennis interest through artificial measures like the Champion's Cup.

So how could promising talents be persuaded to continue to play tennis? In 1970, the association distributed brochures and posters with a slogan: "Do you want to travel around the globe in tennis shorts?" The only way to produce strong players was to toughen them in an international environment. It would take time. It would cost money. But after selecting the best juniors and offering them to play internationally for five years, an assessment of the progress could be made.

Kjell Johansson received the offer and accepted, as did Håkan "Granaten" Zahr, a player from southern Sweden with a wicked forehand, and Tenny Svensson from the western coast of Sweden. Now the association needed a mentor, too.

"I'll take care of it", said Lennart Bergelin and packed himself and the young players into his car, a red Volvo 164 without power steering. Bergelin would make funny comments about how he hated that car. Swedes couldn't make cars. "So nice to leave old Sweden," said Bergelin when they got to the ferry down to Helsingör, Denmark.

"Look!" said Bergelin when they whizzed down the Autobahn with hills and valleys stretching out in all directions. "This is what it should look like! This is what a nice landscape looks like!"

Kjell, Zahr, and Tenny enjoyed Bergelin's stories and jokes. They each bought a tape recorder, asked Bergelin questions, and recorded his answers. The trip took them to the French Riviera, a familiar spot for Swedish tennis players. That's where many players would welcome spring and prepare for the clay tournaments and the Davis Cup in May. Bergelin drove the entire way.

The young players loved being on the road. They loved Labbe, and Labbe loved being a father figure to them.

"Just get your asses in there," said Labbe. That meant: work hard, fight, don't pay attention to how you feel.

Between practices and matches, during lunches and car rides, Bergelin fed his pupils simple, down-to-earth truths and hammered home the harsh reality of playing the game of tennis.

"Boys, you have ten years. After that, it's over. When you hit thirty, you might as well quit."

What he told them stuck, lodged in their minds, and would pop up as reminders much later in their lives.

"Boys, get yourself a freaking rock-solid physique. That's the most important thing."

"Sure, Labbe, sure."

"I'm serious. Without a rock-solid physique, you have no chance. You have to get your asses in there."

Rock-solid physique was a matter of attitude.

For the first generation of Swedish tennis talents traveling around the world with Labbe, his nagging went in one ear and out the other. But the following year, a junior player joined the group. With him, there was no need for Bergelin to nag.

The association received a blue VW bus and personalized it with lettering painted on the sides: "The Swedish Tennis Association." Bergelin walked around the bus every night, making sure there were no scratches. The kids weren't allowed to place their feet on the dashboard. Bergelin received 5,000 kronor a month from the association. He slept in the bus. That was typical for him.

Björn was the youngest and sat in the very back of the bus. He was the quietest in the group. But he made sure to get a rock-solid physique. When he wasn't out on a tennis court, he was out running.

Aside from his attitude about training, Björn stood out in another way, too. He had a way of saying that he expected to win his matches, which was something the other players weren't used to. Kjell Johansson was brought up to sit in the backseat, bow to the pastor and custodian, and not to grab things for himself. Björn wasn't afraid. He said: "I'm going to beat this guy, that's just the way it is." Bergelin wasn't afraid, either. In 1971 and 1972, when Björn won against internationally established players like Pasarell and Gimeno, the older Swedish players were thinking: *What the heck, I'm at least as good as Björn in practice, so I should be able to win, too . . .*

But the feeling that they were as strong as Björn only occasionally struck the other players. Usually, they felt that he was a different kind.

"We were in Johannesburg for a tournament," recalls Kjell. "That's pretty high above sea level. You won't hit a shot inside the court the first week you're there. The ball shoots right for the fences, there's no air resistance whatsoever. You'll get beat by the janitor the first few days. It was raining one day, and me and Björn and the Spaniard José Higueras decided to go for a run instead. We went over to a soccer field. Björn always carried his Slazenger cover with him. He put his watch and a little money in it and carried it as he ran. We ran around the soccer field, just ran and ran. I quit first. Björn and Higuera continued. Björn ran carrying his cover. Higueras, who was really skinny, stopped after a while. He was completely exhausted. But Björn ran five more laps. With his damn cover. I'd never seen him go for a run before. I knew Higueras could run like hell, but Björn. . . . He was absolutely phenomenal. He was crazy. We were so impressed by him, he was unbelievably disciplined."

Björn noticed that he trained harder than his older pals on the national team but didn't find it strange that they didn't follow his lead:

"I think you must have a certain attitude and personality and mental strength to be able to train as hard as I did. You can't just say: 'I'm going to start training super hard now.' A lot of people just can't handle it, or only to a certain degree. For me, I could keep going because I enjoyed it the whole time. I could keep going no matter what. Both on and off the court."

Björn came along for the trips when he wasn't in school. When he was in school, he kept getting more and more fatigued. He didn't have the energy to focus. After his ninth-grade fall semester, it was clear he could no longer keep up with his schoolwork.

One day, his geography teacher lost her patience and yelled at him in front of the class, claiming he was both lazy and stupid.

"You're right, I know nothing," said Björn.

He wanted to quit school. "A fifteen-year-old can't quit school, it's impossible," said the principal. But Björn argued his case with the same conviction he used to endure baseline battles out on the tennis court. He nagged his parents. He asked for help from the Swedish Tennis Association. And the association was able to take advantage of the antiauthoritarian winds of change that had undermined the school system as a social institution. Ten years earlier, it would have been inconceivable for a sports association to advocate so actively and openly for the early removal from the school system of a young boy from modest circumstances, for the sole reason that he was good at sports.

The association's education director visited Björn's school, Blombackaskolan, in Södertälje and spoke with the principal and with Björn's homeroom teacher. Mats Hasselqvist was present, too: "We'd like for Björn to be exempt from the rules and be allowed to quit school, so that he can participate in the tennis tournaments in Europe this spring."

"Is there a real reason to push for this kind of commitment to tennis so early?" said the homeroom teacher. "Boys aren't mature at this age, neither socially nor emotionally."

Hasselqvist didn't even bother to respond to this argument.

"It's possible to make a living as a professional tennis player nowadays, it should be fine to let Björn leave early."

No one at the school had experienced this situation before, this pressure by another social institution to relieve a student of mandatory schooling. The principal took Björn aside and said: "What happens if you cross the street, are run over by a car, and hurt your arm so you can't play tennis?"

Björn gave him a very serious look: "If I'm not among the world elite players before I'm eighteen or nineteen, I'll give up tennis and get the education I need."

Björn was excused from the last semester of the ninth grade. In late winter, he boarded a plane and arrived for the spring season in southern Europe. There, he won his first match as a professional against Janne Lundqvist, who was in yet another one of his comebacks.

Mats Hasselqvist, chairman of the Davis Cup committee, selected Borg to Sweden's first Davis Cup match in 1972, against New Zealand in Båstad. As the team's captain, Bergelin's plan was to have Ove Bengtson play first singles and let the practices determine whether Kjell or Tenny would get the second singles spot. Björn was there to observe and learn.

Kjell and Tenny played on one practice court, Björn and Ove on another, adjacent court. Bergelin picked up balls and spun his Tretorn racket around, watched the play on both courts, and acted as referee to Björn and Ove, who were keeping score. Ove made a double fault, but Bergelin called the second serve good. Björn stopped dead in his tracks:

"You're calling it for Ove so he'll win!" he shouted.

"No, I'm not!" said Bergelin.

"Yes, you are," said Björn.

"Listen here, you little shit!" said Bergelin, who picked up a package of balls and held it up as if he were going to throw it at Björn.

"Okay, come on . . .," said Björn, who dropped his racket and stepped up to provocatively face his team captain head-on. Bergelin threw the package of balls in Björn's face. This scared Björn, and he ran up in the stands, Bergelin in hot pursuit. Bergelin caught up with Björn and grabbed his shirt, making Björn tumble and end up on his back. He got up and escaped just to be caught in a different trap, a green fence that separated the stands from the center court. Bergelin smashed his racket into the ground with all he had. It bounced back up, a centimeter or so from Björn's face. Björn began crying and ran off to call his parents at home.

Rune and Margareta hopped into their brown Toyota and drove down from Södertälje to Båstad—about a five-hour drive. They spotted Kjell and Tenny outside the courts. Margareta lowered her window:

"What's going on? Has Bergelin gone crazy?"

Björn and Bergelin didn't speak for two days. The practices continued, but Bergelin had made his decision. Björn wasn't ready to make his debut in this kind of important event.

However, Hasselqvist had other ideas. He spoke with Bergelin and made his case strictly in tennis terms: "Ove has barely won a clay court match in his life." He could be rather blunt. The players felt that Hasselqvist truly believed that no other Swedish tennis player aside from Janne Lundqvist was capable of playing the game.

"Ove will play," said Bergelin.

Hasselqvist decided to speak frankly: "This is where we are. The PR value of having a fifteen-year-old play in the Davis Cup is more important than the result. This match is about maintaining what keeps Swedish tennis alive, the general public's interest for the Davis Cup. Us having the world's youngest Davis Cup rookie might compensate for the team being weak. At least it would create added buzz for tennis."

It was as clear as could be. Bergelin walked down to the court, where Kjell and Tenny were playing for the second singles spot.

"That damn jerk . . .," he snarled. "He should just stay in his office in Stockholm and not meddle in my job. He says Björn should play. Should we put out a stroller, too?"

Bergelin selected Björn and Ove Bengtson to play the singles. That Friday, the rookie was matched against a world Top 20 player, Onny Parun, who won the first two sets. Björn played well, and everybody was happy. He put up a better fight than could've been expected. As Bergelin wiped off Björn's racket during a third set changeover, he said, "It's too heavy for you," and gave the youngster a lighter racket. Björn turned things around and won the match. The result made headlines across the world. In Sweden, it raised the question if fifteen-year-old Björn was already the best tennis player in the country.

A few weeks later, it was time for the Swedish Championships. The fifteen-year-old had now turned sixteen, and he arrived directly from the Swedish Junior Championships in southern Sweden's Smålandsstenar. The Swedish Championships were held closer to Stockholm, in Västerås. A player who misfired a shot might see the ball end up in the backyard of the home of Curt Nicolin, the CEO of ASEA (a major Swedish industrial company, now known as ABB), which was situated right next to the court. Nicolin had just given Kjell Johansson a sponsorship contract in the amount of 1,500 kronor a month, which sufficed to cover his rent, meals, and snacks. But Björn went on to defeat Kjell in the semifinal and Ove in the final. Björn was now the best player in Sweden, and it was clear he had the capacity to become a player of international caliber.

"I had come a long way in a short amount of time," he says. "I might not have been invincible, but it was very difficult to beat me, especially on clay. I knew that one day I'd hit a plateau, that I wouldn't be able to continue to constantly improve, but those years I was still getting so much better very quickly. Before the 1973 season, when I began playing on the ATP tour, I set up clear goals. I wanted to advance far enough in the tournaments so that I could play against and get a feel for as many of the really big names as possible. I wanted to play as many matches as I possibly could against the best tennis players in the world."

Björn had the opportunity to face a number of the top players in a short time span. During the first six months of 1973, he faced four of the world's best players. The world's number-one player, Ilie Nastase, in the final of Monte Carlo's clay tournament; the number-two player, Manuel Orantes, in the Davis Cup; the number-eight player, Adriano Panatta, in the round of 16 in Paris; and the number-three player, Stan Smith, in the semifinal in Båstad. Björn wasn't even close to winning any of the matches. Instead, he received proper tennis lessons and experienced how great tennis was played. He realized he had a long way to go. Against Nastase, he ran out of gas as early as the second set. Björn commented that he never had a clue where Nastase's shots would land. Against Smith, he realized he was all but a lightweight against a player who put that kind of weight behind his strokes.

"I wasn't surprised that I lost, but that the best players were so good, they played at a level I barely knew existed. But I also thought there were moments in those matches when I was actually able to keep up, and this was something I took with me—I'd come this far and I actually played against these players in the semis and final rounds."

Wimbledon in 1973 was played without the best players. Eighty-four professional players boycotted the tournament, in a measure of support for the Yugoslav star Nikola "Niki" Pilić, who served a suspension for not playing the Davis Cup. Björn entered the tournament, and, in the absence of the pros, he was seeded sixth. "You're so sweet!" screamed a teenage girl in the crowd to Björn after his win against Premjit Lall of India in the first round. This cry opened the floodgates of passion. The next day, about a hundred teenage girls gathered outside Björn's hotel. And the day after that, most of the bleachers by the side court where he played were filled with girls who swarmed around him when he walked off the court after his match. After the third and fourth rounds' long and uncertain matches, it was obvious that Björn, regardless of the match result, was more than a tennis star. He was a pop idol. When they caught a glimpse of the Swede with the long legs, blond locks, and sweet smile, girls screamed with excitement until their voices turned hoarse. At night, they'd knock on the door to his hotel room. They wanted to meet Björn.

Bergelin would come out and push them away. "Björn can't be disturbed," he said.

"Take it easy," said Björn. "It's not that bad. Come on, they can come in, can't they?"

"All of this is getting to your head," said Bergelin.

The rest of the week, Labbe woke Björn up early every morning and made him go for long runs. In the quarterfinals, Björn faced the home player, Roger Taylor, and lost. This didn't stop his fans from storming out on the court and throwing themselves at the Swede.

"I didn't get it at all," Taylor has said. "I'm the only remaining home player. We haven't won here in 40 years. I live so close to the arena that I can hear it from my bedroom when they cut the grass on the courts with their nail scissors before the tournament. I win a quarterfinal—and the crowd storms out on the court and swarms my opponent, trying to kiss him to death and wanting to follow him home. I walk off the court and nobody cares. What am I missing?"

The reports about the Beatles-like hysteria around Björn reached Sweden around the same time that the newspapers' business pages reported that Sweden had passed the United States as the world's richest country, measured by GNP per capita. The processed wood like IKEA's furniture, the skilled engineers and metal workers who built crash-proof cars that were shipped out from the ports. . . . What could be more logical than at the same time, from Sweden's modern airports, brilliant sports stars with beautiful hair would also be lifting off? Ulrika Knape from Göteborg spun around and twisted as she dove into the swimming pool from tall heights, more elegantly than any other. Ronnie Peterson from Örebro drove a race car faster than all other Formula 1 aces. Börje Salming from Kiruna was tougher than any other North American hockey player. Ralf Edström from Degerfors headed the soccer ball in ways that got all of Europe talking. Stellan Bengtsson from Falkenberg toyed with ping-pong-playing Asians. A quiet army of ordinary and friendly young Swedes, all of whom always let their achievements do the talking.

In the amazement of young Björn's fast progress with a racket and balls, there was also a sentiment that he was part of a deeper trend, which was commonly called "The Swedish Sports Miracle" and was explained by the belief that interaction between different parts of society benefited sports. The fact that sports had many supporters among elected representatives and influential people in society played a part, as did the country's prosperity, which provided athletes with the safety net they needed to commit to their sports. But more than anything, the key was the welfare infrastructure with its many volunteer leaders and officials, and the close coexistence between mass and elite. In the world of sport, the latter manifested itself annually in competition races such as *Vasaloppet* and *O-ringen*. The mass participation was a condition for the elite sports. The many tennis courts that had been built gave everyone a chance to play tennis at a low cost. But the courts quickly filled up. The communities responded by building more courts.

When Björn Borg arrived in Båstad after Wimbledon, he was met by admiring looks. The crowds applauded his winning passing shots, although it was inconceivable that entire sections of the stands would break out in screams as soon as he entered the court. Björn was at home—back in the country where people, just like him, kept their emotions in check and didn't expose themselves to the risk of losing their grip and letting what bubbled within them begin to work against them. Björn advanced to the semifinals, and afterward, the Swedish crowd returned home in their clean and tidy cars.

Between his matches in Båstad, Björn spent time in negotiations with two pro leagues. They were representatives of a commercial tennis world that, after Björn's promising results—and especially after the excitement at Wimbledon—wanted to get him on board. One of the actors was the WCT pro league, which was played during the winter months and didn't conflict with Sweden's Davis Cup matches or the Swedish tournaments. WCT offered Björn big money to sign a contract for the period January to May the following season. Björn's other option was to join WTT, a team tennis circus in the United States. WTT offered even more money than WCT, but signing a contract with WTT would mean that Björn wouldn't be able to participate in either the Davis Cup or the tournaments in Sweden.

Björn consulted with his parents, with Bergelin, and with Percy and Ove. The Swedish Tennis Association saw what was happening. Its investments over several years to produce a high-caliber tennis player was about to end in an anticlimax. Mats Hasselqvist, an employee of the SEB bank—when he wasn't busy with the tennis association—turned to his boss, who himself had played in the Davis Cup.

"I called Marcus Wallenberg and asked if we couldn't match WTT's offer, give Björn free air travel. Wallenberg said: 'Call Hagrup at Scandinavian Airlines, SAS!' I did so later that day—I knew that Wallenberg had talked to Björn by then—and we presented a contract with SAS, which gave Björn 425,000 kronor per year plus free air travel around the world. This was a huge break for Björn. In turn, Björn would wear SAS labels on his clothing, and he would participate in the Davis Cup and the big Swedish tournaments. Also, he would visit the SAS office to say hello to the staff in each city he visited. Formally, Björn was employed by SAS as an intern, with the assignment of learning the organization of the company."

Björn declined the WTT offer, and, during the final days in Båstad, he signed his name to the contract with SAS. The American negotiators felt like negotiating with Björn was like negotiating with the Swedish government; representatives from the association or other parts of Swedish upper society stayed in the hotel rooms on either side adjoining Björn's room. The richest actors in professional tennis weren't able to match the counteroffer from the world's richest country.

Björn bought his parents a summer house in the Möja archipelago of Stockholm. He also bought a small grocery store; Rune's dream had always been to work for himself. Björn's season had brought him more money than he could've imagined in his wildest dreams, but still no international titles.

At the Stockholm Open that November, he reached the final.

"I played Tom Gorman, and as you know, we Swedes are always very sportsmanlike to foreigners. We were expected to be polite and nice. I was up, 3–1, in the decisive set's tiebreak, and then he hits a double fault that's out by this much, yeah, 20 centimeters, I should have led 4–1. 'No,' says the referee, 'it's good.' So, I lost that final, 7–5 in the decisive tiebreak, but had I gotten to 4–1, I doubt I'd have lost. We were expected to be good hosts, it was a bit like that. You could say that I was pissed off. I tried to think: *Come on, it's history, there's not much you can do.* But the Stockholm Open was special for me and important for the Swedish audience. It was important to keep these tournaments going. In Båstad and at the Stockholm Open, you're expected to play and do well, that's just how it is.

In December, Björn and Kjell Johansson traveled to the next stop on the tennis tour, Buenos Aires. As always, Björn was expected to brighten the day of the SAS staff with a visit. He didn't think it was superinspiring.

He looked at Kjell. "What the hell should I do?"

Kjell said: "You'll have to at least go over there."

Björn: "You can come with."

They arrived, each wearing a Fjällräven jacket, said hello, had a cup of coffee, and left.

"I was shy and liked having company when I visited the SAS offices," says Björn. "In the tournament, I played Vilas in the final and led, 2–1, in sets, and 3–3 in the tiebreak, when I slipped and crashed into the referee chair and hurt my back. I had to withdraw from the match. That's when I met Vilas for the first time."

Vilas brought Björn, Kjell, Panatta, Tiriac, and Bertolucci with him out on the big streets of Buenos Aires, where they cruised around in Vilas's green MG with the top down.

"It was all very exciting, but I was incredibly annoyed that I didn't win that finals match, and that I didn't win in Stockholm. And I was exhausted. I'd played every week, and I realized I needed to slow down a little, schedule some recovery weeks. Kjell and I went to Rio after the final. It was a great trip. I realized that I needed to expect to have slumps in 1974, that all players have them."

In the days between Christmas and New Year's, Björn flew to the Australian Open. He was more or less ordered to go there by the Swedish Tennis Association, which wanted him to promote Swedish tennis in Australia. At that time, and for another decade, the Australian Open was an insignificant tournament without prestige or big prize money. No journalists accompanied Björn there. After every match, Björn was expected to call the newspapers back home to report the results. He made two such phone calls, but after his loss to Phil Dent in the third round, there was no report.

CARRYING SWEDEN ON HIS SHOULDERS

"Labbe always talked about how bad things were in Sweden. The taxes, the mentality, how Swedes can't do anything and don't understand anything."
—KJELL JOHANSSON

A few days before Björn's departure for his first WCT matches, he was practicing with Percy in the SALK hall when Lennart Hyland, the television program host, showed up with a film team and asked to hit some balls with Björn. Standing at the net with Björn next to him, Hyland explained to the Swedish TV viewers: "Here we have one of the most peculiar products ever produced in Swedish sports. He's seventeen years old, and he's almost world-class in the difficult game that is tennis, maybe one of the two or three most difficult games there is. You might know this, Björn?"

Hyland was the people's television star of the times. He was a butcher's son from Tranås, in southern Sweden, who in the '40s had fought his way to a job among the academics at Swedish Radio, where he'd introduced a folksy approach. Hyland recognized himself in Björn's challenges, and his fatherly empathetic tone reflected how many viewed Björn. Although the kid had already practically secured his future, he was still seen as just that—a Swedish kid on his way out in the big wide world. Caring was one of the homeland's more prominent characteristics. Hyland asked the kid what his parents thought of "now having a boy who travels around the world."

"In some ways, it gets a little boring," said Björn. "I'm an only child and I want to see my parents as often as possible, so whenever I have a chance I like to come home to them, even if it means taking a huge detour."

"Don't you think they worry about your future? How it will end?"

Björn nodded.

"Yes, maybe they do. It's up to me how many tournaments I need to play. I might have to schedule around two or three months per year for recovery. Last year I played every week and that was silly of me, I felt a bit fatigued at the end of the year."

"Do your parents ask you what you're going to be when you grow up?"

Björn laughed.

"No, they don't. I hope, and they hope, that I'll become a tennis player."

"Have you learned how to eat and drink?"

Björn gave Hyland a quizzical look.

"Yes, and I think I knew how to do that before, too."

"So, what do you eat?"

"A big steak before my matches and I also drink milk. That's what I like best."

"And you read comic books?"

"Yes, I think they're a lot of fun to read, actually. If I have time, I like to read *The Phantom* and [sports comics]. I like them a lot."

"And what about your education?"

Björn scratched his arm. "Well, I hope I won't have to go back to school or any other education program, I hope I can support myself with tennis."

"And you're a bit of a pop idol, too. Those curls . . . don't they get in the way a little?"

Hyland ran his fingers through Björn's hair. Björn put on a brave face, but his muscles tensed. He wasn't going to cut his hair. Hyland mentioned the girls in England chasing him. Björn said they didn't bother him.

"Don't you ever worry about your future?"

"No, I don't."

"Not even that you might get tired of all this jet-setting when you're twenty-five . . . ?

"No, not at all . . ."

". . . to engage your will and your nerves every single day, time and time again . . ."

Björn shook his head.

"You want to do this, it's your life?"

"Yes, I do, I want to take the opportunity."

The encounter had a symbolic significance. Sweden was an ultramodern country at the time, and one of the world's most secular countries. But it was also small population-wise, and situated on the outskirts of the world. You didn't need to be an anthropologist or a social scientist to sense a tribal mentality.

A tribe worships itself. It strengthens its collective identity by calling on its god or its totem. It wasn't difficult to see in Björn Borg the youth the tribe had selected as its chosen one—the golden boy who'd been given a free apprenticeship with the tribe's most knowledgeable leaders, the boy who'd received the economic chief's blessings to travel around the world at no cost. When Hyland ran his hand through Björn's hair like a medicine man, the apotheosis was complete. At the same time, it was obvious that the young tennis player hadn't been sent to realize his own individual goals, but to make the tribe that had selected him continue to worship itself. Hyland's talk with Borg had all the ingredients of a surrender ritual.

The boy himself was too young to worry about, or simply too crazy about tennis to understand, the collective pressure that rested upon him. In early 1974, nobody had a problem with the still-concealed conflict between the individual and the dull undercurrent of unspoken collective expectations. For Björn Borg, it was simple. He played only for himself, not for anybody else.

"It was, of course, a big change in my life when I began traveling around the world being just seventeen," says Björn Borg. "But I knew that if I wanted to get really good at tennis, I had to travel a lot. I had to meet other players, see other styles of play. Otherwise, I'd never improve. I knew that, too. And I liked to travel, that's the life I wanted to live. That's what I had trained so hard for and dreamed about in front of the garage door."

The Philadelphia Spectrum in mid-January became for Borg an introduction to everything that had made pro tennis big in the USA: 17,000 daily visitors in the stands in the A-hall and 13,000 in the B-hall. Film teams and TV cameras. An engaged and loud audience. The arena was built for basketball, but for a few years it had also been the stage for the

BJÖRN BORG AND THE SUPER-SWEDES

American Indoor Tennis Championships. It was the world's largest tennis tournament under a roof, and it was organized by the WCT, World Championship Tennis, the mightiest and best organized of the various pro tennis leagues. The WCT was owned by Lamar Hunt, a billionaire from Dallas. Hunt, a tennis enthusiast, had inherited an oil imperium from his father, and when prize money entered the sport in 1968, Hunt quickly concluded that the time had finally come to popularize tennis and capitalize off of it. The key to success was television, and Lamar Hunt saw in the television companies' sports scheduling an opening that, like newly discovered oil resources, was just waiting to be exploited: the January to May time period. That's when the American football season had ended and the tennis calendar had not yet started to fill up with the International Tennis Federation's (ITF's) many Grand Prix tournaments and the major championships in Paris, Wimbledon, and Forest Hills.

Lamar Hunt repackaged the sport of tennis for the TV companies and their large audiences. Rather than traditional white, the players were urged to play in colorful shorts and shirts that looked good on color television. Instead of time-consuming long sets, the tiebreak was introduced, a directly decisive game where the first player to get to seven points with a two-point lead won the set. Instead of a crowd of rich people who paid big money for their tickets and conversed in whispers like embarrassed library patrons, the WCT's arenas were filled with spectators who only paid a few dollars for their seats and who were urged to get involved in the matches. A series of classic matches were played right away in the first seasons. And every year, the WCT organized more tournaments and signed more pro players. The tennis boom originated in the United States and was spreading around the world. Most of the world's new courts were built in the United States. In 1974, the WCT had signed 90 of the world's best players, who were divided into three groups, each of which toured around the world in the spring, playing tournaments for money and points. The season then concluded with playoffs in Dallas featuring the eight players who had earned the most points. Björn ended up in the green group together with players like Arthur Ashe, Rod Laver, Roscoe Tanner, Mark Cox, Jan Kodes, and Ove Bengtson. The green group gave themselves the internal nickname "the Yo-Yo Group," because "we fly around the world twelve times in four months," as Arthur Ashe put it. But before the three groups set out on their tours, everyone gathered at the Philadelphia Spectrum to play for the season's first title. CBS paid what was, at the time, an incredible sum of $300,000 for the rights to broadcast live from the event.

Björn stepped out onto the court in a red shirt and proceeded to immediately lose in the first round to the Australian veteran and volley specialist, Tony Roche. Any rookie could have been plagued with doubts for less, but Björn was mostly annoyed because he'd been careless on some important points. He got himself on the first SAS flight back across the Atlantic and quickly jumped back into the thick of things at another tournament.

The Scandinavian Indoor Championships at the Njord Hall in Oslo the next week was a journey back in time to everything Björn was about to leave behind: red-colored wood floors, sparsely populated bleachers, and a draw filled with Swedish amateur players. Björn won the tournament and received 16,000 kronor in prize money, paid in 1,000-kronor bills. He stuck them in his black boots—8,000 in the right and 8,000 in the left—and hopped on the next flight, to Bologna, for the second leg of the WCT tour. There he suffered another loss in the first round.

Björn didn't bother to reflect on the loss. He packed his bags again and went on his way. At the Royal Albert Hall in London, he won his first pro tournament in spectacular fashion. In the final, he saved six match points against the local favorite, Mark Cox. In addition, Björn won the doubles with Ove Bengtson.

"That's when I thought, *time to celebrate*," says Bengtson. But it ended with us—Björn, my wife Lotta, and me—sitting on the floor in our hotel room eating sandwiches. The morning after, we were off to the USA to play. It wasn't always glamorous. But I was happy to eat a sandwich in the middle of the night."

The top players in the Yo-Yo Group began speculating about how good the young Swede could become. His game was perplexing. All he did was smack the ball. All out, no holds barred. As if each point were the last. Björn's service returns felt like a sledgehammer in your stomach, said Ashe. Cox philosophized that the Swede was an idealist in the true spirit of sports, who gave it his all on every point.

"As for the rest of us," said Cox, "we have a tendency to save our best efforts for the critical points."

Laver offered Björn the advice to be careful, not so much for the sake of his physique, but for his psyche. "If you play this hard, your mind will be drained, you'll burn out in seven years."

BJÖRN BORG AND THE SUPER-SWEDES

Perhaps Björn put more strain on his body than the other players. But he also received treatments. Bergelin gave Borg a massage after every match. This wasn't anything for shrinking violets. Labbe applied as much pressure as he could onto Björn's back and leg muscles. Björn's body got used to it. Other Swedish players were terrified of Bergelin's treatment. After a Davis Cup match in Ireland, Tenny Svensson had a sore back and needed a massage badly. But Tenny wasn't keen on Bergelin treating him, so instead he found a big Irish man, a massage therapist, at the club where they played. Tenny laid down on the bench, and the therapist went to work as Bergelin watched.

"You massage way too gently," said Bergelin. "I'll show you how to do it."

"No, Lennart, no!" pleaded Tenny.

"Lie still, kid!" said Bergelin.

"No!" screamed Tenny as he tried to escape.

"Hold him!" ordered Bergelin, to the Irishman.

The next day, Tenny Svensson's back was black and blue with obvious signs of major bleeding in the back muscles. "He's just weak, not used to massages," concluded Bergelin.

The rumors about Bergelin's massages spread in the tennis world and attracted a mixture of horror and curiosity. Often, players from other countries looked up Bergelin and asked to have a variety of ailments addressed. One of them was the Australian Barry Phillips-Moore, who needed help with a hip that was giving him trouble. "I'll fix you up," said Bergelin and massaged the Australian player, who after the treatment was unable to walk for three days.

In Barcelona, Björn played harder than ever before and defeated his childhood hero Laver in two straight sets. He then went back home, won the Swedish Indoor Championships, took the next plane across the Atlantic, and won the tournament in Sao Paulo. When the winter season was over in late March, Björn had played 41 matches and had won 31 of them. He had entered 12 tournaments, won two, earned $76,645 in prize money, and qualified for the prestigious WCT playoffs in Dallas. The red and blue groups' top names, Newcome and Nastase, had collected the most points, but nobody had played as much tennis as Björn. His competitors asked themselves if the Swede ever had time to sleep.

Björn recalls: "You had to catch some z's whenever you could. And I got used to it pretty quickly. There were new tournaments every week. I could sleep anywhere, often curled up in airplanes. It could be hard, of course, but I loved the lifestyle. You've got to love what you do. And I really did. If you don't, it just won't work. I liked to go out on the court and play tennis, and I liked all the rest that came with it, too."

For "the Exclusive Eight," the eight tennis pros who'd come to Dallas to play for the WCT title—one of the five biggest in the tennis year—in yet another basketball arena, the Moody Coliseum, the mingling evening event at Lamar Hunt's French-style mansion was mandatory. The guest list also included billionaires from Dallas high society and tennis journalists from all over the world.

The players each had a white Cadillac luxury car at their disposal, personalized with their name. Lennart Bergelin drove the Cadillac with Björn's name, with Björn sitting in the passenger seat. When the vehicle was allowed entry through the large gates to the mansion on the outskirts of Dallas, a garden opened up, or rather a large park. Huge fountains and pools were scattered along the road leading up to the mansion. At yet another swimming pool, men in white shirts appeared and instructed Bergelin to stop. The men took the car keys and gave them a parking ticket. Cajun food was sizzling on the grills. Paintings by Goya hung in the mansion.

The Dallas ladies ran up to Björn, who wrote autographs and answered questions about himself. He was surrounded for over an hour, smiled, scribbled his "BB" signature, and exchanged a few words with everyone.

In the past, he would have snuck away from things like this, thought Bergelin. A bit later, Björn was called up onstage for a talk with the MC, the leading actor from Ben Hur, Charlton Heston. Bergelin thought that Björn was paraded around like a circus animal, but the Swedish star brought down admiring laughs and applause with his simple answers that showcased his limited school English.

"Could you even win this tournament?"

"Wait and see, gentlemen!"

Lennar Bergelin had come to Dallas to practice with Björn, keep him company, and help him with the logistics. After a tight relationship spanning four years, Bergelin had learned that his main task was to create peace and quiet around Björn. Lamar Hunt's party was a challenge, and those challenges were becoming increasingly common.

Tommy Engstrand had traveled to the Moody Coliseum to report live for Swedish Radio. Engstrand was placed at the very top of the arena, a few meters below the ceiling, without radio cables, and reported via telephone. The matches were played at nighttime, Swedish time. Four million Swedes, half the country's population, stayed up and listened. For those who couldn't stay up, a ten minutes-long summary of the match highlights was provided at 6:30 the next morning. After every match, Björn, soaked in sweat, climbed up the steps through the crowd for lengthy interviews with Engstrand. The telephone, which for several hours had been glued to the reporter's sweaty face, was soaking wet.

"Do you run laps up here while you yap on the radio?" asked Björn, whose victory over Ashe in the quarterfinals had turned all other news into fillers.

The minister of finance, Gunnar Sträng, was going to address the oil crisis with an aggressive stimulus package, including lowering the sales tax, lowering rents, lowering prices on meat and milk, and paying out an extra child allowance in early May. These measures had led to a spring-time Christmas-like rush, but tennis was more exciting. And Björn Borg turned things around and beat Jan Kodes in the semifinal. Sifo, the Swedish Institute for Opinion Surveys, showed that the Social Democratic party, now in its 42nd year of straight government power, was climbing steadily in the voter standings.

As for Lennart Bergelin, he was mostly pondering how his prodigy could return to Sweden as soon as possible following the tournament. A Davis Cup match against Poland awaited, and Björn needed both rest and practice hours before then. Bergelin flipped through the itineraries. The variants of the flight routes were plentiful.

Björn looked at Labbe and said: "Talk to Lamar! He takes care of everything. He has a private plane we can borrow."

Bergelin hadn't heard that kind of talk from Björn before. And he didn't like it.

Before Björn's final against John Newcombe, *Svenska Dagbladet*'s tennis writer, Sune Sylvén, made a promise to Björn that, if he won, he'd be awarded the newspaper's annual Gold Medal Award for Outstanding Sports Achievement, *Bragdguldet*, the following winter. Björn didn't win, as Newcombe's game was too much. Björn was sad over the loss, but still proud of what he'd accomplished. He'd broken through into the global tennis elite. He couldn't hold his tears back at the prize ceremony, and he later collapsed on a bench in the locker room. Labbe entered.

"Hurry up, kid! We have to be at the airport in 15 minutes."

Lamar Hunt had arranged a Cadillac. But the flight route that Bergelin had found wasn't the most direct. The first stop was Seattle on the West Coast. From there, they flew via Canada across the North Pole to Copenhagen.

When Björn finally set foot on Swedish ground again, there were no doubts about where he was. Posters with bold letters told the story: BJÖRN BORG IN BÅSTAD. Further down, there was information about the occasion being a Davis Cup match. One headline revealed the secret behind his success: ELVIS HELPS BJÖRN WIN. Vendors were hawking shirts with his name.

Björn was totally exhausted when he stepped out onto the practice court with Kjell Johansson. He missed easy shots, threw his racket into the clay, and mishit a ball, sending it high up into the treetops.

Meanwhile, the Swedish people acted the same as always: admiration from afar, warm smiles, appreciative nods. The young kid had just fulfilled his duty and made the citizens love their country even more. During the Davis Cup matches that followed on two consecutive weekends in May 1974, against Poland and the Netherlands, the Swedish crowd applauded Björn's many winning shots as politely as it applauded the occasional nice shots hit by unknown opponents like Rolf Nowicki of Poland or Tadeusz Thung of the Netherlands.

At the Foro Italico in Rome, Mussolini's still-gleaming white marble athletes oversaw the two long-haired tennis players who were playing at the Italian Open and the crowds of people who were strolling between the espresso bars and tennis courts. Suddenly, Björn's name blared from the speakers. The masses were set in motion. At the Center Court, the kid with the golden locks began his tireless rallies. When the opponent, the Chilean Pinto Bravo, hit the match point out of bounds, throngs of people rushed the court and surrounded Björn. Young people grabbed at him, clung to him, pulled at his copper bracelet, pulled off his sweatband, stole his gold chain, and were about to pull the shorts and shirt off of him, before the guards finally caught up and could help Björn escape and run for cover to the locker room. What happened didn't bother him, he assured the Swedish newspapers, and then he returned to his hotel and his routines: rise at nine, breakfast, leave for the Foro Italico for a two hours long practice, lunch . . . In the afternoon, he sat in the bleachers and let his eyes rest on someone else's match, although in reality he was just inside his own mind.

Ove Bengtson tried to get him to visit the Coliseum and St. Peter's Basilica. Björn said he didn't have the energy. Winning in tennis required total focus. Didn't Ove understand that? Björn won against Riessen in the round of 16, against Tom Okker in the quarterfinal, and against Vilas in the semifinal after five tough sets. Ilie Nastase waited in the final.

Nastase had first appeared on the international tennis scene in the mid-'60s. He'd first become known to the Swedish audience at the 1969 Stockholm Open, where he reached the final. Back then, he'd looked like an altar boy, a timid and skinny young man with short hair combed to the side. He'd learned to play tennis as a child on the courts in Bucharest, where his mother and father worked as janitors and the Romanian Communist Party's dignitaries spent their free time. Nastase's fast rise to the top of the pro tour in the early-'70s had made him Europe's best player after the Second World War, based on achievements. It was hard to say if his successes had changed Nastase's personality, or if tennis had emboldened him to let his true self out. Nastase let his hair grow and developed a severe sex addiction. He had new women every night, in every city. His game, too, included all ingredients of the art of seduction: catlike hits, aggressive ulterior motives, and passionate moments when his black magic with his racket enthralled the crowd and made his opponent dizzy.

Still, he was popular among the players, despite the fact that any player who faced him in a match never knew quite what to expect. Also, many of the young players who were trying to make it in pro tennis saw Nastase as the most approachable person in a world where the jargon was all about keeping the newcomers at bay, keeping them down. Two years earlier, a few hours before his Wimbledon final, Nastase had hit with the sixteen-year-old Björn, who'd just won the junior singles final. Kjell Johansson had also felt welcomed and nurtured by Nastase, as had Rolf Norberg. The latter became Nastase's temporary doubles partner, after Nastase had asked Bergelin for suggestions. Norberg had been very nervous before his and Nastase's first-round match in a tournament in Morocco. "What do I do?" asked Norberg. "Just make sure you hit the ball over the net and I'll take care of the rest," was the answer. The pair won the tournament.

In Sweden at this time, it was Nastase and not Borg who was the favorite player of two young boys, Anders Järryd and Mats Wilander, when they hurried to the tennis court to play each summer morning, in Lidköping and Växjö, respectively.

What Nastase saw of Björn Borg during the final in Rome was his big blond hair, his long legs that never stopped, and balls that came back in the same monotonous manner throughout the entire match. If Borg by chance missed a shot, he just walked back to the baseline and started over, seemingly without irritation, anger, or any other identifiable feelings. The world's number-one player found nothing inspiring in that.

Nastase called Björn a martian: "Björn plays like a pawnbroker. You get nothing for free from him. He must be cheap in business, and he never gets nervous; I don't understand how he does it," said Nastase afterward.

"My composure was something I learned," says Björn. "I'd built it up for many years. It was a front. I cursed and raised hell on the court when I was young. I cheated, yelled, threw rackets. I still had all those emotions inside me my entire career, but I'd decided not to show them. To never become annoyed. If I could keep my anger over missed shots and incorrectly called shots inside of me, I'd become invincible. It was as if the calm built up my strength from within and gave me new opportunities. Not even when I'd missed a shot would I stand there like other players do and follow through in the air the shot I just missed. As if they've forgotten how to play. You can't do that. Never in my life."

Björn had won his biggest title and had earned 400,000 kronor. The Swedish press asked him what he was going to do with the money. "The money will go to paying taxes," said Björn. "Eighty percent goes to [the minister of finance] Sträng." A reporter pointed out that Björn would still have a lot of money left. Björn didn't respond.

Björn celebrated his finals victory at a restaurant in Rome, where he got food poisoning from a piece of sausage. While the rest of the tennis elite traveled to Paris to play the French Open, Björn was laid up in Rome. He then jumped on a plane back home to Sweden and the apartment in Södertälje.

"I don't know why I went home. It really wasn't good timing. But I was so happy to win in Rome against Nastase, and I didn't think much about Paris . . . or . . . I guess I thought *I won't win in Paris anyway*. That kind of preparation for a Grand Slam tournament, it's just not what you do. I was back at home training with Percy in the morning the same day I was scheduled to play in Paris. Percy stood around and fiddled with his keys after the practice. I saw that he had a sleeve with French francs. I remember wondering, *Why does he have French francs? He doesn't need those. I need them, I'm going to Paris, but he doesn't need any francs.* I said, 'Bye, Percy' and left."

When Borg arrived at Arlanda Airport, there was Percy again. Björn didn't get it. He said, "Bye, Percy," again and boarded the plane.

"And there was Percy again. 'I'm coming with you to Paris to practice with you,' he said. 'It's an 18th-year birthday present from the Stockholm Open, and it was supposed to be a surprise.' I was happy, of course, but when we got to Paris, we rushed over to the stadium, and I started my match immediately. My opponent won the first set and was winning, 4–0, in the final set. I managed to win it, 6–4, but I could just as well have lost. I don't know why I planned it that way. I was caught up in some sort of haze after the Italian Open. I wasn't thinking about Paris much. Rome back then was a huge tournament, almost as big as the French Open, so I was still consumed by it."

Björn received about a hundred calls a day at the hotel where he was staying. He used the simplest of tricks, asked the receptionist to answer all incoming calls with the phrase: "No, Björn has left the hotel and won't be back." Meanwhile, Björn was in his room resting as much as he could. It was a matter of taking advantage of the downtime. He was booked for four extensive interviews every day. He could have said no, but he believed that the journalists had a job to do, too. Björn also trained with Percy and his doubles partner for the week, the Russian Alex Metreveli, at a furious pace. And the tournament turned out to be physically demanding, with long matches that Björn won, strictly thanks to his pure stamina. Percy got bored of sitting in the stands and went back home after the quarterfinals. Lennart Bergelin replaced him.

For Björn, Percy and Lennart were both important, in different ways: "There's never been a better technique coach in Sweden than Percy. Even today. Percy can watch a player for five minutes and he'll see what the player is doing wrong or what needs to be changed. He's incredibly good, and that's well known not just in Sweden, but around the world.

"Lennart was different, he could take care of me as a player in a totally different way. That was the difference between them. They're both incredible coaches, but specifically when it comes to technique training, Percy is extremely important for a player in the junior age group, which is when you need to learn that. Lennart Bergelin became almost like a second father for me, someone who took care of the daily operations. Lennart handled everything, from logistics to sparring partners. And he made sure I could focus my concentration where I needed it, on the court. Tennis is that kind of sport. To be successful, you must have a clear mind and be able to concentrate only on the game."

In time for the final, a heatwave gripped Paris. Björn's opponent was Orantes, who from the start unraveled Björn's baseline game with a mixture of short, sliced backhands and unexpected attacks at the net.

As Bergelin watched Björn hit a backhand out and Orantes stroll toward his chair after having won the first two sets, he thought: *Orantes will win this, his game is too big, he's winning the important points.* But Björn glanced over at his opponent during the changeover and saw a face in agony. He thought: *I'll win this easily now.*

Björn had built his game on simplicity and control. He'd learned that at the garage wall, the thoughts that had shaped a behavior: keep the ball going . . . long enough . . . win the point. In the heat, Björn kept feeding his heavy topspin forehand. Tennis was about not missing, just gliding across the dry red clay, not hitting the ball out. Safety wasn't just Björn's motto, it was also a Swedish export success story that had turned a car maker and a lock maker into billion-dollar industries. It was a thought pattern that had built the entire welfare state. Match point: a heavy forehand deep to Orantes's backhand side, a desperate attempt at a passing shot from the Spaniard that landed in the doubles alley, a Swedish racket up in the air.

Björn had won his first big championship.

Foreign tennis experts and journalists who had witnessed Björn's achievements in Dallas, Rome, and Paris were just as curious about Björn's play and maturity as Nastase had been. They described Björn as an exceptional human being, as an entity that didn't exist in the real world. In *Sports Illustrated*, Curry Kirkpatrick wrote that Björn probably wasn't eighteen years old, but in fact a mature forty-eight-year-old, a wizard from Södertälje who'd gone off to the mountains a long time ago and now had just woken up and discovered miracle drugs, hair dryers, and color television sets with a lot of channels, and had now realized that with a bit of effort and a double-handed backhand, he could embark on a looting spree in tennis, the World Bank, and some select record stores.

BJÖRN BORG AND THE SUPER-SWEDES

The Swedish newspapers stayed away from that sort of playful journalism. There, headlines, articles, and analyses were hammered home in a patriotic smugness. Björn was a winner, thanks to his Swedish characteristics—diligence, persistence, cool, and reticence. BJÖRN IS MAKING MILLIONS BUT IS LEADING A DULL LIFE, read one headline in *Expressen*, which also published pictures from his parents' photo albums. That's where Björn's ideal life was. It could only be lived in Sweden. In the archipelago. On a boat excursion with his parents across dark-blue waters between dull-green forest islands. A quiet, calm, and natural life.

NOW HE CAN FINALLY COME HOME, read another headline after his victory in Paris.

Yes, Björn was coming home. To get his driver's license.

At a press conference in Madrid 110 days later, following early losses at Wimbledon and the U.S. Open, Björn declared that he was moving from Sweden to take up residence in Monte Carlo.

"There are two reasons for why I'm leaving Sweden," he said. "The taxes, of course, and that I'll be able to spend much more time with my parents."

To date that year, Borg had already earned 735,000 kronor from playing tennis. Of that, just over 80 percent had gone to paying taxes. In Monaco, he wasn't going to have to pay one krona. Bergelin attended the press conference looking somber, but he said that he completely understood: "Sweden will lose its greatest athlete ever. We'll lose him before he's even started his career. But I understand Björn. If you have to pay that kind of scary sums in taxes, you're going to try to get away. Then, your only chance is to leave the country."

Björn said that his parents were going to move into an apartment next door. They were going to start a company together and open a tennis shop where Rune and Margareta would work. "It'll have Björn's name," said Margareta.

The reaction was fast and furious. Björn was called a tax dodger and Monaco refugee. If you were to believe one evening newspaper's survey of five people, three of five Swedes were furious and viewed Björn as a traitor who was running away from his responsibility to the country and its regeneration of new sports talent.

Björn was too young to remember when the question of sports' place in society had first come to the forefront, at the time of Sweden's Davis Cup match against Rhodesia in 1968. Then, the questions to the tennis association's higher-ups had been a clear-cut moral choice: Should we participate in sports with a country that is subject to UN sanctions? Now the moral questions were posed to Björn, an individual athlete and a Swedish private citizen. The questions touched the people's soul: You're not going to take the money and run, Björn, are you?

The news of the move also opened things up for criticism against pro tennis and its raw commercialism. Behind the planning was Björn's financial agent since a few months back, Mark McCormack, a Yale-educated attorney who'd founded the International Management Group, a corporate name that, when pronounced in full, brought thoughts back to an Orwellian surveillance society. The company was more commonly known as IMG, which, according to many tennis players, was short for "I'm greedy."

IMG's business concept was to sign contracts with top athletes to manage their affairs. McCormack had found the apartments in Monte Carlo and had laid out in black and white how much more of his money Björn would keep by moving there. To move capital to places where politicians couldn't get their hands on it was McCormack's specialty. The company was a kind of an early storm troop for globalized capitalism in the '70s, when a different set of ideals still ruled. If the WCT had made the tennis pros known to the general public, IMG had turned them into merchandise. As an example, Björn had recently signed a clothing contract with Fila, which resulted in IMG refusing to let the Swede play in a Jockey shirt when he was in Sweden, as had previously been agreed.

Björn Borg became a homeless tennis player. Sweden was no more his country than Monaco. He believed the Swedish reactions reflected the well-known "royal Swedish envy," that the Law of Jante was trying to suffocate him. According to Kjell Johansson, this was an opinion that Bergelin helped him nurture.

"Labbe always kept on with that jargon when we're traveling abroad, talked about how bad Sweden was. The taxes, the mentality, how Swedes can't do anything and don't understand anything. He talked about it constantly, and if you're a young person who hears this all the time, of course it's easy for you to start thinking the same way."

BJÖRN BORG AND THE SUPER-SWEDES

Björn felt misunderstood. First, journalists had nagged him about how risky it was to jeopardize one's future by leaving school. Then, they whined when he was successful, even if he didn't cause anyone else harm. "All hell broke loose, they claimed I was disloyal to the society which had raised me, that I was selfish and money hungry," said Borg in an interview in the book, as told to Gene Scott, *My Life and Game*, in 1980.

However, the vocally strong journalists who hunted Björn down with their questions believed they were only doing their job and were in line with the times. In Sweden in 1974–75, the political radicalism that in 1968 was portrayed as avant-garde now became generally accepted. Striving for an all-equal society was the socially accepted norm.

During the six months that followed his announcement about leaving Sweden, Björn rarely played up to his standards from the spring. He lost in the semifinals at the Stockholm Open. The Masters tournament followed in Melbourne just before Christmas. Swedish Radio again broadcast live overnight for an audience of a million, but Björn was eliminated in the group rounds. Björn ended the year ranked number three in the world, but he had clearly fallen behind the new number one, Jimmy Connors. Vilas, the Masters winner, was considered the only real challenger to Connors. Vilas had a game that resembled Björn's but was much more aggressive and with even harder-hit strokes.

During the 1975 WCT season, Björn mixed random tournament wins with unexpected losses. He didn't care much about his relationship with Sweden, but when he played in Johannesburg in South Africa, he knew he'd be asked questions about it.

One week in April, the WCT tour made a stop at the Johanneshov arena in Stockholm. The same day that Björn landed in Stockholm, *Aftonbladet's* columnist "Macke" Nilsson reminded the readers that the news programs that week had reports about the national idol Björn Borg, "who emigrated to Monaco to avoid paying taxes, including for Swedish sports facilities." Nilsson argued that Borg just had played WTC tennis in South Africa and that the tennis pro circuit ignored all sanctions and as a result collected money from the racist regime in Johannesburg: "After having entertained South Africa's upper class, the tennis circuit can now make a stop here and rake in its millions."

Björn responded with his poorest showing of the year, a quick loss to his countryman Tenny Svensson in front of a dead-silenced crowd that felt cheated. Tenny knew that the moment he hit the match point winner, the organizers lost all their would-be profits in ticket sales. Björn left the court accompanied by boos and whistles. "Are you finished now, Björn?" asked a reporter but received no response. Björn hated those kinds of questions. It wasn't enough that journalists questioned everything he did, they also demanded an explanation for each loss. They didn't understand how tough the pro circuit was, didn't understand that losses were part of it, that losing was how you learned.

Arthur Ashe, who ended up winning the tournament in Stockholm, was upset over how the press and the Swedish sports audience treated Björn. Ashe pointed out that Connors had refused to play in the Davis Cup for the USA, and that Connors always demanded money under the table to play. Ashe told the Swedish crowd: "You should thank Björn for having played in every Davis Cup match and for playing again this year. Without demanding a krona in compensation. That's hardly how we Americans are. But Björn always comes to play. He likes Sweden. Appreciate that!"

In the early summer, when Björn defended his title in Paris by defeating Vilas in the finals, it didn't stir up as much excitement in the Swedish media as the previous year. The kid's steps and actions during the eight months that preceded his win in Paris had chipped away at the tribe's love for him. Rather than trying to continue to adore themselves through Björn, people were forced to contemplate difficult issues about sports and politics, tax morality, and the individual's loyalty to the collective that had produced him.

As for Borg, he believed that the reduced interest was because the player lineup in Paris was weaker than the year before. He declared that he would go to Wimbledon and win on grass, too. "This year, I'm ready to win."

In 1975, British bookmakers had Björn Borg as the third seed, after Connors and Ashe, in the world's most prestigious tennis tournament. To win the real big money on Björn, you could bet on which day of the tournament the girls would mob Björn, tear his clothes off, and carry him away naked from Wimbledon's center court.

That year, Björn was closer to being stripped by the girls than winning the tournament. Young girls were waiting for him everywhere, in parking lots and outside locker rooms, hotels, and players' tunnels. In the fourth round, Björn injured his thigh and then had no chance against Ashe in the quarterfinals.

A few days later, Ashe and Connors met in the final. Ashe's statements in Stockholm in April, about Connors's refusal to play in the Davis Cup, had resulted in Connors suing Ashe for slander in the week before Wimbledon. Connors demanded three million dollars in compensation. After that, everyone who had an interest in tennis followed the two Americans' progress through the draw and wondered what a match between them would look like. Perhaps a judge wearing a wig and a black robe should keep score? Never before had a Wimbledon final been played between two players who at the same time were involved in a legal dispute against each other.

Connors had built up an almost invincible aura around his tennis persona. He'd reached the finals without losing a set. In the semifinals, he'd crushed the world's hardest-hitting server, Roscoe Tanner. Connors had looked like a wild dragon who took in with one breath what the opponent with all his might threw at him—then spewed everything back engulfed in devastating flames.

Ashe, whose style of play was identical to Tanner's, albeit with a bit more rhythm and finesse, watched Connors's massacre from the stands and realized what was in store for him. After consulting with a close friend, Ashe decided to try a new style of play, which was in complete contrast to his natural instincts.

Every stroke of Ashe's was a shot that was thoroughly planned and softly placed, a sliced short ball or a high spinning slow ball. Spin after spin, Ashe deconstructed the massive hit machine that was Connors, like a methodical engineer. Finally, the only thing remaining was putting away a high volley and raising a fist in the air.

Ashe's tactical triumph inspired tennis players all over the world. In Växjö, a city in southern Sweden, Mats Wilander watched the match on live TV. Immediately afterward, he ran outside and tried to imitate Ashe's style of play. At the U.S. Open later that summer, Borg tried the same tactics in his semifinals match against Connors but wasn't at all comfortable with it—hitting soft balls was not part of his game. Connors won in straight sets but fell hard the following day in the final against Orantes, who applied Ashe's tactics 100 percent.

Later that fall, Björn was given another chance in the semifinals at the Stockholm Open. But not even in front of an encouraging home crowd in the Kungliga Tennis Hall was he able to crack the code; the varied game systemized by Ashe and Orantes didn't suit Björn. In the Stockholm Open final, Connors was defeated by a player who knew how to get it done, Adriano Panatta. The final was considered the best match ever played on Swedish soil. The Swedish tennis audience—more knowledgeable and less patriotic when it came to the pro tour—could, after the Masters in December, conclude that the pendulum at the tennis top had swung the other way. Four of the five major titles in 1975 had been won by players from a generation preceding the hard-hitting and masochistic youth trio of Connors, Borg, and Vilas, who with great fanfare had seized an equal share of major titles in 1974. The year 1975 marked the comeback of the classically schooled tennis game—the triumph of tactics and touch over the youthful power game.

For Björn, what had happened around and after his move to Monaco meant that he'd been relieved of the role as a godlike sports fetish. In 1975, this role was taken over by the slalom skier Ingemar Stenmark. Björn Borg had embarked on a more complex relationship with his home country, whose love and deep admiration was changing in character. What remained was something more lasting, a deep interest for tennis. What also remained was a critical, judgmental view of Borg. It said: We like you and we root for you, but we reserve the right to criticize you when we believe you're being too egotistical.

A ONE-MAN TEAM
IN A COLLECTIVE TIME

**"My thing was to do something on my own. I think that's what
motivates every athlete in an individual sport."**
—BJÖRN BORG

In just a few years, the tennis world had expanded, with major stars now
originating from several more countries. But in one respect, everything
remained the same: either Australia or the USA had won every Davis
Cup tournament since 1936. At the sight of the gleaming Davis Cup
trophy, a number of top players from other countries had been struck
by a condition that resembled delirium, which caused them to lose their
self-control as well as their tennis game. That had been the case in the
1972 final, when the experts had agreed that Romania, with Nastase
and Tiriac at home on clay in Bucharest, would triumph over the USA.
Gigantic posters with the Romanian stars' faces adorned the Communist
capital. Bakeries sold pastries in the shape of the trophy. But out on the
court, Nastase was barely able to hold onto his racket and became easy
prey for the Americans.

But in 1974, the USA without Connors was eliminated early on by
Colombia. And two Indian brothers, Vijay and Anand Amritraj, had
caused a tennis fever in the world's second-most populous nation, by defeating Australia and leading India to the final, where they would face South
Africa. But India never came to play, in protest of the South African regime's

apartheid politics. South Africa won by default and thus became the first country to drive a wedge in the American-Australian dominance.

At the time, the UN urged its member countries to boycott all sports relations with South Africa and Rhodesia. The International Tennis Federation settled for moving South Africa to the Latin American zone before the 1975 tournament. It didn't help. South Africa slithered its way through the draw like a poisonous snake that nobody wanted to touch. Colombia didn't come to play in the first round, and Mexico refused to play in the second. Without returning one single serve, South Africa reached the final in the Latin American zone, where Chile awaited. Chile's dictator, Augusto Pinochet, declared that it would welcome the apartheid state. Sports and politics were closely interwoven, and nowhere was this more obvious than in the 1975 Davis Cup.

For Sweden, the Davis Cup tournament began against Poland. Because Kjell Johansson was injured, Birger Andersson and Björn Borg would play the singles. As if this weakening of the team weren't enough, Björn's pro career also complicated matters. He'd once again qualified for the WCT playoffs in Dallas and as such was required to attend Lamar Hunt's mandatory garden party. The last connecting flight to the United States from Heathrow in London departed at 6 p.m. The Swedish Tennis Association leased a private plane, which would depart at 3:30 p.m. to take the Swedish superstar from Warsaw to Heathrow. Sweden received approval from the Polish team to move up Björn's match on Sunday against Poland's number-one player, Wojtek Fibak, from 1:30 to 12:30 p.m.

It was still going to be tight. Björn had to beat Fibak in two hours.

And Fibak was a player who didn't rush between points. He'd defeated Birger Andersson in straight sets on Friday, but it had taken three hours. On Sunday against Borg, the king of long rallies, there was nothing to indicate that this match would be any quicker. The Swedes asked the Polish team to move Fibak and Björn's match up another hour, but their request was denied.

A moral dilemma loomed for Bergelin. Should he be loyal to his responsibilities as captain of the national team and demand that Borg play, or loyal to his role as Björn's coach with a mission to ensure his prodigy had optimal preparation? Bergelin prioritized the latter and announced that he'd remove Borg from the court if he risked missing his flight to Dallas.

Leading up to Sunday, Sweden was up, 2–1, and needed one more victory.

Ove Bengtson recalls:

"Everything was so rushed. A lot of money was involved. There were private planes and stuff. Bergelin was supernervous, Björn took it easy. We were a fun group, different personalities. Before the match, we told Björn, 'on the first changeover, you'll have to ask Labbe what time it is.' The match started. After the first game, Björn walked over to the changeover with unusually hurried steps and said: 'Labbe, Labbe, what time is it?' Labbe didn't find that kind of stuff funny."

Fibak strolled around leisurely between points and tried out quirky stroke variations, like hitting drop shots off Björn's second serves. His play earned him thunderous applause. Björn still won the first two sets, but the players kept even in the third: 4–4, 5–5, 6–6. Then Fibak hit a drop shot that Björn wasn't able to run down. It was getting close to 2:30 p.m. And rain had begun to fall. The Polish coaches got up to ask the umpire to stop the match. But Fibak waved his arms, "Let's keep playing," he said. A few minutes later, Björn put away the match point and rushed off to his private plane. Bergelin sighed with relief. He'd been wearing long johns in the damp weather. With the victory secured at the last minute, the captain became superstitious and decided that the long johns would be a constant the rest of the season.

"I want to say they had a lion theme," says Rolf Norberg.

Björn made it to Dallas in time. In the semifinals, he played his young life's best match to date, beating his childhood idol Laver in five sets. In the final against Ashe, Björn was totally drained and seemed dejected from the start. When he landed in West Berlin a day or so later for the next Davis Cup battle, against a strong West German team, he asked to be excused from the doubles match. "Ove and Rolf are just as good a team," he said. This awakened the prey instincts of the Swedish journalists. Borg's requests were called diva behavior.

This rubbed Björn the wrong way. He was annoyed. With Sweden. With the journalists. With the entire situation. And with the role in which he found himself. His victories for the national team were taken for granted. He barely received recognition for his victories anymore. When Borg won the opening match against Karl Meiler, his efforts on the court were described in terms such as "Borg fulfilled his duty and gave Sweden the lead." Björn was becoming the unsung hero of the tennis national team, a team that hardly shone bright in Berlin during the first two days. Birger Andersson had no chance against the German number-two player, Hans-Jürgen Pohmann, whose most prominent talent was how elegantly he twirled his racket between points. The newly formed doubles team, Bengtsson/Norberg, lost by the merciless score of 2–6, 3–6, 1–6. In all practicality, Sweden had been eliminated. Björn indeed fulfilled "his duty" and tied the match with his victory over Pohmann on the third day. But this victory, too, was noted with almost purely academic interest, since everyone knew how Birger Andersson's match against the skilled German number-one player, Karl Meiler, would end.

Ove Bengtson remembers the solemn mood: "People left and went home. Articles had been written. We were eliminated in advance."

Paradoxically, many newspapers put the blame on Björn Borg. They said he no longer cared about the Davis Cup. It was implied that this was because the tournament lacked prize money, that it wasn't enough for him to represent his country.

Today, Björn says, "My thing was to do something on my own. I think that's what motivates every athlete in an individual sport. But at the same time, I loved it when we played the Davis Cup. The team spirit, it was great."

Nothing creates a better breeding ground for that team spirit than when, in the midst of misery, there is suddenly a glimmer of hope. Such as when your opponent is affected by the Davis Cup delirium. Jan-Erik Lundqvist, who'd been hired as an expert radio commentator for the weekend, hit some balls with Birger that morning and visited the players' hotel at lunchtime. There, he saw Karl Meiler sitting at a table, staring at his food without taking a single bite. The rumor spread. Bergelin urged Birger to just keep the ball in play. Then he took his captain's seat wearing his tennis track pants with his blue and yellow long johns underneath. While the warm May sun colored the clay court red, Meiler was pale as a ghost out on the court. His shots hit the nether regions of the net or way outside the lines. Birger Andersson stuck with his game plan, and his self-confidence grew with each point won. After he won the first set, the rest was quick history: 7–5, 6–1, 6–2.

Ove Bengtson still doesn't quite understand what happened. "Of course, everything really started with Björn. But everything just fell into place with Birger, too, in a curious way that nobody could've imagined."

Birger became "Miracle-Birger." When the new hero was hoisted in the air by Ove, Rolf, and Björn, the image of Björn as a loyal team player helped the Swedish people forget his move to Monaco and the doubles match he'd declined to play. Those things weren't worth arguing about anymore. He was just a regular guy.

That summer, Sweden played several matches away from home. After having defeated the Soviet Union, 4–1, the Swedish team continued on to Barcelona. On paper, Spain's team was stronger than Sweden's. In 1975, Orantes's results were as good as Borg's. The highlight was his U.S. Open victory on the Forest Hills clay. José Higueras was one of the world's ten-best clay court players, and the Spanish doubles team was the best in the world. The Davis Cup match in Barcelona progressed in a similar way to Sweden's match against West Germany earlier that spring:

Orantes–Andersson: 6–1, 6–3, 6–4.
Borg–Higueras: 6–3, 6–1, 6–1.
Orantes/Gisberg–Borg/Bengtson: 6–4, 6–3, 6–1.
Borg–Orantes: 6–4, 6–2, 6–2.

Björn's win over Orantes was a sign of strength, but for Sweden the situation was as grim as it had been in Berlin. Birger's chances were considered non-existent. Higueras was a tireless ball blocker who practically never missed a shot, and he could stay out in the oppressing heat forever. Birger had no killer weapons. During the warm-up, Birger couldn't find his rhythm and shook his head in resignation. Meanwhile, Bergelin sweated bullets in his long johns.

During the changeover after the first game, Bergelin checked Birger's rackets and asked why he hadn't changed the strings on them. Birger said that he had, but that he'd probably grabbed the wrong bag when he left the hotel. Bergelin asked Ove to go back to the hotel and pick up the right rackets. Meanwhile, Higueras took the first set.

"The hotel was completely dead, and I couldn't get into Birger's room," says Ove. "Finally, I got a hold of a cleaning lady, who reluctantly let me in. I hurried back, and Birger had the rackets he needed in the second set."

Right away, Birger began hitting the ball cleaner. Higueras noticed the difference and got nervous. When Birger won the second set, 6–4, the

Davis Cup delirium started to seep into the Spaniard's bloodstream. There was no turning back. Birger won the third set, 6–3, and easily took home the fourth, 6–0. Sweden had advanced to the semifinals.

Chile was next. The fascist Pinochet's team had eliminated prime minister John Vorster's South Africa. The Communist President Gustav Husak's Czechoslovakia and the democratic country Australia were the other semifinals teams. Husak, who just a few months earlier had been called "the dictatorship's creature," announced that the country wouldn't play in a potential final against Chile, in a protest against the military junta's crimes against human rights.

In Sweden, that point of view was also gaining momentum.

The Swedish government declared that it didn't intend to get involved in the matter. Tommy Engstrand, the sports reporter for Swedish Radio, interviewed Prime Minister Olof Palme and asked if the reluctance to interfere was because the government believed that sports and politics didn't belong together.

Palme answered: "I meet people everywhere who say that sports and politics don't go together. In the next breath, they ask for much increased benefits from the state and local municipalities. The annual contribution from the state is more than one and a half billion kronor. This means that sport is an important and valuable part of society and can never entirely isolate itself from politics."

"Are we asking too much of a single movement like sports? We often ask it to be at the forefront of these kinds of situations," Engstrand questioned.

"Yes, but independence has a price," said Palme. "It's nice that sports are independent. But this also means that difficult decisions need to be made. You can't expect others to make these decisions for you."

Palme's announcement meant that the Swedish Tennis Association's decision to play against Chile had been confirmed. "Sports and politics do not belong together," said the association, which selected Båstad as the location for the match. In response to Palme's statement that "difficult decisions need to be made," the tennis association's programmatic comment appeared tone-deaf.

Chile's best player, Jaime Fillol, sympathized openly with Pinochet's military junta. In the week leading up to the match, the police announced that a death threat had been made against Fillol by Swedish opponents to the match. This prompted the Chilean star to decide to stay at home, but Pinochet then summoned Fillol to his presidential palace and persuaded him to go.

The Swedish players discussed the situation. They were informed by the police that vague death threats had also been made against Borg and Bengtson. A decision was made to send 1,300 police officers, several helicopters, around 60 horses, and twice as many dogs to Båstad.

The Swedish Chile Committee, which comprised basically the same people who for the last ten years had protested America's war in Vietnam, decided to travel to Båstad to attempt to stop the match, similar to the events around the match against Rhodesia in 1968.

A gang of greasers announced that it would help police maintain order.

"I'm terrified of greasers," said Rolf Norberg in an interview.

The Social Democrats, who sensed that Palme's refusal to make a decision about the match was a plausible reason for the mobilization, decided, as a compromise, to organize a demonstration with the former Prime Minister Tage Erlander and the Swedish Ambassador to Chile, Harald Edelstam, as main speakers. The demonstrators would present arguments for the reasoning behind playing the match but at the same time appeal to the Chilean government to release political prisoners.

Still, approximately 150 active athletes demanded that the match be stopped. In a manifesto, the wrestler Pelle Svensson and the soccer players Roland Andersson and Reine Feldt argued that stopping the match was the only way to show solidarity with the Chilean people. Two sports heroes from an older generation, Sixten Jernberg and Gunnar Nordahl, also joined the debate. They argued that the match should be played and the demonstrators' growls ignored.

Bergelin picked Björn up in Copenhagen. Margareta and Rune drove from Monte Carlo. On Thursday, 1,000 demonstrators supporting the Social Democrat Party marched through Båstad. The protest ended with a gathering at the town square, where Erlander delivered a speech against fascism. Chilean singers performed. Later, in the darkness of night, Ambassador Edelstam, whose bravery had saved the lives of many Chileans at the time of Pinochet's military coup, was up on the stage dancing with the female singers.

On Friday, police helicopters buzzed in the air. Pinochet sent encouraging telegrams to Fillol. Around one hundred police officers, plain-clothes and uniformed, were in the stands. Among the journalists was a writer from Uruguay who, when the Chilean number two player, Patricio Cornejo, took the first set from Borg on a wet court that was heavy from the rain, noted that Cornejo likely felt right at home surrounded as he was by the uniformed and armed police officers who were positioned all over the stands.

Björn Borg complained. The heavy balls in the autumn chill annoyed him. His shots fell short. "So typical of Sweden", he screamed when one of his shots landed on the baseline but was called out.

Björn won in the end, but at the press conference, he was in a sour mood: "I really don't enjoy playing tennis in Sweden anymore. I won't play here again. The newspapers write too much crap."

Birger was sluggish and had no chance against Fillol. The first day's results pointed to a Chilean victory. Its doubles team was one of the world's best.

The leftist groups, which were planning to gather for a joint demonstration on Saturday morning, prepared in different locations around Båstad. KFML(r), the Soviet faithful, gathered down by the Malen saltwater pools in the eastern part of Båstad. The instructions from the party leaders, who otherwise advocated for an armed revolution in Sweden, said that nobody should be provoked to violence. The Trotskyists—a group of young Swedes who claimed that the problem with the Russian Revolution and society in general was that the Bolsheviks in the Soviet Union in 1922 had deviated from the course of the Red Army leader, Leon Trotsky—in 1975 consisted of a group of skinny intellectuals who'd made themselves famous by their way of talking politics at all the parties, without ever actually accomplishing anything. Now, according to rumors, they had gathered at a secret location in Båstad, armed with meter-long bats, helmets, heavy boots, protective goggles, and gauntlets.

As the large demonstration began to come together, the Left Communist Party distributed flyers saying that the Trotskyists and another leftist group, the Communist Federation—which had distanced itself from Stalin and Trotsky but leaned somewhat toward Lenin—both had weapons. One of the armed members of the Communist Federation was Anders Carlberg, who'd led the occupation of the Student Union in Stockholm in the spring of 1968. He assured that the reason for the bats was only to protect themselves from the greasers and the purpose of the protective goggles was to protect themselves from the teargas from the police.

BJÖRN BORG AND THE SUPER-SWEDES

The doubles match had already started when the protesters reached the town square. The police were kneeling behind barricades surrounding the arena, while the protesters created a thick sound wall of slogans, sirens, drums, and whistles. Out on the court, however, it was quiet, or, like Jan Guillou wrote in the magazine *Folket i Bild/Kulturfront*: "a different world, [with] only the sound of the tennis ball."

The protesters listened to Tommy Engstrand's commentary through portable radios. Occasionally, the slogans about "crushing fascism" were interrupted by exclamations like *"yeees!"* A moment of silence was held for the victims of the junta, before the protesters released balloons decorated with the names of murdered Chilean junta opponents. At the stadium, the spectators turned their eyes away from the match skyward, where the red balloons bobbed like blood splatter against the gray sky.

Ove Bengtson played the doubles match of his life, and Birger once again won his Sunday singles match over a much stronger opponent. For once, Björn could play a singles match without having to carry the weight of a must-win match on his shoulders.

Sweden had advanced to the Davis Cup final.

"Should we play tennis against a team whose players are representatives of a country governed by 'the dictatorship's creature,' which is what you called the Czechoslovak political leaders back in the spring?" asked Tommy Engstrand of Sweden's Prime Minister Olof Palme before the final.

"Yes," answered Palme, who himself played tennis at the Kungliga Tennis Hall every week, with the Swedish Film Institute's then-director, Harry Schein. "The tennis association has decided that we are going to play. Its decision stands."

The Swedish tennis fall season had been hypnotic. Before the final, which would be played two weeks after the Masters tournament in Stockholm, the Swedish team checked in to Foresta Hotel in Lidingö. There, the team could focus and prepare at a safe distance from the temptations of Stockholm's nightlife. However, the newly appointed assistant national coach, Ilie Nastase, didn't express a need for peace and quiet. He once again checked in to the Grand Hotel at the Swedish Tennis Association's expense.

"The reason he was there was not for us to engage socially with him at night," says Ove Bengtson. "He ran his own race, and it suited him perfectly. But I have to give him credit. He did an excellent job. He was always on time. He was there in the locker room. He practiced with us, but he never took over. He liked us, he liked Sweden, and he was fond of the ladies. It worked out well."

Björn Borg recalls that he liked the idea of Nastase as a coach:

"The association asked him, I didn't. We'd always had a good connection with Nastase, and he was really fired up about the job. He and I were competitors among the world's top players, but at the same time there was, both with him and with most of the other players. . . . Maybe we weren't pals, but there was a level of respect. So, he came to Stockholm and served as our sparring partner. He played singles and doubles with us, it was great to get us up to speed, and it served as an incentive."

Nastase stayed out until the wee hours, but when he and Rolf Norberg played doubles against Björn and Ove, Nastase was in tip-top shape. Bergelin decided early on to change the winning lineup from the summer's successful clay court matches. Birger was out as a singles player. Ove Bengtson would take his place.

"I wasn't bitter about it at all, says Birger. "The Kungliga Tennis Hall's indoor surface was way too fast for me. Bergelin's decision was absolutely the right one. I was relieved I didn't have to play."

Ove Bengtson's match schedule would be tough, including both singles and doubles, just like Björn's:

"Birger was better than me on clay, but since I was a serve-and-volley player, Bergelin thought I was better suited for the fast surface in the Kungliga Tennis Hall. The point was that I would get a feel for it and be ready for the double, not be rusty in the doubles match. Everyone knew the doubles match would be the decisive factor, since Björn's two singles wins were considered a given."

In the days before Christmas, there was no longer room for discussions about sports and politics or about tennis's responsibilities. All focus was on the match, in the Kungliga Tennis Hall, where Gustav V's spirit lingered and where a modest jazz trio played on the court while the spectators—who'd been waiting in line for hours—took their seats and the officials marched in with flags and banners. Marcus Wallenberg, who'd played in Sweden's first Davis Cup match exactly 50 years earlier, was honored in the stands.

BJÖRN BORG AND THE SUPER-SWEDES

The concern that Björn may have lost his self-confidence following his loss in the Masters tournament was gone after only a few points. Björn played with fury against Jiří Hřebec, attacked the net, put away volley winners, and lost only four games in the entire match. In four close sets, Ove managed to put pressure on Kodes, who'd won both Wimbledon and the French Open. This was promising, but also a matter of concern. What if Ove had wasted his best efforts in a match he wasn't going to win anyway? What if he had a reaction in the doubles and then be completely burned-out in his final day's singles match?

The Czechs' big doubles specialist, Vladimir Zednik, already soaking wet from nervousness, started out the doubles match by making three double faults in the first game, which gave Sweden the only break it needed to win the set. In the second set, the same scenario repeated itself: Zednik faltered in one game, and Sweden played inspired and won the set. The pattern continued in the third set. On this afternoon, the hapless Zednik more or less handed Sweden the victory. This meant that Sunday could see Björn Borg win the Davis Cup for Sweden for the first time. After South Africa's "pretend victory," Sweden had the chance to become the first country to actually break the United States-Australia hegemony.

That's when the cool Borg suddenly began suffering from nerves. Was it the Davis Cup delirium? After all, he was still a teenager.

"I didn't get any sleep before Sunday's match against Kodes. I played the match through in my mind over and over all through the night. I won every time. I need a lot of sleep, but one night like that is fine," Borg explains.

Once out on the court, Björn played with a focus and presence while seeming completely unfazed by the moment's historic significance in sports. He attacked the net, returned masterfully, and ran down everything Kodes tried to throw him off his rhythm. After closing out the match point, Björn threw his racket up in the air, jumped over the net, and was immediately mobbed and hoisted up in the air by his celebrating teammates. It was Björn's moment, after a season when he, like a loyal blue-collar worker, had performed his job in silence and let other players, usually Birger, borrow the spotlight.

A few days later, on Christmas Day, Björn spoke to the Swedish people from Monte Carlo. Swedish Radio broadcast an hour-long program in which Björn spoke with journalist Arne Hegerfors via telephone. Björn chose the music and talked about the tennis year. An audience of a million interrupted their Christmas celebration to listen in. Björn began the program by selecting Elton John's "Funeral for a Friend," a song choice that could be seen as a commentary on the Swedish people's attitude toward him during and after his move to Monaco. But Björn made no such connections in the program; he simply said that Elton John's record was one of the best ever made. He also said that for his part, the annoyance with Sweden was a forgotten chapter. Björn asked the Swedish people to understand that he always wanted to do his best, that he was very grateful for his achievements to date, and that the Swedish people and tennis fans must understand that things like his loss at the Masters also were part of tennis life. Nobody can win all of the time, as the competition is supertough. After that, Björn put Barry White's "You're My First, My Last, My Everything" on the turntable. He said that when he and the guys in his WCT group used to go out dancing, they'd request this song from the disc jockey. The radio listeners could now imagine one of the world's most eligible bachelors smoothly walking up to the DJ booth in a trendy hot spot to request that the most sensuous bass-baritone voice of soul music be played from the speakers.

But reality for Björn Borg wasn't always what the general public imagined.

"I was with him one of those times," says Kjell Johansson. "It was an evening in Munich. The disco was completely deserted when Panatta and Björn and I arrived there. We just stood there and stared. Björn said he didn't have the nerve to go up and request the song. Panatta did, the song started playing, and Panatta said: 'Come on, let's dance!' But Björn and I thought it'd be embarrassing to get up and dance alone in an empty disco. So Panatta had to dance all by himself. Björn and I watched, we started to shake our booties a little where we were standing, but mostly we just felt embarrassed and shy."

DESIRE, WINS, AND WIMBLEDON

"Nastase was the favorite; me being there was more of a shocker. I know Nastase looked at it that way, too."
—BJÖRN BORG

Allan is sitting at his desk counting. Judit walks in through the door; she's wearing summery clothes, a short dress, braid against her back, her hat in one hand, tennis racket in the other. She stops in the doorway. Allan stands up, serious and respectful.

Judit (serious but friendly): Why don't you come out to tennis?

Allan (shy, fighting emotion): I'm too busy.

Judit: Didn't you see that I leaned the bike against the oak tree, not away from it?

Allan: Yes, I saw that.

Judit: So, what does that mean?

Allan: It means . . . that you want me to come out and play tennis . . .

The play Ingmar Bergman was rehearsing at the Dramaten theater in Stockholm wasn't a new, original contemporary commentary on the Swedish tennis boom, but rather the opening scene in the second act of August Strindberg's *The Dance of Death*. It's a drama that revolves around a husband and wife who are ostracized by their friends and acquaintances after having engaged in intrigues, foul play, and slander. The dance of death that the couple and their friends are pulled into is a relentless transformation from being chosen to becoming rejected and denied atonement. The characters are morally and financially submerged. Their only way out is hate, contempt, and self-imposed isolation.

Tennis, lies, and broken friendship ties . . . The rehearsals with Margaretha Krook, Anders Ek, and Jan-Olof Strandberg on this gloomy, late January morning in 1976 were suddenly and without advance warning interrupted by the theater's executive secretary, who rushed in and announced that a police officer wanted to speak with Bergman immediately. The scene that followed could have been taken from a rehearsal of a play by Kafka on another stage in the theater building.

The famous director follows the secretary to an office. There, a gentleman wearing a dark overcoat and a floral shirt, with dirty fingernails, introduces himself as a police officer.

The director: What's going on?

The police officer: Your tax affairs. You have to immediately come with me to a hearing.

The director: I don't understand.

The police officer: You're suspected of tax evasion, and you must immediately come with me to a hearing.

The director (unsure): In that case, I must bring my lawyer.

The police officer: Your lawyer is involved and also summoned for a hearing. You'll have to immediately come with me.

In his autobiography *Laterna Magica*, Ingmar Bergman describes, 11 years later, how he felt: "Finally, I'm out on the street. It's dusk, there's a light snow fall. Everything is very clear, but black and white without colors, raw like a Xerox copy. My teeth are chattering, every thought or feeling is numbed."

On the same day, in a hotel room in Philadelphia, Sweden's other international celebrity, Björn Borg, had wondered how he, the chosen one with a tennis racket, was going to take the next step up. The player who'd given him the most trouble to date was waiting for him in the finals at the American Indoor Championships. The one player who seemed to prevent him from taking the last step up on the tennis throne, Jimmy Connors, had beaten Björn three times in a row. Björn turned into a boy when he faced Connors. Throughout 1975, the older guard—Ashe,

Orantes, and Nastase—had shown that the remedy against Connors was soft shots and a varied game. But in his hotel room, Björn decided on another strategy. Just like the couple in *The Dance of Death* are offered an opportunity to break out of their misery but opt not to, Björn was going to reject the tips from his player colleagues. Instead, he was going to use his fists to hit his way out of his prison. He was going to play hardball, an eye for an eye.

At 5–2 in the first set, everything seemed to go according to Björn's stubborn plan. After wiping his racket during the changeover, Borg rose from his chair and stepped out on the court in his rolling gait, ready to serve home the set. At the same time, Connors got up from his chair, cursing at himself. He hit his head with his racket, slapped his palm against his thigh, and muttered: "Now it's crunch time, damn it. Get yourself together. You're going to win this."

From that moment on, Björn didn't win any of the important points. The final score, 7–6, 6–4, 6–0 to Connors, had ruined Björn's mood. In the end, he didn't even enjoy playing. To be on the same court with a player who hit the ball so hard and so deep and possessed such an impervious "I'm the best" attitude was a challenge whose solution thoroughly eluded Björn.

In Stockholm, the police's interrogations with Ingmar Bergman dragged on. After two months, all criminal charges were dropped, but the investigation into whether there was unreported income continued. By now, Bergman had had enough.

In an open letter, he wrote that he'd decided to leave Sweden: "I am leaving all my assets in Sweden, to the disposal of the National Tax Administration. I've been a convinced Social Democrat. With genuine passion have I embraced this, the ideology of the gray compromises. I believed my country was the best in the world, and I guess I still believe that, possibly because I have seen so little of other countries."

If the simple tennis player Björn Borg's exile the previous year had awakened a complex anger, a feeling of betrayed love, this exile by the intellectual artist Ingmar Bergman was met with open contempt. "Leave, Bergman, we won't miss you!" screamed one editorial headline. While the leftist groups felt that Bergman was too bourgeois, the bourgeois felt he was too difficult, too nonnoncommercial. The image of Sweden that Bergman depicted in his films was different from that of the politicians and newspapers. In Bergman's films, the welfare state's souls were not happy and content with politically tangible and practical solutions. Rather, they were suffering from existential despair, anxiety, and thoughts on God and truth.

Björn Borg, who was raised in the city of Södertälje, a traditional stronghold for the Social Democratic Party, had finalized his plan for the year 1976 even before his loss to Connors. His plan was built on foolproof shots for money and glory. He would achieve the glory by focusing 100 percent on Wimbledon and the U.S. Open in Forest Hills, the two most important tournaments. To have a nineteen-year-old openly declare that his goal was to win the world's two biggest tournaments was unusual. In particular, it wasn't the typical way for Swedish athletes, who'd always preferred to play the role of the underdog and keep their innermost dreams to themselves. But Björn was never afraid to say exactly what he felt. It gave him goals and a purpose.

The problem was that the tennis world's highest level was filled to the brim with all sorts of brilliance. Björn had recently been reminded of two of the sorts: Nastase at the Masters and Connors in Philadelphia. Also, Björn couldn't be sure that his development curve would continue upwards. On the contrary, he realized that at some point he was sure to hit a plateau, and that his ambitious goals would require even more work.

Also, there was money to be made everywhere. Björn was the busiest of all players in terms of exhibition and challenger matches, which these years started to make up a greater part of the professional tennis calendar. Less than a decade after tennis had opened its floodgates to prize money and professionalism, it moved at a high speed toward an unbridled capitalism that foreshadowed the general societal development.

In late February, the day before the challenger match between Borg and Laver, which early on had been marketed as a benefit for cancer sufferers, Borg was sitting in the press room along with the promoters, Curt Hageus and Carl-Axel Hellqvist. At his side, he had IMG's Jan Steinmann. Someone asked Hellqvist if the money went to cancer sufferers.

"No one believes that the spectators have purchased tickets to help cancer sufferers," he said. "People have paid up to 100 kronor per ticket to see Björn Borg and Rod Laver, the greatest of all, fight for half a million kronor."

The Scandinavium arena was almost sold out. Hellqvist said that 750,000 kronor had come from ticket sales and 250,000 kronor from advertising. A reporter noted that it was a good business deal for Hageus and asked if cancer sufferers could expect a contribution. "No, I'll keep the profits," said Hageus. "To cover what I've lost previously, in other events. And to keep it going for the next time."

Björn said that he'd arrived at four in the morning on a flight from another challenger match, in Hawaii. Laver hadn't arrived yet. He was playing WCT tennis in Rotterdam that same week. He'd won his quarterfinal on Wednesday and was to arrive on a flight to Göteborg later in the afternoon. Directly after the match, he was going to return to Rotterdam to play his semifinals match.

Björn was asked whether the match against Laver was important to him in terms of his athletic career. "Not really. But I play for 500,000 kronor."

Björn's response was too provocative for the marketers of the challenger match. Steinman grabbed the microphone: "The match is extremely important to Björn, because if he wins he has the chance to meet the winner of the Connors-Orantes match in a World Cup match later this spring."

"If Björn wins, his match against Connors is practically a done deal," added Hellqvist.

"And then we're talking even bigger money," said Steinman.

The next day, the arena was filled with a crowd that enthusiastically applauded the nineteen-year-old Swede. Björn was jetlagged but able to keep up the power in his heavy topspin strokes. He crushed the thirty-eight-year-old Laver. The Australian wobbled around on the court on legs that seemed to barely hold the weight of him. And Björn pocketed another half a million kronor, the equivalent of ten annual salaries for a Swedish laborer. Although the winner didn't take it all. The loser received his share as well, to the tune of a few hundred thousand kronor. The only ones left out in the cold were the cancer sufferers.

Two weeks later, there was another sign that the country that Björn Borg and Ingmar Bergman had chosen to leave was in the process of changing, in the process of taking its first step into a future that more resembled the world of professional tennis. The children's book author Astrid Lindgren published a fairy tale in *Expressen*'s arts and culture section. The title of the article was "Pomperipossa in Monismanien." The author had borrowed the latter name from the Swedish filmmaker Kenne Fant, who about a year earlier had made a drama film about a futuristic totalitarian one-party society. The film's storyline follows a teacher who is persecuted when he tries to teach his children to think independently.

Astrid Lindgren described how Pomperipossa happily and for a long time had wanted to contribute and pay so that everyone in Monismanien could get their share of the welfare cake. She wrote that the leaders who'd called the shots for more than 40 years had created such a great society where nobody needed to be poor. But one day, one of Pomperipossa's friends told Pomperipossa that her marginal tax rate was 102 percent. "'You're kidding,' said Pomperipossa. 'There aren't even that many percent.' But yes, there were, because in Monismanien there was an unlimited amount of percent."

Astrid Lindgren's criticism was not only a protest against her own personal financial tax situation. It questioned deeper layers in the construction of the welfare state. In her story, Astrid Lindgren incorporated a poem:

You create a value, this society cannot accept,
the squabbling of the bureaucrats, in this you must participate.
You must help Castro drive his war in Angola,
or else, off to the old folks' home for therapy you go.

Gunnar Sträng, the finance minister, couldn't hold his tongue: "The author is clearly good at writing fairy tales, but she has no clue about taxes."

That answer revealed an arrogance by a political party that had been in government for 44 years. A few weeks earlier, the newspapers had published photos of the president of the transport workers' union, who was vacationing in Spain in the midst of a political boycott. He was shown with his exposed potbelly, wearing sunglasses, and smoking a cigar. The public opinion, which had been sympathetic to the Social Democratic Party up to the late winter/early spring of 1976, began to turn. It wasn't that people were suddenly questioning the heavy tax burden or the welfare state, but that other parties, especially the Center Party, were offering an alternative that seemed closer to people's everyday life—less bureaucratic and more small-scale—while still maintaining the welfare and social safety nets.

To the extent professional tennis offered a vision for the future of society, Björn Borg was the picture of the tireless traveling salesman. A simple man who, through hard work and diligence, was able to dig for gold for himself. The week before the WCT playoffs in Dallas, which was another of the major titles he wanted to win, Björn left for a tour of exhibition and challenger matches. Wednesday: Copenhagen; Friday: New Jersey; Saturday: Chicago; Sunday: Oakland; Monday: arrival in Dallas. Covering a distance of 46,340 kilometers in five days was not ideal preparation for a tournament, but it did make you richer.

"You've declined in the last year. The spark is gone. You play too much," Janne Lundqvist told Björn when he saw him at one of Lamar Hunt's parties.

"Easy for you to say," said Björn. "There are so many exciting tournaments."

Bergelin and Sven Davidson were there, too, but it was Janne who kept pushing: "All that rushing around to challenger matches is affecting your game. Your play hasn't changed since last year. The last few matches, you haven't even taken a set from Connors. You need to improve your serve-and-volley."

For once, Bergelin agreed with someone who criticized his protégé. "The challenger matches are a curse," he said. "I'm trying to make Björn cut down on them."

Janne Lundqvist said that tennis probably was at a lower level technically than it had been ten years ago. The players hit shorter returns, the shots weren't deep enough. Björn didn't agree. He thought it was better to play a simple game than to play beautifully and technically correctly. His experience had taught him that conservative more often beat brilliant than the other way around. What it looked like didn't matter. A short ball that bounced up high was more difficult for an opponent to handle than a deep, flat shot.

"You should try to mix things up with a drop shot every once in a while. Even if you end up losing the point, you'll create confusion in your opponent," said Janne.

"They're already confused because my game is exactly the same all of the time," said Björn. Janne said that you could get as far as Björn had done with that style of play, but never reach the absolute top. To be among the best players, a larger repertoire was required.

This year at the Moody Coliseum, baseline players were in the majority. Connors, Nastase, and Panatta weren't there. The two best players of the topspin school met in the final, Vilas and Borg. Vilas, the poet, had just learned that the second edition of his book had sold out. One of the book's poems in particular had become very popular. The first lines, more than any others, set the stage for what was to follow:

Guillermo, where are you?
Someone shouts my name.

I search anxiously among the people
but find no one.
Guillermo, where are you?

Vilas the poet's introspective question might have been aimed at Vilas the tennis player, he who had developed a habit of always losing to his friend Björn. Stroke by stroke they matched up evenly. What decided their matches became obvious to the spectators once the ball had passed back and forth over the net for some time. It wasn't that Vilas was an unfocused player, but that Björn's killer instinct was stronger and won out over Vilas. Björn was an underestimated tactician; he knew his rivals and when to tighten the screws. In those moments, he didn't hesitate to abandon his usual game.

In the Dallas final, the moment arrived with the score being 1–1 in sets, 5–5, and 30–40, Vilas serving. When the players' rackets had made contact with the ball 44 times each in an uninterrupted string of heavy topspin shots, and with a few lobs and drop shots thrown in, Björn rushed forward and hit the ball right at Vilas. That was enough to create a moment of hesitation. Vilas had an opening, but he was flat-footed and unprepared and whisked his passing shot long. Björn got to lift up the first big trophy of the year, before rushing off to the next big thing. Yet another challenger and exhibition odyssey waited before the start of the French Open: Hawaii, North Carolina, Düsseldorf. . . . In the book *My Life and Game*, Björn says that all the rushing around between the challenger matches was supposed to make him more focused in the major tournaments. For him, the decision was simple, being one of four or five players who received many invitations. It was a good way for Björn to make money without having to play long tournaments where he risked facing good players early. Björn said: "The tennis season is not like the football season, with a long break between seasons. We have to play year-round. We don't get paid if we get sick. And you don't want to come to the major tournaments knowing you have to play well for the money."

Björn had come to Paris to make history by taking his third straight title at the French Open. In the quarterfinal round on a scorching-hot center court, he faced Panatta, who was in peak form. His low backhand shots, concrete-like hard serves, and an enormous reach at the net became too much for Borg. The Swede walked off the court with his head hung low. He realized that the loss was the price he had to pay for all his traveling around the world. But once the disappointment began to wear off, he told himself that perhaps this was the best thing that could have happened.

Television viewers around the world felt that they knew the best players in tennis. They observed how Connors always consoled himself by fiddling with his necklace on his way back to the baseline after a lost point. How Björn stared at the ground after points both won and lost. How Panatta gazed unhappily into space after having put away an unhittable drop shot, as if he realized that the beauty was worth nothing unless he repeated the same thing in the next point he played. How Ashe, in the moments before he got ready to return a serve, dropped his shoulders and let his arms and racket hang down along his body while his gaze looked straight ahead but nowhere. Members of a large worldwide audience felt as if they actually got close to the top players' inner selves.

But perhaps the ability of professional tennis to keep its large audience was hidden within other, even deeper, layers. The tennis-playing Judit in Strindberg's *The Dance of Death* shows up and wants to remove Allan from his soul-destroying accounting work. What does accounting have to do with real life? Tennis is the enticing opposite of everything that is soul-destroying. Not only because it is a pleasure, but because in tennis, the individual is given an opportunity to express his true and real self. In 1976, Woody Allen made *Annie Hall*, the film that came to be his most beloved and commercially successful. It won four Oscars at the Academy Awards, including Best Picture, under the nose of the first *Star Wars* movie. *Annie Hall* tells the story of people who, despite the fact that they have language, education, money, and an abundance of close friends, can never find their true selves. The focus of the film is the love story between Alvy Singer, played by Woody Allen, and Annie Hall, played by Diane Keaton. The key scene is their first meeting, on a tennis court together with two other friends, where the camera follows the otherwise neurotic, fickle, and chatty characters when they for a few moments are quiet and absorbed by what they have their eyes and heads set on—forehands and backhands. Everyone plays well but has completely different styles. On the tennis court, they don't have to talk to one another, their hands aren't tied behind their backs by the convention of language. Yet they express enough of their personality, and Alvy and Annie fall in love.

During the breakthrough years for professional tennis, the matches often seemed to be about something more than just the championship title. The relatively cool interest for the matches between Borg and Vilas was probably because the battle was all about desire, and the outcome, like in the 1976 Dallas final, was predictable. However, the Connors-Borg matchup left few untouched. On the surface, it was a duel between an arrogant egomaniac and a quiet lone wolf, but what the crowd really experienced as they watched Connors's flat, deep shots attack Borg's defense—consisting of high shots and relentless saves—was a battle between boldness and safety. The choice between taking chances and letting one's fate be decided by one's own volition and risk taking—or relying on the safety of doing the same thing time after time, with an ever-growing level of perfection. The crowd immediately decided, consciously or unconsciously, where their sympathies lay, based on what they themselves were or aspired to be.

Borg-Nastase on the other hand, was pure desire against talent—the contrast between the moral insight that success in life requires a rock-solid desire to submit to hard work and discipline and the aesthetic dream of beauty and artistry as the happiness and meaning of life.

In hindsight, it's easy to see that Borg and Nastase were an obvious Wimbledon final in 1976. Not only because they both had good spring seasons behind them, but because both, at the same time, wanted to supplement their respective massive amount of desire and talent with something more. When Borg and Nastase came to Wimbledon, they had analyzed themselves and realized that continued success would require a correction of weaknesses.

Thus, Björn arrived in England early. Within his "perhaps this was the best thing that could have happened" insight after his loss to Panatta in Paris was the realization that it would allow him more time to prepare for Wimbledon. Now, arriving in London in his fourth year as a professional, he knew that the change from a hard clay court, with its high bounces and heavy balls, to Wimbledon's often wet grass and fast, low bounces, required other qualities than those he'd been able to utilize in Paris so successfully.

Before Borg had left the French capital, he'd taken the time to call the Romanian tennis star, Mariana Simionescu, who was a friend of his ex-girlfriend, Helena Anliot. Björn asked Mariana out on a date and fell in love. He'd been saying for a long time that being in a relationship was impossible for a world-class tennis player, but now he was willing to compromise. At the same time, he knew all too well that tennis would have to come first.

In his relationship with tennis to date, Björn Borg had chiseled out an impenetrable defensive game that couldn't be found in any instructions manual. He had fast feet and put an explosive spin on the ball, and he could keep going forever. Wimbledon required him to dig deeper within himself to investigate if he had any other talents, like an aggressive game that would work on the fast grass. He was prepared to put in the required work. His appetite for tough training was insatiable.

In London, Björn met up with Vilas, who brought the Swede and Panatta to Hampstead in the northern part of town, to a small club with around 1,000 members. The club had a nice groundskeeper, a cook who prepared light, delicious lunches, and courts that were often available. The three world-class players trained hard there for two hours each morning. In the afternoons, Björn worked on fine-tuning a new, harder, and faster serve. Anyone who has practiced serves at a quick pace knows how tiring it is—after ten minutes, most players are completely exhausted. Björn worked on his adjustments for two and a half hours each day. He changed the positioning of his feet so that his ball toss let him hit the ball in front of his body, throwing his body weight behind the serve. He kept working on it until he found his rhythm, power, and precision.

"I've been asked many times whether it was Labbe or Percy or someone else who suggested the changes to my serve. But I made the changes all on my own. I just kept grinding, hour after hour, until I was satisfied," says Björn today.

When he arrived at Wimbledon in 1976, he simply said: "I serve and volley big now."

Nastase had played in a charity tournament in Nottingham, where he'd gained the upper hand against Connors in a well-played final, before a rainstorm interrupted the match and caused the two buddies to share the victory in true brotherly fashion. The Romanian then went to London, where he met up with his brother, Konstantin, who'd come to prevent Nastase's attention from being directed at the linesmen, the crowd, or the women who waited for him in scores everywhere. Nastase's schedule outside of the matches was strict during this year's tournament. No discos, no excesses. His wife, Dominique, had accompanied him to London, and she and

Nastase checked into the same quiet hotel where Björn was staying, and had stayed for a few years.

Björn wanted to win Wimbledon because it had always been his dream. Nastase wanted to win because it was the remaining blank spot on his résumé. He was too good a player not to have won there. He'd reached the final and lost in a close match in 1972, but after that he'd wasted his chances. Now during the tournament's first week, as Nastase walked from the courts after his easy wins, he had the usual throngs of female admirers following him around. But this year, he gave them angry looks and hurried back to his hotel.

The other top players didn't prepare with the same methodical purposefulness. Connors brought with him a team consisting of a new girlfriend, a new doctor and massage therapist, and his well-known mother, Gloria. Connors wanted to gain new respect by convincing the world of his new "serious image." This meant, for one, that he limited his strange behavior of placing the shaft of his racket in his crotch simulating masturbation. As for Arthur Ashe, he had a difficult time coming to terms with being the reigning champion: "It's frustrating to hear that you're the champion every day when you come out to play. It doesn't exactly make it easier to play," he complained before he lost a 2–0 lead in sets against Vitas Gerulaitis and was eliminated from the tournament with a bang. Panatta was tired and unfocused after winning the title in Paris. His sad eyes were looking for something other than tennis. He found it in the third round, in the shape of a baby bird puttering around in the grass by his baseline. Panatta bent down, picked up the bird, gave it to someone in the crowd, and was knocked out of the tournament. Vilas griped about the draw. If he reached the quarterfinal round, he'd face Borg.

The temperature reached over 100 degrees Fahrenheit for most of the first week. Signs inside the arena pointed out that shirts were mandatory. One day, 500 people collapsed. Strange headgear was seen throughout the stands: folded newspapers, Napoleon hats, and tropical helmets. The officials were allowed to call the matches in short-sleeved shirts. The courts were dry and hard. Out on Court 2, Björn banged home his serves against Colin Dibley, who barely had time to blink. The serve gave Borg the victory in two more matches. Before the fourth round, an abdominal muscle began to bother him, screaming: Stop this now! The tournament physician prescribed medications, which didn't help. Björn gritted his teeth, served his way past Brian Gottfried, and found himself having reached the quarterfinals. But his pain was so bad that he concluded he wasn't going to continue playing; even tossing and turning in bed was painful.

Bergelin called a friend: "Björn is so depressed. Can you help us find a specialist? He doesn't trust the Wimbledon physician. If he doesn't get better, he's going to forfeit the quarterfinals." Contact was made with a doctor who examined Björn and reassured him that his injury wouldn't get worse if he continued to play with the help of pain-relieving injections.

After the quarterfinals, the experts' last doubts about who would face off in the final were eliminated. Nastase played brilliantly against Charles Pasarell, and Björn did what he always did in his match against Vilas. He'd reached his first semifinal at Wimbledon. When Connors was eliminated by Roscoe Tanner, Björn knew what it meant.

"I realized that my chances to reach the final had increased. I'd prefer a thousand times to meet Tanner over Connors in a semifinal. I knew that Tanner wouldn't be able to serve this well two matches in a row. I definitely saw that I had a chance. But still, it was such a big deal, I was still surprised. I remember thinking: *Here I am playing a semifinal at Wimbledon*. It felt unreal.

Björn's prediction about Tanner's serve proved correct. To defeat one top player was one thing, two in a row something completely different. Björn won in three straight sets and had made it through to the final. There, he'd play Nastase, who'd toyed with Ramírez in his semifinal.

That same day, a comedy premiered at the Bush Theater, one of London's pub stages. It was called "Blood Sports" and told the story of a Swedish tennis player with long, blond hair, who was very handsome and received everything he wanted in the world. Eventually, he began to make demands. For example, he would only take balls from the most beautiful of the ball boys. The Swedish star's behavior became more and more despicable. The ugly ball boys didn't know what to do, but they felt a need to protest against all the beautiful people who were successful in everything. Those who were born lucky and who made tons of money. The ugly people revolted in the only way they could—they murdered the tennis star.

That Saturday, the two players facing each other in the final had one thing in particular in common: their greatest blessing was their body. Borg and Nastase were the fastest of the world's tennis players. Björn with his dancing steps at the baseline and Nastase with his catlike moves all around the court. Björn's ability to place the balls in the most difficult spot possible for his opponent and his mental strength, which allowed him to hit the same shot hour after hour, made his tennis game unique. Nastase's talent was his ability to predict where his opponent's shots would land. And with a flick of his wrist, he could switch between all types of existing strokes, plus a few more.

"Nastase was the favorite; me being there was more of a shocker. I know Nastase looked at it that way, too. He saw his chance to finally win Wimbledon when he found out he'd play me in the final. He'd beaten me at the 1975 Masters, and this was only six months later. And he'd also beaten me in some challenger matches in Hawaii. Nastase was a genius at the game, he knew every single shot, he knew a thousand different ones. And he played great the entire way at Wimbledon. He hadn't lost a set up until the final, although I hadn't, either. My plan was simple, not giving in to long rallies with the genius. That would have doomed me," says Borg.

Mariana Simionescu was sitting in the stands. She'd spent passionate nights in hotels with Björn, but Nastase was her countryman, and his artistry on the tennis court touched her on a deeper level. In the locker room, Nastase sought to interact with Björn. He combed his hair in front of the mirror, turned to the newspaper-reading Borg, and said: "You ready, keed? You better be ready, keed."

Mariana watched the players come out on the court and rooted for Ilie.

The short version of the final is that Nastase suffered a mental collapse, played poorly, and surrendered. But in the beginning, it was Nastase's mental strength that was on display, while Björn seemed tense.

Game 1. Nastase falls behind but catches up, thanks to his great serves when he needs them the most. And he dares to stick to his game plan—attacking Borg's backhand with sliced shots and moving up to the net. Björn misfires his passing shots.

Game 2. Nastase returns Borg's hard serves in a feather-light manner and moves around the court smooth and panther-like. He runs down everything the Swede blasts at him. Nastase breaks Borg's serve and increases his lead.

Game 3. Nastase starts things out with an ace. The next point ends with Borg hitting his shot out. The third point turns into a baseline rally. Nastase dances and switches tempo between backhand slices and forehand topspins. Finally, he hits a forehand that lands smack on Borg's baseline. It's too good for Björn, whose shot goes out. After that, Björn wins four straight points, which earns him break point. Nastase hits a deep serve to Borg's backhand side, and he handles the sharply hit return with an acrobatic forehand-cross volley. Raw talent and deep concentration in one single motion. Two points later, Nastase is in the lead, 3–0.

Björn recalls what it felt like:

"I was really worried and tense. I began thinking: *This is the worst thing that could possibly have happened.* I was going to get beaten badly, maybe not even take a game. But I told myself all I could do was keep playing and not panic. I think I was more nervous and tense than he was, since he'd played a Wimbledon final before."

Game 4. Borg keeps pressing on with brutal topspin shots and a rush to the net. Nastase makes a spectacular save and hits a shot high up in the air to buy some time. Borg hits a powerful overhead smash, but Nastase pulls out a topspin forehand shot that lands on the baseline. Borg hits out. Nastase has three break chances, which can give him the lead, 4–0, and an easy road to a first-set win.

Every top player has his own routine and strategy when he or she gets into trouble, such as when the opponent has break point. The variations are similar. Most players try to get their first serve in, spinning it to the opponent's weaker side, usually the backhand, and then rushing up to the net. This means an increased risk of being passed, but most players believe that taking the initiative still gives them the advantage. Björn always played like this; he took more chances when he played from behind. Now, he found himself one point from falling behind, 0–4, in a Wimbledon final, against a player who was doing exactly what he did the last time they played—he kept fooling Björn with his daring and unpredictable game. This was worse than the ordinary hardships; this was an acute crisis. When Nastase found himself in these predicaments, he'd usually begin yapping with the crowd and the judges. Yet other players would let the set go and try to find their rhythm for the next set.

It was in this moment that Björn showed what he was made of. He continued to play according to his plan. He served hard, attacked the net, and kept the points short. When Nastase hit a passing shot into the net, Björn could turn the game around. And just like that, he planted a first seed of self-doubt in his opponent, who until that point had played perfectly. Now he lost his next service game and, with that, his advantage. At 4–4, it was clear that Nastase's sudden uncertainty had taken the edge off his game.

On two occasions, he couldn't make up his mind whether to play hard or soft, and this made him miss some easy shots. Björn broke again and served home the first set a short while later. The second set followed the same pattern. Nastase began to stare down Björn, who was busy icing his sore belly with a spray during the changeovers. In the third set, Björn went up an early break and reached match point at 5–4. Only then did the Romanian let go of his inhibitions and temporarily escape from trouble. But Borg continued to play according to his plan, and, a few games later, he earned another match point. Björn blasted a serve. Nastase's return found the net.

Björn's body reacted like a jumping jack breaking free from its restraints. Arms and legs flailed, as he threw his racket up in the air. Nastase jumped over the net and gave him a hug. Björn put his hands over his eyes. Ten years earlier, he'd begun hitting balls against the garage wall; now he'd won the biggest title of them all. At Wimbledon on July 3, 1976, the final result in the match between Desire and Talent was 6–4, 6–2, 9–7. That night, while Björn celebrated his victory at the mandatory black-tie banquet—he arrived wearing a dark-blue velvet jacket, white shirt without a tie, collar outside the jacket—recreational tennis players around the world contemplated an old new insight. As early as 1928, the French tennis player René Lacoste wrote in his book *Tennis* that many players, despite having perfect stroke execution, don't always win, while players "whose strokes and tactics are in no way remarkable win, because they possess what others lack: concentration ability, calm, patience, and a will to win."

At the banquet, Björn praised his opponent, "one of the game's greatest, I admire him." He had cold soup, filet mignon, strawberries, and ice cream before he turned to the ladies' champion, Chris Evert, and said: "Let's go, baby." The couple opened up the dance floor to the brass orchestra playing the year's winning song in the European Song Contest, *Save Your Kisses for Me.* Björn held Chris tight around her waist, and when a new song came on, they began dancing. "It's warmer in here than on center court," Björn said according to a Swedish tabloid, before he left the banquet to sneak home to Mariana.

The impact of Borg's Wimbledon victory, for himself and for the sport of tennis, couldn't be exaggerated. "The Wimbledon win in 1976 made Björn a household name around the world," analyzed Borg's then-financial advisor, IMG's CEO Bob Kain, more than two decades later. "There aren't many athletes in the world who are or have been as big as Björn. He could make money off his name in America, despite not being an American, which is unusual. He could make money off his name in all of Europe, not just in Sweden. He could use his name to sell goods in Japan, he was huge there. Björn was one of very few athletes who could make money all over the world. He became a global superstar. Tennis was popular and the money kept coming in, but thanks to Borg the inflow of money to the sport increased exponentially in the years after 1976. All the tennis players who made big money during those years are indebted to Björn."

Björn's win at Wimbledon was, along with Ingemar Johansson's heavy-weight boxing title, Sweden's biggest sports achievement of all time. But back then, people didn't dance in fountains to celebrate. The best way in which to express one's joy was, of course, to go out and play tennis. As if a signal had sounded a few minutes after the match concluded, the country's many sun-drenched tennis courts, which had been deserted during the afternoon live television broadcasts from London, were once again filled with tennis players of all ages. Everything was business as usual, just a bit more festive, in the tennis-crazy country. Everything was business as usual, but not quite.

Björn Borg the player, who had spread his own and Sweden's name across the globe, had not only showed a new game at Wimbledon, his looks had changed, too. During Wimbledon, he'd grown a beard, and when Swedish television began broadcasting in the second week, the viewers had seen Mother Svea the homeland's cute golden boy with the blue eyes, curly hair, and innocence in his focused stare change into something that more closely resembled a lumberjacking wild man. The squinting eyes in the dark-bearded and narrow face that never betrayed an emotion almost brought to mind a psychopath. No longer was Borg a boy whose hair Hyland could tousle in a live broadcast, a kid with whom people instinctively wanted to cuddle. This awakened a concern that perhaps he was again drifting away from the homeland.

That uncertainty was reinforced when Borg didn't show up for the tournament in Båstad immediately following Wimbledon. No one knew where he was, not even Bergelin, who on his own accord set in motion a minor war against journalists who posed questions such as: Why isn't Björn playing in Båstad? Isn't it a breach of his agreement with the Swedish

Tennis Association? Who does Björn belong to, the tennis association or McCormack?

"Björn feels he is being persecuted by the Swedish newspapers, he's sensitive to crappy articles," said Bergelin.

"Why can't you give us a proper answer? Does Björn have to be released by McCormack every time he needs to play in the Davis Cup?"

Bergelin didn't respond.

"Are you Björn's daddy or the Davis Cup captain? Are you employed by the association to nurse Björn's psyche and rackets? Aren't you abusing your position as the Davis Cup captain, whose job it is to also manage the growth and new additions to the team?"

"You can all relax," responded Bergelin. "Björn is the key to all the success we've had in the Davis Cup. The most important thing is that he gets good service, that he gets what he needs."

When Björn shortly thereafter announced that he wasn't going to play in the Davis Cup, the questions once again came to the forefront.

"Is it reasonable that the superstar never receives any criticism?"

"What you do to Björn is not criticism," Bergelin shot back. "You call him a tax dodger and a traitor. I'd like to see the one of you journalists who wouldn't split if you saw your wallet begin to swell. I have the right to yell at you dogs in the press, it's not your privilege."

"Why doesn't Björn answer himself? Is it easier to win Wimbledon than answer questions?"

"We might never see Björn in Sweden again. The kid has become too big for this country," Bergelin said.

Björn joined the Davis Cup team in Rome, but he didn't play and he didn't speak with the press, except for a brief statement: "I'm tired of Sweden. I've received so much false criticism from Swedish newspapers, which has made me lose all interest in coming home again."

Björn still felt as if he were measured by another measuring stick than the other Swedish sports hero of the '70s, Ingemar Stenmark: "I was a tax dodger, it was just horrible, terrible, that I moved. But when Ingemar did the same thing, it was like: 'Good luck!'"

The Swedish superstar's absence and silence marked the beginning of a lengthy break with the homeland. In 1976 and 1977, Björn didn't play in either the Davis Cup or Båstad. The only glimpse of him that the Swedish people got to witness during those years was a weak performance at the 1976 Stockholm Open. Björn lost early and didn't speak with the press.

Kjell Johansson recalls, "In terms of the Davis Cup, we accepted his withdrawal in 1976. He'd played with a pulled abdominal muscle at Wimbledon and was mentally exhausted. But the situation was different in 1977. There was a lot of talk that Björn didn't play because he demanded to get paid a lot of money. We reacted rather strongly. I remember I told him: 'Come on now! We need you!' At some point the gap becomes too big."

The tennis crowds act differently in different countries. In Paris, spectators come to admire the technically most aesthetic professionals. That's why players like Nastase and Federer have always been the French crowd's favorites. At Wimbledon, people gather to socialize, mark their social positions, and admire the most well-behaved players. As such, the British audience has always been fascinated with Björn Borg, with his exemplary conduct and mystical calm, to a greater extent than any other player. At the U.S. Open, people want to see action. If you don't get what you want, you can always do what you can to make it happen. No crowd can, like the New York crowd can, smell blood and like a mob direct its attacks at the player who reveals weakness.

Borg-Nastase and Connors-Vilas were the two pairs in the semifinals at Forest Hills in 1976. The following had happened earlier in the tournament.

Nastase-Pohmann, second round: Nastase, still unsettled after Wimbledon, protests a call for the tenth time. The crowd whistles and boos. Nastase spits out a mouthful of orange juice in the direction of the crowd, yells: "Fuck you all!" The crowd yells: "Fuck you, Nastase! Go to hell!" Nastase swings his racket toward the photographers and makes a masturbation gesture toward the crowd, holding his hand around his racket shaft. The crowd applauds Nastase's misses, shouts when he tosses up the ball to serve, throws tennis balls out onto the court. Pohmann suffers cramps, and the umpire calls for a doctor. Nastase screams so it can be heard across the entire court: "This isn't football, we don't have timeouts." Pohmann staggers up to standing. Nastase self-destructs, and the German earns himself match points. Nastase saves them all and wins the match. Pohmann refuses to shake hands with him. "Son of a bitch," screams Nastase across the net.

The umpire also refuses to shake Nastase's hand. Nastase swings his racket in a threatening manner in the umpire's direction and runs after Pohmann into the locker room. "Fuck you, Hitler!" he yells after the German. "You're an animal." "Fuck you, animal!" yells Pohmann back at Nastase. Nastase grabs a shower hose and starts spraying at Pohmann, who yells that he's going to sue Nastase. Tournament officials and other players scramble and are able to separate the two.

From that day forward, the crowd turned against Nastase in each of his matches. Booed him and tried to rile him up and psych him out. Nastase said that he felt like he was being persecuted. Gerulaitis offered his support: "If Nastase wins this tournament despite this crowd, it's the sports achievement of all times." Connors, on the other hand, took the crowd's side and argued that the customer is always right. "The crowds in New York want to see blood, it's our duty to give it to them." If Borg had faced a tense Nastase at Wimbledon, at the U.S. Open he faced an exhausted and broken player. Just like at Wimbledon, the Romanian seemed uncertain of how to play, hard or soft. Often, he made the wrong choice and missed his shots altogether. The semifinal was played the same week in which Palme and Fälldin participated in the great televised election debate at the Scandinavium arena in Göteborg. Palme possessed the language tools, but Fälldin won the debate with his calm confidence. The same thing happened at Forest Hills; Borg won in three sets.

The final at the 1976 U.S. Open signaled the start of an era when the two hard-hitting baseline players Borg and Connors left the rest of the tennis elite behind. This was also when the older-generation players, led by Ashe, Nastase, and Orantes, unequivocally lost their grip on the world tennis elite. Between 1976 and 1978, Borg and Connors faced each other in five major finals:

The U.S. Open 1976:	Connors–Borg	3–1
Wimbledon 1977:	Borg–Connors	3–2
The Masters 1978:	Connors–Borg	2–1
Wimbledon 1978:	Borg–Connors	3–0
The U.S. Open 1978:	Connors–Borg	3–0

Connors hit the ball at its highest point. Björn ran from side to side, hit everything back, and had a powerful serve. No one in the crowd was unmoved by what they saw, even if they didn't find it beautiful. In the 1976 U.S. Open final, Björn won the most points, but Connors won the title. With set point in the tiebreak in the third set, Björn became cautious and Connors crushed a brutal backhand that landed on the line. After that, he never let go of his grip on the match. Björn was just as lost and disappointed as he'd been after his loss in Philadelphia early in the year. But he'd lost "like a man," played the game he believed in, and had shown Connors that he'd have to be at his very best to keep Björn behind him.

As the tennis year of 1976 was summarized, Connors was ranked number one in the world, partly because Björn stuck to his original annual plan and didn't play in many tournaments after the U.S. Open. When there were no major tournaments, he spent his time playing exhibition and challenger matches. In just over two months, he played 23 such matches, in three different parts of the world.

It was symptomatic that Borg broke his streak of losses against Connors in an exhibition match in early 1977, in a tournament called the Pepsi Grand Slam. The seasoned American commentators noted that the winner made more from this match than the newly sworn-in president of the United States, Jimmy Carter, made in a year. The 1977 Wimbledon final was decided in the fifth set when Connors, after having caught up from a deficit of 0–4 to 4–4 and a 15–0 lead in his own serve, double-faulted and then fell apart completely.

The pace between tournaments was so high that, for the best players, everything but tennis suffered. Before the Masters final against Connors in January 1978, Björn isolated himself at the Roosevelt Hotel in New York City. The American journalist Peter Bodo describes in his book *Courts of Babylon* the sad state of Borg and Bergelin's hotel room, with its empty bottles of beer, curtains drawn tight, half-eaten fruits, and two men as pale as apatic ghosts. And then: "The Swedish idol's face was unwashed, and his hair hung in oily strands. His eyes were sunken deep in ashen sockets. You could always tell how important a given tournament was to Borg by the number of blemishes on his face, and the Masters had produced a bumper crop. He looked less like the greatest tennis player on earth than the unhealthiest man alive, with Bergelin in close pursuit."

Parallel to his close battles with Connors on the fast outdoor and indoor courts, in 1978 Björn also regained his position as "King of Clay," a title he'd let Panatta and Vilas borrow in 1976 and 1977. In Paris, Björn lost only a handful of games, and when he crushed Connors at Wimbledon three weeks later, it meant he was the first player since Rod Laver to have won "The Channel Slam." When Björn lost to Connors at the U.S. Open, it didn't affect the feeling that he had widened the gap, that what had happened after Philadelphia in 1976 was that now it was Connors who had to overachieve to beat Björn.

To emphasize that his loss at the U.S. Open was only a minor glitch, Björn flew to Tokyo, where he demolished Connors in the final. He came to the Stockholm Open to fulfill yet another goal—winning his home tournament. Wearing a gold-colored shirt, he advanced to the semifinal. There, on the other side of the net, stood a younger player Björn had never faced before.

FAST FEET VERSUS GOOD HANDS

"Is Björn trying to psych me out or get me to relax?
Or . . . is he just a nice guy?"
—JOHN McENROE

The guy across the net walked around between points, scratching his curly head of hair and making grimaces he didn't seem to be able to control. The grimaces gave the impression that he was having a monologue with an inner nemesis:

"You idiot!"

"You should've placed that shot better."

"Your game sucks!"

"Why do you even try this?"

"You can't play tennis, you're a loser!"

The paradox was that the scolding to which the player subjected himself didn't reflect what was happening on the court. It was Sunday night in the Kungliga Tennis Hall, semifinals at the Stockholm Open. The young guy who was nineteen had Björn Borg, twenty-two, against the ropes.

The Swedish world number one gave him a look, but not the usual steel-hard look, void of expression. Rather, this look was exploring. Who was this kid who was so skilled with the racket and played tennis with such deft hands?

Björn bounced the ball, kept his eyes on the floor. With another glance, he seemed to think: *Okay, you've outplayed me so far, but can you finish it?*

I'm pretty tough when it comes down to it. His opponent met the gaze with one of his own that said: *Come on then! I know I'm at least as good as you are, I can do whatever I want with whatever shot I want. Don't think I'm going to start trembling now.*

Björn hit a service winner; his opponent returned it into the net. The acute crisis was averted, but the scoreboard revealed that the next moment of crisis was just a few points away. Björn Borg–John McEnroe 3–6, 4–5. It was McEnroe's turn to serve.

The spectators did their best to help Björn get out of trouble, stomping their feet so hard that the old wooden bleachers shook. But there was never any real liveliness behind the ovations. What they'd witnessed so far was difficult to comprehend, but also fascinating. Just like to Borg's game, there were homespun elements to McEnroe's, idiosyncrasies that defied all classic instruction books. The young American hit many of his ground-strokes from the baseline without a real backswing. And he used the dated continental grip on both his forehand and backhand side. This technique required an extraordinary touch and feel for the ball to create good shots, and this guy's shots were often unreturnable.

The most curious was the serve. McEnroe positioned himself one meter from the center line, turned his back to Björn and the net, tossed up the ball in the air, twisted his body half a turn, and hurled off a shot that was nearly impossible to read—and which flattened with a low bounce way out on Björn's backhand side in the ad court. If the Swede was able to return the serve at all, he'd be far out off the court, and when the ball passed over the net, McEnroe would already be there waiting for it. At the net, McEnroe's wrists made other tennis hands seem amputated. Seven points were all that Björn won in McEnroe's service games the entire evening.

When the American had hit the match point in for a winner, thanked his opponent with a quick handshake, and hurried off the court, he didn't look happy at all. It was as if everything were like it's supposed to be, as if nothing unusual had happened.

But it had, of course.

One person who'd followed the match on TV was fourteen-year-old Mats Wilander.

"It had gotten to that point with Björn, he was so superior that it was almost boring. You knew he'd beat whomever he played. But as soon as you saw McEnroe, you realized that here was a player who had the game to beat

Björn. It wasn't that Björn needed to have a bad day and McEnroe needed to overachieve. It was about McEnroe's game, his way of forcing Björn far off the court."

For the first time in his life, Björn had lost to a younger player. Afterward, he was exhausted: "I tried to get my legs going, run, do something to get to him, but nothing worked."

McEnroe's friend and doubles partner, Peter Fleming, asked McEnroe, whom he called by his nickname "Junior," if he was going to go out and celebrate the victory over the Swedish legend. McEnroe said no, he had a final the next day to think about. Then he smiled: "What do you think? I've beaten Björn Borg. Damn well I'm going to celebrate." The two stayed out until four in the morning.

Fleming had reserved a court for the next afternoon. McEnroe barely hit a shot over the net, but a few hours later he was again standing on the court, where he followed up his easy win over Björn with an even easier win over the American Tim Gullikson in the final.

The match between Borg and McEnroe in Stockholm in November 1978 was the first in what was to become the most famous rivalry in tennis. It was also young McEnroe's first indication that he was on the right track, that what he knew he had the talent to achieve wasn't that far off.

He had introduced himself to the tennis world as an amateur in the summer of 1977, when he received $500 from the United States Tennis Association to go to Europe and gain some experience in the French Open and Wimbledon junior tournaments. McEnroe tried to qualify for the main draw instead. In Paris, he won all his qualifying matches for the main draw and proceeded to defeat his opponent in the first round in straight sets. In the second round, he faced Phil Dent, the experienced Australian Davis Cup player. If any shots were questionable on young McEnroe's side of the court, without exception McEnroe let Dent replay the point—two balls. With respect to questionable shots on Dent's side of the net, the Australian wasn't as generous—he took the point without a replay. At the net, after having won in five sets, Dent told the eighteen-year-old: "Kid, this is the pro circuit. Here we don't give away points for free."

McEnroe stored this statement in his memory and went on to London to try to qualify for Wimbledon as a simple proletarian. He stayed in a hostel, rode the subway to the qualifying tournament in Roehampton, and won his three matches—he was ready for his first Wimbledon. There, the young American with the grumpy, arrogant demeanor won match after match. In the second round, he threw his racket in anger after having missed a shot, causing the crowd to turn against him. Then McEnroe questioned a call, and the crowd's boos increased in power. Wimbledon's chairman, Brian Burnett, went to speak with McEnroe after the match. Burnett had graduated from Oxford in 1934 and had been a pilot in the Royal Air Force during the second world war. Now, his hair had specks of gray. He explained to the eighteen-year-old that his thrown racket would cost him $500 in fines. McEnroe protested. Burnett listened patiently and told McEnroe he'd play better if he controlled his emotions. McEnroe nodded and promised not to let it happen again. Burnett tore up the ticket. "A big mistake," Burnett admitted later.

John McEnroe made it to the quarterfinals, where he again faced Phil Dent. In the second set, the American threw his racket into the grass in disgust over a missed shot. The crowd booed; you don't show your sulkiness so publicly at Wimbledon. McEnroe kicked his racket to see what would happen. He had the crowd against him, and for the rest of the match, he questioned all doubtful calls. He also came back from a 1–2 deficit in sets to win against a furious Dent. The tournament that was celebrating its centennial had its youngest semifinalist ever, and the first to win eight matches, three in the qualifying rounds and five in the main draw.

The Wimbledon crowd became more and more conflicted. People were annoyed by McEnroe's explosive temper but admired his talent. It took the world's No. 1 player, Jimmy Connors, to stop the newcomer in his tracks. Everyone who had seen the prodigy's game was convinced that he'd jump on the pro circuit immediately. Instead, McEnroe went back home to the US. He was planning to continue his academic career and enrolled at Stanford University outside San Francisco. However, his life was mostly about tennis. During the spring semester, McEnroe only studied parapsychology. He won the NCAA Men's Tennis Championship and decided to turn pro in the summer. In August, he reached the semifinals at the US Open, and in the following weeks, he won tournaments in Hartford and San Francisco.

Not since Björn Borg's breakthrough in the spring of 1974 had tennis seen such a quick climb to the top. After his win in Stockholm, McEnroe went on to London, where he won again. This prompted America's Davis Cup captain, Tony Trabert, to select him for one of the singles spots in the Davis Cup final against Great Britain. McEnroe took on the important task and lost only five games in his first match and just as few in his second. Consequently, he broke Bill Tilden's and Björn Borg's record in terms of lopsided wins in Davis Cup finals. "No one has ever made me look like an idiot on the tennis court. Not Borg, not Connors, no one—not until I played McEnroe today," said John Lloyd after the match.

McEnroe's season finale qualified him for the Masters tournament in New York, which he won following victories over players like Connors and Ashe. Ashe had match points in the third set, but McEnroe escaped.

The youngster had won his biggest title to date and afterward, Ashe noted: "McEnroe can hit any shot you can imagine. I've never seen anyone with as much talent. He has no weaknesses. Within two years, it'll all be about Connors, Borg, and McEnroe. He's already passed Vitas and Vilas. His potential is limitless. Playing against Connors and Borg feels like you're being beaten by a hammer, but this guy is a switchblade.

Thus, Björn Borg had been warned. To stay on the tennis throne he'd just recently seized from Connors after so much hard work, he now had to deal with a new and even more dangerous rival. In his first tournament of 1979, Björn already found himself standing face-to-face with McEnroe, in the semifinals at Richmond's WCT tournament in the US. At first, the match resembled the one in Stockholm. After winning the first set 6–4, McEnroe earned four match points, leading 6–2 in the second set's tiebreak. Then Björn hit four amazing shots from positions way off the court and turned the set and the match around. Afterward, Björn was completely drained, but he could console himself with the fact that his unlikely turnaround was front page news in Sweden.

In New Orleans a few weeks later, Björn won the first set, 7–5, McEnroe the second, 6–1, and in the third, the players kept pace to 5–5. Then McEnroe became increasingly annoyed with himself and his surroundings, and in a ten-minute period, he threw his racket following a lost point, complained about calls, and cursed at the crowd and himself. Borg watched as the fiery American kicked his racket. Borg motioned with his finger to

McEnroe to come to the net. McEnroe stared at him. Björn said: "Come up to the net, John!" McEnroe stopped for a moment and thought: *What the hell? Is he going to tell me I'm the biggest jerk of all time?* But he walked up to the net. Björn looked McEnroe in the eye, put his arm around his shoulder, and said: "It's okay, it's a great match."

McEnroe was speechless. Thoughts rushed through his head as he wandered back to start the next point: *Is Björn trying to psych me out or get me to relax? Or . . . is he just a nice guy?* McEnroe figured it must be the latter, and his admiration for the Swede, who was already his idol, grew. He gave Björn a look and a surreptitious smile and prepared to serve. Björn remembers the moment:

"He was going totally crazy in the beginning of the third set. When I talked to him, I earned his respect, because he could see I had respect for him. He gained a special feeling for me as a person, not just as a tennis player. And it was mutual. Since that very match, we've both had great respect for each other."

Björn knew that McEnroe's feelings on the tennis court were the same feelings he himself had.

"I'd learned the hard way to keep my anger inside, when the Södertälje Tennis Club suspended me for six months after I'd acted like an idiot. After that, I kept my mouth shut out on the court, even if I sometimes boiled inside. That had become my winning weapon. If I showed emotions, I didn't play well. With McEnroe, it was exactly the opposite. He played better when he was angry. Some of us are like that. He had to make something up, find his rage, to play really well. That's a strength, too. But I had to remain calm."

The match in New Orleans went to a decisive tiebreak, in which Björn had match points, but this time it was McEnroe who turned things around and won the match.

After McEnroe won in Milan the following week, Björn and Vitas Gerulaitis invited him to go out with them in the evening. McEnroe almost burst with pride; to be invited to go out with "Broadway Vitas" and cool Björn was as big as beating them at tennis. As McEnroe writes in his autobiography: "I marked the occasion by indulging in something I'd never tried before (never mind what)—and the next thing I knew, Vitas and Björn were carrying me back into the hotel. I felt sick but wonderful: I had passed the initiation. I was part of the gang." McEnroe also noted that while Vitas copied Borg in certain ways, when they were out on the town, Borg followed Vitas. Vitas set things up and decided where they'd go, which restaurants, which dance clubs, and the women they'd talk to.

A week later, Borg and McEnroe faced each other in the WCT final in Rotterdam. Björn won in straight sets and felt for the first time that he controlled the events, that the outcome of their matches didn't entirely rest upon McEnroe's racket.

These matches between Borg and McEnroe at small venues all over Europe and the US during spring 1979 laid the foundation for an expectation of even more to come. Tennis fans looked forward to experiencing their battle with their own eyes, on location or via television from one of the biggest tennis arenas.

McEnroe returned to the USA and won in San José.

Björn stayed in Europe and won in Monte Carlo.

Then both of them traveled to Dallas and the WCT playoffs.

All the best players were there. But it was the youngest one that attracted the most interest, just like it had been with Björn five years earlier. "He's the best I've ever played," said John Alexander after having lost to McEnroe in the quarterfinal.

Björn defeated Gerulaitis in his semifinal. In the other semifinal, McEnroe would play Connors. If Björn and McEnroe were a positive and a negative pole who liked each other's company, McEnroe and Connors were a short-circuit waiting to happen as soon as they stepped out on the court.

Connors wasn't going to accept being overshadowed by his younger fellow countryman.

McEnroe wasn't going to stand still and bow his head.

Björn Borg remembers his two competitors' meetings.

"I think they were glad to have me in the middle, so to speak. For a while, they didn't speak when they saw each other. And they're from the same country and were incredible players. It's a good thing they had me, because all three of us met in fantastic matches. It was good that it was us three, different personalities, and good for them that I could separate them a little. That was some of the charm with tennis at that time, the different personalities. Both of them were pretty wild on the court, and I was calm."

In May 1979, McEnroe didn't give his opponent more than a few games. Connors stormed off the court in a rage, skipped the press conference, and left Dallas in a private plane. McEnroe didn't mind adding insult to injury.

He pointed out that he'd controlled Connors the entire time, that he'd known he was going to win.

Thus, Borg and McEnroe would meet in the final, on a slower surface and with heavier balls as compared to Stockholm, something that should benefit Björn. At 1–1 in sets and 2–2 in the third, Björn had sharpened his serve and looked to be the stronger player. Then the American slowed the pace of his shots. He went from hitting deep, sliced shots to Björn's backhand to throwing up high moon balls. At the same time, he began mixing up his twist serve out to Björn's backhand with a serve down the middle. Björn became insecure, and by a score of 7–5, 4–6, 6–2, 7–6, McEnroe took home his greatest win ever.

After the match, Borg admitted feeling sluggish and always late to the ball: "If you play against John and you're not at your very best, you'll lose. I don't even want to think about playing him again. Not in the next two weeks anyway. He's very good, he can do anything. He serves well, runs fast, hits hard, and has a great feel for the ball. But come back this fall, and we'll see who's the best in the world. That's when we'll know the results from the three biggest tournaments."

McEnroe was humble in a way that contrasted his statements about Connors: "Björn is still the best in the world. Nobody can beat him on clay, all results count."

McEnroe withdrew from the French Open with an injury, and Björn easily advanced through the tournament. An unseeded player waited in the final, Victor Pecci from Paraguay. It drizzled in Paris and the crowd of 17,000, the largest crowd ever to see a tennis match in Europe, gave the Paraguayan a standing ovation as the players came out on the court. Pecci was a big man, 6'3" and heavyset. He resembled Rocky Balboa, Sylvester Stallone's boxer hero. He wore a diamond in one ear and had a hard, flat serve. Borg wasn't surprised by the crowd's support of Pecci. He thought it normal that the crowd wanted to see a new winner, and he was prepared to play against the crowd.

Pecci tried to use softly hit, short shots against Björn. Drop shots and chips. But Björn ran down everything and got to the net with so much time to spare that he could hit outright groundstroke winners off the drop shots. He rarely missed a first serve. After two hours, the score was 6–3, 6–1, 5–2, advantage Björn, who'd played magical tennis.

But just like Rocky Balboa, who withstood round after round of heavy knocks and kept coming back, Pecci continued to play, unsteady and exhausted but brave. He began playing like McEnroe, with fast attacks to the net and spectacular volleys, and forced Björn to hit increasingly difficult passing shots. When the Paraguayan broke back, the large crowd exploded in chants: "Pec-ci, Pec-ci, Pec-ci!" The set went to a tiebreak, Pecci attacked every single point, and eventually Björn misfired.

In the fourth set, Pecci continued to attack the Swede's backhand, and the players kept pace. But Björn's double-handed backhand was calibrated, especially the cross, and incredible passing shots kept swishing by the brave "Tennis-Balboa." When Björn had finally put away an angled drop shot for the win and the title, he turned to Bergelin, raised his hands in the air, and breathed a deep sigh of relief. It was his fourth win in Paris. Not since the French musketeer Henri Cochet from the era between the two world wars had anyone won the physically demanding clay court tournament so many times.

"Paris is the toughest tournament of all," says Björn today. "You have to be able to stay out on the court hour after hour. It's not only physically hard, it's even harder mentally, knowing you'll have to be out there that long. Everyone knows it. I was always completely drained when I'd played in Paris and won. Everyone was. Anyone who denies it is lying. That's why it's so difficult to come directly from Paris to Wimbledon. The differences in the game is so great, and you're so tired, body and mind. I knew that if I could only get through the first matches at Wimbledon, I would usually get stronger and start playing better again. But the first matches at Wimbledon were always scary, you never knew what would happen."

Borg had been in trouble in the early rounds of Wimbledon both in 1977 and 1978. Now the crisis occurred in the second round, against Vijay Amritraj of India, an elegant and talented player who would become famous for a new audience a few years later, when he used his tennis racket to help James Bond in a rickshaw keep villains at bay. Now, Amritraj won two of the first three sets and went up, 4–2, with a breakpoint in the fourth. The popular Indian, who was dating the actress Farrah Fawcett, returned Björn's serve deep, rushed up to the net, and saw that the Swede moved to the right, so he angled his volley to the left side of the court. Borg was off balance and Amritraj knew the Swede wouldn't be able to get to the ball. He turned around to prepare to serve home the match at 5–2. But Björn had made a sharp turn in the air, made a dive for Amritraj's ball, and thrown his racket after it. The ball hit the frame, sailed slowly back over the net, and landed unreturnable for the Indian. The save defied gravity, and Amritraj never recovered from the shock. Björn held his serve and broke Amritraj's serve in the next game. He was never threatened after that.

While Björn was able to get himself out of the trouble he'd known would come in Wimbledon's first week, McEnroe got tangled up in his own problems. He'd won the Queens grass tournament the previous week, was seeded second and filled with confidence, but he stumbled and lost in the fourth round at Wimbledon, annoyed with everything and everyone. After Björn destroyed Jimmy Connors in the semifinal, only Roscoe Tanner stood in the way of the Swede lifting the Wimbledon trophy for the fourth straight year. Tanner grew up in Tennessee and had won the 1977 Australian Open. He'd played unevenly in 1979, and now he also wore his hair in a short perm. The change brought some amusement to the growing number of people worldwide who followed tennis and everything around it.

The interest in tennis had only grown bigger. In 1979, for the first time, the National Broadcasting Company, NBC, broadcast live from Wimbledon. The program was called *Breakfast at Wimbledon,* and NBC had looked forward to a final between Borg and McEnroe, and a historical record television audience for tennis in the US. McEnroe with the capacity to challenge and defeat Borg, had contributed to the increased interest, but the Swede could sell the sport on his own. Aside from that, Tanner was also American after all. NBC's biggest problem before the final was that there was no time for commercials prior to the match, as Wimbledon adhered strictly to traditions and would begin exactly at 2 p.m. local time, when the royals were expected to arrive. To still have a chance to time its broadcast, NBC asked Tanner to hide out in the bathroom. He did as he was told.

Wimbledon's officials knocked on the bathroom door and said that the royals had taken their seats and it was time for the players to make their entrance. Tanner muttered something about not feeling well and that he needed a few more minutes. The organizers were forced to keep the royals waiting, and NBC had a chance to get in a first commercial break in their programming. When the match began, Tanner was as pesky as ever. He played extremely aggressively, attacked the net on both his first and second serve, and played defense with a backhand he varied by hitting it either with topspin or flat. It was a risky style of play, but from Tanner it looked unusually controlled. And it brought him a 2–1 lead. But Björn was the superior player from the baseline. He hit numerous outright forehand winners, won the fourth set, and after hitting a couple of crushing backhand passing shots, he was up an early break in the fifth set. But Björn was becoming increasingly nervous playing in the lead, as he was closing in on his fourth straight title. Tanner secured breakpoints at 3–4 and outplayed Björn completely, but he then hit a forehand out instead of just safely angling it inside the lines. In the tenth game, Björn charged ahead and earned three match points. When Tanner saved the match points and caught up to deuce in Björn's service game, the Swede was convinced he was going to lose. "If Tanner had won one of those break points, there's no chance I'd have won the match," he said afterward, when he'd won his fourth straight Wimbledon title after keeping his nerves in check.

The next day, there was only one headline on *Expressen*'s front page: HE'S THE GREATEST. Borg's fourth Wimbledon title was monumental. He was now regularly ranked as one of the world's five greatest athletes overall. He'd left Connors behind and had erased the edge McEnroe had held after his winter and spring season. Moreover, Björn was playing better tennis than ever. Most important, his passing shots were even sharper, and he felt that he finally had a real chance of winning the US. Open. He bought a house in Sands Point on Long Island and trained hard with Gerulaitis during the weeks leading up to the tournament.

In the warmup tournament in Cincinnati, Borg proved that his fine form was intact. McEnroe's low shots didn't bother him, and Björn won their final in two sets. Their head-to-head record now stood at 3–3.

At the U.S. Open, Björn won his first matches handily, but he knew the quarterfinal was going to be tough—against Tanner in an evening match under the artificial lights. All top players had to play evening matches, in the same way that all players at some point have to play on the outer courts at Wimbledon. Bergelin didn't like any of it and had managed to get Wimbledon to make an exception for Borg, referring to the crowd pressure. However, the organizers at the U.S. Open didn't budge. From the start, Borg had a negative attitude toward the match, and Tanner and his serve destroyed the Swede's U.S. Open ambitions in four sets. In the last set, Tanner broke the net with one of his serves. The semifinals were all American. McEnroe won easily over Connors in one, and Gerulaitis came back from two sets down to beat Tanner in the other.

McEnroe went on to win the 1979 U.S. Open with a score of 7–5, 6–3, 6–3 in the final. He became the youngest champion in more than 30 years. He'd now won his third major title of the year and could match Borg's triumphs at Wimbledon and the French Open. This meant that the Masters in New York in January 1980 would be the deciding factor for who'd be on top of the world rankings for 1979. At the Masters, the two superstars battled it out in a semifinal that had it all: blazing shot exchanges, quick thinking, and heroic saves. The crowd of 15,437 responded to what they were witnessing with constant eruptions. In the first set, McEnroe's quick wrists were a wonder of timing. In the second, Borg's extreme topspins were unrelenting. The third set went to a tiebreak. Björn won it and the match, 6–7, 6–3, 7–6, but one month later, McEnroe climbed to first place in the world rankings.

Björn took it back after just one week.

The rivalry between Borg and McEnroe became a worldwide drama and contributed to tennis catapulting from a major sport to the world's most popular. Borg and McEnroe were known around the world, and the fans were split between them. McEnroe appealed to an unholy alliance of intellectuals, artists, punk rockers, psychologists, and tennis purists, all of whom loved his explosive blend of raw talent and uncontrolled temperament. Early in his career, Borg had upset the sport's leading representatives with his two-handed backhand and exaggerated topspin. Now, he was the darling of the conservatives. But also Björn was the nice and quiet guy in this battle, and he awakened the dreams of everyone who wanted to see common courtesy and a down-to-earth decency end up on top. The tennis world was looking forward to finally being able to see a match between the two stars at a major tournament like Wimbledon or the U.S. Open.

On July 5, 1980, the day had finally come. All preliminaries had been taken care of. Things had gone according to plan: Borg had won in Paris, for the fifth time, after having given up only a few games to Gerulaitis in the final. McEnroe had won at Queens and had battled his way to victory against Connors in the semifinals at Wimbledon, where the crowd had booed him for his behavior. Now they were standing in the locker room, ready to be escorted out to center court. The entire world was waiting. Nelson Mandela was sitting in his cell on Robben Island listening to the radio. Västervik, Sweden, was hosting a Junior European Championship match between Sweden, and West Germany, but there was no match play on Saturday afternoon. Thus, Sweden's fourteen-year-old Stefan Edberg and Germany's twelve-year-old Boris Becker could sit down in front of the TV and watch the match together. The expectations were so high and the interest so great that the match had been declared a classic even before it started.

Borg and McEnroe were escorted from the locker room and up the seven steps to Centre Court, past the trophy for which they'd be playing, past the mahogany doors bearing Kipling's famous words: "If you can meet with Triumph and Disaster, and treat those two impostors just the same . . ." They entered the waiting room, furnished with a few chairs and a sofa. On the sofa were the blankets intended for the royal box.

Björn was calm. The year before, in this same room, he'd tried to break the silence by talking to Roscoe Tanner. This year, he remained quiet. McEnroe was nervous and couldn't get a word out. He'd never before been in this room. He just wanted to get out on the court and play. Finally, the referee appeared and signaled that it was time. McEnroe walked half a step ahead of Borg. "This is live," screamed Bud Collins in the NBC live broadcast, which got rolling at exactly the same moment. "Wherever you are, rub your eyes and watch! You might never see anything like it again!"

The crowd cheered for Borg and booed McEnroe. Never before had a Wimbledon final started out with such an obvious expression of sympathy from the crowd. Peter Fleming watched on his TV in London. He was still there, because he'd played in the doubles final with McEnroe the day before. "Björn was Mr. Nice Guy," he said later. "He didn't belong to the establishment at all, but he was the hero of the English middle ground. Everyone loved him. He was surrounded by that aura—everything that had to do with him was worth loving. With Junior, things seemed to be the opposite—everything that had to do with him was worth hating. But now here he was, and he did have his fans."

The players came out on the court, both wearing white shorts, red tracksuits, headbands, and big hair. Borg's facial expression didn't change.

McEnroe was pale and smiled nervously when the camera focused in on his face.

"It's cold Nordic blood against New York arrogance," said the BBC commentator. The styles of play were in sharp contrast, too. Borg's feet versus McEnroe's hands. The players started warming up.

The first set went by in a flash. McEnroe's lefty serves cut through Björn's defense. The American's deep volleys forced Borg to run, lob, and take chances with desperate passing shots. McEnroe's tempo and feel for the game were too much for Borg. The American put away a beautifully angled backhand at the net, making the score 6–1. McEnroe's advantage continued in the second set. He won 14 of 41 points in his own serve through aces or serves that Borg was able to get his racket on but couldn't return.

The television audience, the crowd around Centre Court, the players themselves . . . everyone sensed that McEnroe was the better player, and that he was well on his way to destroying Borg. For McEnroe, this feeling concerned him. *When you have an obvious edge against a player like Björn without putting much effort into it, that means something isn't right*, he thought. Björn tried to focus on the psychology of the game and told himself: *Hit some returns back and give him the message that "I'm here, I'm going to pass you." Make sure to get some returns back . . .*

The situation was urgent. McEnroe threatened in each and every one of Björn's service games, getting himself one breakpoint after another. Björn's back was up against the wall. Late in the set, McEnroe missed an easy volley. In the next point, Björn capitalized on his passing shot and was up, 15–30. Two points later, he'd won the set. The score was tied at one set apiece, but it didn't at all reflect the match. McEnroe looked ready to have a breakdown. He'd clearly been the better player for over an hour, but now everything was back to where they'd started.

Björn took advantage and broke McEnroe's serve at the beginning of the third set. But McEnroe wasn't going to quit. Down 4–2, he had five chances to break back. The game was 20 points long, and when it was over, Borg had held serve. In the fourth set, it was as if Borg's ability to stand his ground, to get himself out of every difficult situation facing him, left McEnroe only one option—surrendering. Björn stood at the baseline, ready to serve for the match at 5–4. He got to 40–15. McEnroe restlessly shifted his weight between his feet in anticipation of the serve. It was a bullet, but McEnroe managed to get it back over the net. Björn pushed him back with a heavy forehand to McEnroe's backhand and rushed up to the net to finish the match, but the American found the only existing gap with a backhand down the line. First match point saved. Björn stepped back to again serve for the victory. After another hard serve, he put away a volley cross that seemed to be an outright winner, but McEnroe floated across the court and chose an impossible shot, a forehand drive volley on the run. Two points later, after some whipping backhand returns, McEnroe had evened the score. The crowd that up until this point had been booing him now cheered. Two games later, the set would be decided in a tiebreak.

Mariana tried to look calm for the TV cameras, but she was a nervous wreck. In the first point of the tiebreak, McEnroe followed up his serve with an athletic smash, 0–1. Borg served, unreturnable, 1–1. And then another, 2–1. McEnroe served and put away a forehand stop-volley, 2–2. McEnroe served down the middle, out of reach for Björn, 2–3. Borg served and hit a forehand stop-volley, 3–3. Then, he hit a serve that made the chalk fly, 4–3. McEnroe served, Björn mishit the return, 4–4. McEnroe served, Björn crushed a backhand return, minibreak Borg, 5–4. Now Björn could secure the title with his two serves. The first serve was a rocket; McEnroe took a step forward and returned it right at Björn, who blocked it back with a half volley, and the American ran forward and whipped in his backhand cross, 5–5. The minibreak had been erased. Borg served, ran up to net, and hit a volley winner, 6–5, match point number three.

Please, let it happen now, said Bergelin to himself. McEnroe missed his first serve, and Björn took a step forward into the court, ready to demolish whatever the American threw at him. The crowd leaned forward. McEnroe hit his second serve to Björn's backhand, and the Swede ran around it and hit a forehand cross, which shot off with missile-speed in the direction of the abandoned half court. But McEnroe managed to reach the ball with his racket and hit a forehand volley winner, 6–6. "He'd been passed but was somehow able to block the ball back," noted Tommy Engstrand on Swedish Radio.

McEnroe served to Björn's backhand, then followed it up at the net with an angled volley that Björn returned past him with a phenomenal backhand. It was 7–6, match point number four.

Björn to serve, McEnroe stood behind the baseline. Björn served and volleyed, McEnroe kept his passing shot low and hard, and Björn couldn't get it over the net, 7–7. "Unbelievable drama," said Engstrand. "We've already seen it all, nothing else can happen," exclaimed the BBC commentator.

The crowd was in a frenzy, and, suddenly, McEnroe had the support of the majority.

Borg saved two set points before going up, 10–9, his fifth match point.

The drama was now so thick that some of the spectators had trouble breathing. Others stood up and screamed and were hushed by the chair umpire. Björn blew into his fingers. McEnroe twisted a serve that landed as far out on Björn's backhand side as was possible. There was nothing Björn could do, and the score was now 10–10. "Yes, this Wimbledon final will obviously become a classic," said Engstrand. Another serve for the American, another volley, a passing shot from the Swede that was too hard for the American to handle, and he sent the ball into the net, 11–10. Match point number six.

"Silence, please."

Björn served, and both players hit cautious groundstrokes from the baseline. McEnroe sliced a backhand that bounced off the net cord and landed on Björn's side, 11–11. "McEnroe got lucky there," said Tommy Engstrand.

There were more set points for McEnroe, and a seventh match point for Björn.

McEnroe hit a first serve and attacked the net, and then Björn hit a passing shot winner. But the American's serve was called out, and Björn didn't protest. McEnroe hit a second serve and followed it with a drop-volley winner; set point. Björn hit an ace, 15–15.

"I've never seen anything like it," said Ove Bengtson, Engstrand's expert cocommentator. The players looked confused. What was the rule? Should they change sides? As they strolled to the opposite sides, the crowd yelled out their names in scattered, desperate bursts.

"Boorrg . . . McEnroe! Borg! . . . . McEnroooe . . ."

Bengtson and Engstrand commented that this tiebreak was the most excruciatingly exciting event that had ever occurred in a sports arena.

Borg hit his serve, McEnroe his return, Borg a volley-cross, McEnroe reached and hit a forehand passing shot down the line, and then his own momentum took him up in the stands. He groaned "pleeaase" as he realized that he had another chance to win the set, his sixth.

"It's absolutely phenomenal what he can do," cried Engstrand.

McEnroe served but hit a sloppy volley out, his worst stroke in the entire match, 16–16. Björn hit his next shot out, 16–17. Björn served, McEnroe returned low, Björn couldn't control the ball, 16–18.

2–2 in sets.

The crowd was in an uproar. Engstrand described the moment with an understatement: "It's a bit scary for Björn. This must leave a mark on his psyche."

In fact, Björn was devastated when he sat down on his chair between sets. He felt like he'd been sitting there for ten minutes. He thought: *I have to forget it and move on.* But it was difficult. He was sure he was going to lose. McEnroe was just as convinced that the victory was his. Now the crowd was clearly on the New Yorker's side. Björn served first in the set and lost the first point, 0–15; lost the second, 0–30. *Calm down,* he said to himself. *Don't tense up.*

Out of nowhere, his body and thoughts were waking up again. Not until the ninth game would he lose another point on his own serve. McEnroe, on the other hand, had to fight his way through his service games, increasingly tired. In games two and eight, he came back from 0–40. The doubles final and the tough match against Connors the day before, when Borg didn't play, began to show. But he kept pace, point by point. 5–5 became 6–6. Björn held serve to 6–7, McEnroe served, and Björn earned two more match points. "Remember how expertly McEnroe handled the previous match points," said Engstrand.

But this time, Björn's backhand whizzed by McEnroe. Björn fell to his knees on the grass. "He's done it again! He's done it again! I'd all but given up," said Engstrand.

In his deep voice, Ove Bengtson proclaimed: "He's performed a feat that no other human has done before and probably never will do again."

Borg still believes that his Wimbledon win over McEnroe is his greatest moment.

"First, you're winning, then you're losing, then you come back again and win it. If you look at the match, it was the most fun of them all. Or . . . I shouldn't exaggerate and say that it was fun to play, because during certain moments it was anything but fun, just painful and so damn hard, but when I finally won. . . . That final had it all, excitement, great tennis, incredible twists and turns."

The previous years' longing for great finals between Borg and McEnroe was realized in 1980 and 1981. Both Borg and McEnroe had to work hard to get to the U.S. Open final. The quarterfinals were virtual wars. Borg fell behind against Tanner, 1–2 in sets and 2–4 in the fourth set, but clawed himself back in a familiar manner. McEnroe outlasted Lendl in his quarter-final. In the semifinals, Borg came back from 0–2 against Johan Kriek while McEnroe, who played the late match on Saturday night, had to fight against a born-again Connors for four hours, before winning the fifth set's decisive tiebreak. "Now all I want to do is get some sleep before the match against Björn tomorrow," gasped McEnroe afterward. Björn said: "Everything has worked for me so far. If I'm ever going to win the U.S. Open, it's now."

The match was broadcast live on both television and radio in Sweden, with a program start of 10 p.m. A Swedish audience of a million people, and a gigantic tennis audience across the world, took their seats and expected a replay.

McEnroe stole the first set from Björn in the same way Björn had stolen the second set from McEnroe at Wimbledon. And in the same way Björn had sailed through the third set at Wimbledon, as if a result of the theft's negative impact on the opponent, McEnroe now sailed through the second set: 7–6, 6–1. Then, he got an early break in the third, but Björn was able to turn things around and won the set in a tiebreak. In the fourth set, both players played dream tennis, but McEnroe seemed to start to slow down. When Björn broke McEnroe's serve to 7–5, his body jerked in a spasm of happiness that the entire stadium could see. Everyone was convinced the Swede would finally go all the way at the U.S. Open.

McEnroe was exhausted, but just like Björn had done in the final set at Wimbledon, he told himself he just needed to keep playing and not think.

The level of tennis kept improving. The American TV's commentator said that the jury was still out on what had been the best match ever, the Wimbledon final earlier in the year or what had been seen in the match here so far.

Borg had never lost a match that had gone the distance; he'd been the victor in 13 straight five-set matches. Now he was battling drop shots and volleys hit with a godlike touch and whip-like ground strokes. McEnroe spun his racket around in his hands like a gunslinger. Borg stared him in the eyes and thought he saw red fire. In the stands, Henry Kissinger and Jack Nicholson kept their fingers crossed for the American, but most people hoped for a Borg win. He was mythological, beloved, and admired in a way that the American wasn't yet.

At 3–3, McEnroe crushed a forehand return that Borg didn't play, but the ball was called good. Borg stared at Bergelin and Mariana. The ball was good. Borg served a double fault. Break point. Björn did what he always did when he played from behind—he attacked. McEnroe chanced it and rushed up to the net, but Borg hit a passing shot by him. McEnroe attacked the next point, too, Björn lobbed, and McEnroe put away an overhead, setting up another break point. McEnroe whipped a cross-court passing shot that Borg couldn't reach. "Yes!" McEnroe screamed. All he needed to do now was to hold his serve two more times. That would mean he'd send Borg back to the world of mortals, where everyone else resided. In the next game, Borg did it all, but McEnroe was phenomenal at the net. "Fantastic play by John McEnroe!" yelled the American commentator in a falsetto voice when McEnroe finished off a blazing shot exchange at the net by putting away a volley that landed smack on the line.

One game later, McEnroe handled Björn's high return like a starving wolf and destroyed it, cross-court, hard, and screaming out in relief. Björn had been defeated. The King of London had been dethroned in New York. McEnroe had defended his title and proven that he was ready to take over the world's number-one spot.

"Ahhh!" shouted the American when he got the mic.

"I have many years left. It was a great match. But there will be even better matches in the future," said Borg before he quickly left the arena without signing any autographs.

During six weeks in March and April 1981, Björn played only sporadically. He was beaten by McEnroe, by a German named Rolf Gehring, and by Victor Pecci. He took two months off, saying that he had to tend to his injured shoulder. Rumors became speculation, which became gossip. His shoulder was dislocated. Borg had become lazy and indifferent. Borg wanted to quit tennis. Borg wanted to have kids with Mariana. Borg had become senile. Borg's nails had started to grow and he'd smuggled liquor with divers on his island in the Swedish archipelago. Borg's response was radio silence. When he arrived in Paris, he looked normal. He said he had doubts about the physical shape he was in, that he was rusty from not having played matches. But he'd practiced hard for two weeks and said that he felt strong and could stay out on the court for a long time if he needed to.

It wasn't needed. This spring, the rain fell over Paris, but it always held up for Borg's matches. At times, the Swede was two rounds ahead of everyone else in the tournament. It could have been because he won so quickly in the first three rounds, he lost on average two games per set, against low-ranked opponents. But in the fourth round, a real test awaited: Terry Moor, ranked 37 in the world. The final score ended up 6–0, 6–0, 6–1, after Borg had slowed things down at 5–0 before solidifying the victory. After winning his only game, Moor celebrated as if he'd won a Grand Slam. The Parisians in the stands waved their hats. "Borg is on a different level," said Moor. "The worst thing is he looked bored. I don't see how anyone can win a game against that man here."

In the other half, McEnroe lost to Lendl. McEnroe looked bored on the wet clay. "The points go on forever, and that's frustrating," said McEnroe afterward. "I don't think the most talented will win here. I was too lazy, I don't deserve to win here."

The final turned out to be great. Lendl challenged Borg, and the two players hit brutal ground strokes at each other from the baseline. In the last set, Borg went from playing it safe to a more aggressive style of play. He'd been forced to come up with something to win his sixth title, and when he finally won, he threw his racket up in the air and smiled at the whole world. Then he went out and celebrated with his friends—the rock group Fleetwood Mac and the actor Lee Majors—who'd watched the match from Borg's box in the stands.

The next day, Björn, Mariana, and Bergelin got on a flight to London, where they checked in to the 10th floor at the Sheraton Park in Knightsbridge. Björn and Mariana stayed in a suite, Bergelin in a room in the same corridor. The hotel was new that year. Bergelin didn't like it, but Borg thought it was fine. Borg was shy, and the other guests at the Sheraton Park were mostly airline stewards and an assortment of Arab sheiks. If the lobby was crowded, Björn would take the elevator down to the garage and escape through there. He preferred not to go out at all during Wimbledon. He was asked why, and his response was short: "Room service is great."

Borg took a two-day break from tennis. On Tuesday, he visited the racetrack Silverstone, where he shook hands with salesmen from the Swedish carmaker Saab and test-drove a new model. Bergelin received a phone call from the sports journalist Curry Fitzpatrick from the magazine *Sports Illustrated*, who requested to follow Björn around for a few days.

"I wonder if I might speak to Bjorn."

"No, no, he doesn't talk to anybody and doesn't see anybody or do anything but tennis. He tells me dat."

"Could I just watch him practice one day?"

"No, no, he don't want anything but tennis, he tells me dat."

"How about if I just hang around and talk to you?"

"No, no, he don't want ANYthing but tennis, he tells me dat."

Later that evening, the same reporter approached Borg and posed his question. "Sure," said Björn. "No problem."

The preparations started the next day. Björn had received newly strung rackets from Stockholm. He played Stevie Nicks on the car stereo on his way to practice. "Too loud," yelled Bergelin, who lowered the volume and rolled down the side windows for fresh air at every red light.

At the Cumberland Club, Björn said hello to all the usual workers. Bergelin chatted with the groundskeeper about how playable the courts were after the rain that always fell. Borg drank some coffee. Then he ordered up a strange drink consisting of black currants, syrup, and carbonated lemonade. He drank it all in one go, grimaced, and said: "It helps my backhand."

And so began the practice, five hours on the grass. Serve-and-volley, to get used to the surface. Then a few hours of tough match-play against Gerulaitis, followed by lunch, black currant lemonade, warm-up, and then back at it. Borg ran like a madman, but he also applauded Gerulaitis's winning strokes. At night, Gerulaitis went out and partied with Fleetwood Mac, while Björn stayed at the hotel, called room service, and played gin rummy with Mariana.

McEnroe, meanwhile, played and won the Queens tournament. He'd had a better year than Borg and had been the betting firm's favorite. But Borg's win in Paris was such a demonstration of strength that the odds had turned—now both experts and the public believed that Borg would bring home his sixth straight Wimbledon title.

And McEnroe didn't make things easy for himself. In the first round against Gullikson on Court 2, the umpire called a serve from McEnroe a fault. McEnroe slowly walked up to him: "You can NOT be SERIOUS!"

No response.

"That ball was on the line. Chalk flew up!"

No response. McEnroe went back to serve again, muttering loudly: "You guys are the absolute pits of the world, you know that."

The head referee came down to the court.

McEnroe: "I'm not going to have a point stolen from me just because this guy's an incompetent idiot." The crowd booed him. All the goodwill he'd gained in last year's final was gone in a couple of minutes.

But many of the players agreed with McEnroe. They thought that the Wimbledon officials treated players poorly, that the snobbery was too much. Everyone had their own example: Stan Smith's wife hadn't been allowed to take a rest in the members' tea room despite the fact that she was seven months pregnant—because she wasn't a member. Panatta sent a telegram to ask if his first match could be postponed, since he'd played a final in Venice. According to the rules, his request should have been granted, but Wimbledon said no. Connors received a warning for grunting and said: "Rules, rules, my whole life should be disqualified! We don't get anything here. The players aren't worth shit." Connors also complained that everyone except Borg was forced to play on the outer courts.

Borg advanced to the semifinals without any problems. There, he had to battle Connors in five murderous sets before winning. He was ready for his sixth straight final. McEnroe played a semifinal that was easier on paper, but everything became difficult for him. He didn't get his game to click against the Australian Rod Frawley.

"These umpires drive me crazy," he screamed at the beginning of the match. He still won the first and second sets, but he didn't find his flow. A ball was called out. McEnroe screamed: "You're a disgrace to humanity."

Penalty point McEnroe.

McEnroe walked up to the chair umpire.

"I wasn't even talkin' to you, umpire. I was talking to myself."

No answer.

"Before you announce the score, I want to talk to the referee."

No answer.

McEnroe, furious: "What did I say? Umpire, tell me! Please, tell me!"

McEnroe won the match but seemed completely burned out from the pressure he put on himself to dethrone Borg. At the press conference before the final, he was asked a question about his girlfriend, Stacy Margolin.

"You piss me off, are you happy now?" he said and left the press room. An American journalist pointed a finger in the face of the Englishman who'd asked the question. This infuriated the Englishman, and the two reporters started hitting each other. One of them fell down on the floor, the other threw himself onto him. Some other reporters interfered and were able to separate them. The fight reflected a tense atmosphere that wasn't contained within the white lines.

The third major final between Borg and McEnroe became somewhat of a dirty fight. The future Princess Diana sat in the royal box and watched tennis that was as good as last year's, but with one difference: neither of the players allowed himself any bad spells, like Borg had done at the start then, and McEnroe had done at the start of the third set. Now McEnroe created chances for himself on Borg's service game for the majority of the first two sets, but Borg won the first set and had a small advantage in the second, which went to a tiebreak, in which McEnroe proved the strongest. In the third set, Borg was ahead, but McEnroe broke back, and when he saved set points and later won the set in a tiebreak, he had Björn's back up against the wall. He was well on his way to conquer the throne in Wimbledon, too.

The air above Centre Court was stagnant. It was a grittier battle this time—faster, more heated. McEnroe was pale as a ghost but wasn't going to let Borg into the match again.

In the fourth set, Borg played brilliantly. He hit rockets for returns, ran down the most impossible shots, saved volleys on pure reflex. But he only kept up with the American, who did whatever he wanted with his racket and found all the openings on the court. When Björn lost three sloppy points in game nine, it was enough for McEnroe to suddenly smell victory, at 4–5 and match point. Borg served and McEnroe returned deep, right at Björn, who was only able to block the ball back. McEnroe watched the ball hang in the air and moved forward toward the net, knowing that the moment had arrived. He reached for Borg's shot and angled his forehand volley a centimeter or so inside the line.

Afterward, Borg refused to speak with anyone. "Talk to the winner," he said. McEnroe was told that because of his poor conduct, he wouldn't receive membership in Wimbledon's member club, the All England Club, unlike all other winners. He shrugged and skipped the champions' banquet. No other winner had ever done that. "Why should I go there to be with all those old men, I wanted to go out and celebrate with my buddies," he said later.

Was Borg finally defeated? There was no doubt, McEnroe was the best player in the world now. Could Borg come back and oust the new number one? Borg was convinced it was possible. He was going to win the U.S. Open. He was going to win that damn U.S. Open title. He wasn't going to let McEnroe win it for the third straight time. That just couldn't happen.

At the U.S. Open, Borg lost only a few random games in his first three matches. A journalist at *Newsday* wrote that it was like fate had rigged the moment—history demanded that Borg get his revenge at the U.S. Open, that he win it after playing a spectacular final against McEnroe.

Borg was even quieter than usual. When he spoke, it was to refute the impressions he gave. One day, Borg would say that he missed more of his passing shots. The next day that he was getting better every match. He seemed more focused than ever but said, "It's okay to be second behind McEnroe now." He also claimed he had interests outside of tennis nowadays. What they were, he wouldn't reveal.

In the semifinal, Borg played dream tennis and crushed Connors with serves that nobody had seen before. McEnroe barely survived five sets against Gerulaitis.

The fourth act in the McEnroe versus Borg saga had been all set.

Just like today, the men's final in the U.S. Open was scheduled for 4:00 p.m. on Sunday afternoon. But the exact match start time is always vague, because tennis has to wait for the conclusion of the NFL games, which can conclude at 4:00, but just as well at 4:30 or 4:45 p.m. The result is that the final often ends at dusk. That usually creates a spectacular setting, with the long shadows falling on the last major tennis tournament of the year.

McEnroe or Borg—again.

The arena was jam-packed with people. The rich, the politicians, the loudmouths, the hardcore fans, TV-camera people . . . Nobody could escape the feeling that they were witnessing an end of an era. It was the last great tennis event of the old days. The draw was already filled with players using big rackets in new materials, with a bigger sweet spot and a stronger frame that made it possible to hit harder and play with more abandon.

Borg and McEnroe both played with a wooden racket of the same type that Gustaf V had used on his grand tour in 1879. The same type of rackets that had been used by Lenglen, Wills Moody, von Cramm, Janne Lundqvist, and Rod Laver. Borg's racket was strung with high tension, providing control and stability. McEnroe's was strung with lower tension, providing a better touch. There they stood in the sunset, tennis' two giants. Björn was newly shaven, and McEnroe had cut his hair after Wimbledon, but his curly hair had gotten out of hand and was sun-bleached again.

In the minds of the players, there was only this moment. They hit the ball back and forth, fixated on the ball, felt whether the feel was the same as when they'd warmed up. Those things you can never know, that which seems to lie outside one's own control—the small detail in a ball toss or how tension affects one's game.

Borg began brilliantly. He pushed McEnroe back with his shots deep into McEnroe's forehand corner and followed up with rushes to the net. The American was only able to hit a lob, and it sailed long. McEnroe put his hands on his hips and stared across the net. Was this some new Swedish strategy? Taking the net away from the world's best net player? It appeared that way. Björn took the first set, 6–4. A woman was chatting in the stands. McEnroe: "Shut up!"

In the second set, Björn's serve started to falter, but he continued to attack the net. McEnroe couldn't understand why. He kept hitting passing shots and lobs past Björn and won the set handily. Mariana chewed her gum, spit it out, smoked.

What happened next was that McEnroe took his game to a new level. Borg served, McEnroe looked nonchalant, returned with a slice, Borg rushed forward and blasted a shot to McEnroe's backhand side. Almost without moving, McEnroe took a very short backswing and whisked off a backhand that sounded more like a gunshot. Borg wasn't even near the ball; the speed of the shot made it just disappear. Then McEnroe hit two lobs, which showed Borg that he now mastered the Swede's style of play as well or even better than Borg himself. Björn walked back. McEnroe took the set, 6–4.

In the fourth set, Björn won only three games. McEnroe could, for the third straight time, raise his arms as the winner. Borg thanked him for the match and vanished.

McEnroe saw that Borg was empty inside. The cameras followed the winner, surrounded him with microphones. He put his jacket over his shoulders and raised an arm to the sky again. The discussion was over. McEnroe was far and away the best player.

Borg had taken baseline tennis as far as possible; McEnroe had perfected attack tennis. They lifted each other up. They were two regular guys who had different ways of focusing, but who really were quite similar. They demanded respect for their hard work. Borg submitted himself to tremendously hard workouts and lots of sleep; McEnroe submitted himself to his quest for perfection, to always finding new strokes, which required a lot of his focus.

Borg's achievements made him a living legend, even before McEnroe appeared on the stage. In the years after Borg's retirement, McEnroe won major titles and dominated the sport in a way that also made him one of the all-time greats. During the three years between 1979 and 1981, these two stars collided in tennis heaven and gave the world matches that people would remember for decades. And they split the sport's five major titles between them:

	1979	1980	1981
Masters	McEnroe	Borg	Borg
WCT	McEnroe	Connors	McEnroe
Paris	Borg	Borg	Borg
Wimbledon	Borg	Borg	McEnroe
U.S. Open	McEnroe	McEnroe	McEnroe

At Flushing Meadows, the organizers laid out the trophies and rigged the microphones, but the runner-up wasn't there. Everyone looked around. Where was Borg?

McEnroe received his trophy, and since the runner-up wasn't present, the public announcer asked the winner to call his friends down from the stands and arrange a victory party on the court, in lieu of the traditional thank-you speech. For once, McEnroe did as he was told.

"It was pretty nice, says Björn Borg today. I knew it'd be my last Grand Slam tournament, regardless if I lost in the second round or in the final. So, when I lost the final, for the first time I wasn't disappointed. It was pretty nice, and I felt I don't have to stay and speak with the press and say 'nice to see you, nice match' and all of that. I was done. So Bergelin and I, we went out to the car and drove back to the house. We hung out by the pool and went swimming. And then a lot of my friends and family started showing up. Bergelin didn't know for sure that I was going to quit, but he had an inkling."

The decision had grown over the season.

"I knew the entire year. I was entered in tons of tournaments in 1981, and I'd call and say: 'No, I'm injured, I can't play.' Still, that year I won the Masters, and I won the French. And then I made the finals at Wimbledon and the U.S. Open. I also played some other tournaments that I won, so I still had a pretty good year. But I felt that this is it. It was the lack of motivation, it wasn't fun to play anymore. I must have the feeling that I love what I do, and that's not how it was anymore. It felt like a chore to go to practice. After the final, that feeling, to get back home to the house and the pool, it was kind of like I just laughed: 'God, how nice!' It was a relief. I'd made my decision and afterward I knew it was a firm decision. Of course, I could probably have had five more years at the top and won a few more tournaments, you never know. But it's definitely not something I regret."

In the end, Hyland, Laver, Lundqvist, and the others were right in their predictions. Björn Borg's energy had run out, at the age of twenty-five. The constant traveling and playing, " . . . to engage your will and your nerves every single day, time and time again . . .," like Hyland had said, had taken its toll.

The sun's last rays fell on New York, and the tennis world celebrated its new champion. The old champion floated in a swimming pool and knew it was over.

Much later, Arthur Ashe commented on Björn Borg's last final: "I think that Björn could have won a U.S. Open after that. I think he could have won a Grand Slam. But when he left the sport, such challenges meant nothing. He'd become larger than the sport. He was like an Elvis."

THE TEENS WHO COPIED BORG

"Do you have some kind of laboratory for tennis machines in Sweden? Machines you put small heads on?"
—ION TIRIAC

The wind howled outside the windows. The storm from the Atlantic pounded rain against the window panes and tore at the palm trees. The street lights flickered and painted curious patterns on the walls in the strange room. The house cracked, sounding as if parts of the roof were about to come apart.

Mats Wilander couldn't sleep. He got up, wrapped the cover around his body, and tiptoed to the door. He opened it slightly, and when he stepped out into the hallway, he saw that farther down the hall another door had also opened. His friend Joakim Nyström, wearing a t-shirt and briefs, staggered out.

"Damn, it's windy."

"Yeah, shit."

They were quiet for a few seconds, looking at each other and listening to the storm.

Then Jocke said:

"Should I come to your room instead, I can bring my mattr—"

"Yes, do that," said Mats before Jocke had finished his sentence. "Sleep in here!"

Jocke took his mattress, cover, and pillow and carried it all into Mats's room. Together they made room for Jocke among all the tennis clothes, sport bags, and rackets on the floor, while at the same time trying to be as quiet as possible so as not to wake the rest of the house. Eventually, the two youngsters fell asleep.

Joakim Nyström and Mats Wilander had first met at a training camp for elite tennis youth in Båstad a couple of year earlier. The quiet, nice Nyström and the shy but curious Wilander had found each other immediately. Now it was late 1980, soon to be Christmas, and both players had been selected to represent Sweden in the Sunshine Cup, a sort of team World Cup for juniors in Florida. The house in which they were trying to sleep belonged to the Cook family, who were tennis enthusiasts and often acted as a host family to young players from different parts of the world. Mats Wilander was sixteen years old, Jocke a year older. They were still kids, but precocious tennis talents. Mats had already won the European Championships for fourteen- and fifteen-year-olds, and, the year before, he'd taken home the title in a prestigious youth tournament, the Orange Bowl, in the sixteen-and-under division. Back then, his stay in Florida had been painful. Between matches, he'd sit at the dinner table with his host family trying to converse, stuttering in his school English. Then he'd go back to his borrowed bedroom, lie down on the bed, thumb through SAS flight schedules, and dream about blowing everything off and just hopping on a flight home.

Both Mats Wilander and Joakim Nyström liked company and familiar environments more than they liked solitude and tournaments away from home. Mats grew up in the small village of Torpsbruk outside of Växjö in southern Sweden, where he played tennis on the village's asphalt court with his two older brothers, Anders and Ingemar, and their friends. Everyone was seven or eight years older than little Mats, who'd learn how to keep the ball in play against teenagers who were almost grown-ups. When he didn't play tennis, he kept himself busy with ice hockey. He liked the team sport, but he would also get frustrated with opponents who ruined his game with tackles or by chopping at his legs with their sticks. The tennis court was a more pleasant environment. There, he made the decisions, at his own pace.

Jocke Nyström, on the other hand, was crazy about hockey and the club Skellefteå AIK. But he loved tennis even more. So much that he left home as soon as he'd graduated ninth grade.

"I was just fifteen when I suddenly had a studio apartment in Umeå, a town I didn't know, where I stayed during the week. I had to grow up, cook for myself. Or at least heat up the lunch boxes that my mom sent," recalls Jocke Nyström of his new abode, about 90 miles from home.

His mother worked at a grocery store. Every Monday morning, Jocke caught rides with the store's trucks.

In the evenings, he practiced with the tennis club. Jocke soon also found a mailman who was a recreational tennis player, with whom he played in the mornings, and a teacher, with whom he practiced in the afternoons. For a year and a half, he carried on like that. Leave home Monday, go back home Friday. Unless Skellefteå AIK had a home game on Thursday, then he'd go back home a day early.

"It was lonely. I was used to living with my mom and dad and my brother, and I missed them a lot. It was actually a bummer to move to Umeå. But I did it, to get better at tennis."

Jocke was clearly ahead of Mats in his development. He was a player whom Mats Wilander had never defeated, and also never expected to beat. Jocke was the star whom Mats looked up to, somewhat in the same way he looked up to his brothers.

Together, they were unbeatable in the Team World Cup tournament in Delray Beach. They defeated two Spaniards in the final. Jocke didn't lose one single set in the tournament, and Mats lost only two. After the tournament, they moved on to Fort Lauderdale to participate in the Orange Bowl. The team captain Stig Jansson did what he could for the boys to have fun between the matches. After an improvised Christmas celebration, he brought Jocke and Mats to a golf course for the very first time. He contacted the Swedish hockey player Anders Kallur, who got them tickets to a New York Islanders match, and he arranged for the boys to practice on a court that was next to the court where the women's number-one player, Chris Evert, and her husband John Lloyd played.

On the practice court, Jansson tried to perfect Wilander's forehand. Wilander and Nyström were similar players, solid clay court specialists with tactical minds, but Nyström played a more varied game and had an easier time finishing off his battles. Wilander had a nice backhand and a forehand that had a lot of topspin but was soft and monotonous.

Jocke Nyström was so confident in his game, especially on clay, that despite his withdrawn disposition, he became almost arrogant. He easily advanced to the Orange Bowl final. Before the final, Stig Jansson asked him if he'd like some tactical advice. "Nah," said Nyström, "I'll hit a few shots to his backhand and then to his forehand so that he gets to run. And then he'll miss."

That's exactly what happened. Nyström became the second Swede in history, after Björn Borg, to win the Orange Bowl's 18-and-under division. Before returning home to Sweden, he also won a big juniors' tournament in Port Washington. The *New York Times* had a reporter on-site, who described Nyström as the new Borg.

The same comparison was being made in Sweden. When Jocke Nyström's flight landed in Skellefteå, he was met by a delegation from his tennis club and a TV reporter.

"I had no idea they even knew what had happened. But they even had a singer there when I walked into the arrivals hall," says Joakim Nyström.

Nyström's success was welcome. Within Swedish tennis, there was concern for the future. In the generation after Björn Borg, the junior players Per Hjertqvist and Stefan Simonsson had challenged the Czech supertalent Ivan Lendl for the title of the world's best junior. But taking the next step and becoming successful in the main draw tournaments seemed too difficult for them. The drought behind Björn Borg had continued.

Joakim Nyström was the kid of the future. At a Swedish tournament, he was met by a talkative man named Onni Nordström, who closely followed talk with action. He worked with Björn Wagnsson, an attorney who also acted as financial advisor to the skier Ingemar Stenmark and several professional hockey players in North America. Nordström had found his niche in a new and growing industry. He organized events and conventions, was a bit of a sports agent, and was driven by an all-is-possible attitude that occasionally made people around him dismiss him for a flaky chatterbox. But nobody could deny that there was also something very modern about him.

"I want to sign you," said Nordström. "I can get Ramlösa to sponsor you, too, if you sign."

Nordström had no tennis experience, but Jocke thought having a sponsor sounded good, so after Onni Nordström had met his parents, the tennis talent signed a contract with Nordström to be his manager. Shortly thereafter, Jocke signed another sponsorship contract, with the clothing manufacturer Tacchini, which led to envious looks from Mats Wilander when Jocke began arriving to practice wearing cool tracksuits.

About a month later, Onni Nordström and Joakim Nyström were in Dallas for a junior tournament. Nordström got into a conversation with

Patrice Hagelauer, the coach of the Frenchman Yannick Noah, who in 1979 had reached the third round at Wimbledon as a nineteen-year-old. "What can we do to help Jocke?" asked Nordström. Hagelauer responded: "You have so many talented juniors. Why don't you build a team?"

This same thought had crossed the mind of the Davis Cup captain and national team coach John-Anders Sjögren. At Wimbledon in 1981, he had to juggle twelve Swedish players in the different open and junior categories. Just getting practice times for everyone consumed all of his time. There was no time for individual practice, strategizing, or scouting opponents.

Sjögren wanted a small team, and he wanted to design it like a Davis Cup team, with doubles specialists. If there was something the Swedish Davis Cup team had lacked during the years with Björn Borg as anchor, it was a solid doubles team that played well together.

The only question was who was going to finance such a venture. It wasn't within the Swedish Tennis Association's budget—and besides, that's where Sjögren was employed, with other job responsibilities. Sjögren and Nordström consulted with each other, and Nordström, egged on by the spirit of the time, got to work on acquiring the biggest sponsorship contract ever in Swedish sports.

Mats Wilander won the junior title at the French Open in June, and Sweden met Australia in the Davis Cup in Båstad in July. Wilander, who'd signed a contract with IMG, the same firm that managed Borg, got to make his national team debut but lost to both Paul McNamee and Peter McNamara. But the young doubles team, Anders Järryd and Hans Simonsson, surprised everyone by winning the doubles against the same pair of Australian players.

In September, Joakim Nyström achieved his biggest victory to date, when he defeated the Chilean Victor Pecci at Palermo's clay court tournament. After that, it was time for the ATP tournament in Basel. Wilander was going there, too, to play in the junior tournament.

Mats Wilander recalls:

"We arrived at the airport in Geneva, where I was met by one of the IMG guys. He said: 'I have some good news and some bad news. The good news is that you've received a wild card to the main tournament. The bad news is that you'll play Björn Borg.'"

The first time Mats Wilander saw Björn Borg play tennis in real life was in the summer of 1980. Wilander was fifteen years old and sat next to his brother Anders five rows up in the "sea bleachers" at the center court in Båstad. Björn Borg was playing the fourth match in Sweden's Davis Cup match against West Germany. He played Klaus Eberhard, who was ranked around 100th in the world and had lost to Kjell Johansson two days earlier. That Björn was going to win the match was a given. But the way in which he won made a deep impression on Mats.

As he sat in the stands, Mats experienced how something that looked so slow on television could be so lightning-fast in real life. Borg crushed serves that were harder than anything Mats had ever seen before, and when Borg ran way out to his backhand side to hit a forehand, he almost ended up in the stands next to Mats. He saw how Borg moved on the court, fleet-footed and effortless, almost as if he were flying. And then there were the sounds, the singing sounds of Borg's hard-hit groundstrokes.

Björn Borg won the final two sets without losing a game.

"The hair stood up on my arms," Mats describes. "It reminded me of the feeling you have when you're in a car and turn the volume up to max and sing along at the top of your lungs. If Björn Borg had been my role model before that match, from that moment on he was an unattainable hero."

Now this hero was standing alive and well on the other side of the net. It was Björn's first match after his bitter loss to McEnroe at the U.S. Open. Now he was just going to finish off his career. Mats walked out onto the court with a pulled groin muscle.

"Björn served first, and then he hit his shots up the middle of the court. So, there we were, hitting to each other, ten strokes, twenty. . . . And I wondered why he didn't do anything with the ball. After perhaps 30 strokes, I moved up to the net and Björn hit the ball right to me. I didn't understand what he was doing, but I put away the volley and then I broke his serve right away. I thought: *Is this all he does?*"

After that, Björn won ten straight games, leaving Mats in the dust. With the score 6–1 and 4–0, Björn suddenly stopped playing again. When Mats served way out to Björn's forehand side, Björn didn't even bother to reach for the ball.

As Mats describes, "He just turned around and walked with his slumped shoulders over to the other service box. So, he gave me that game, the match ended, 6–1, 6–1. When we thanked each other for the match at the net, he said in his drawl: 'How's your groin, it looks like you're having some problems?'"

Groin problems or not, Mats sensed that he'd never be able to beat his idol. Björn had gifted Mats two games just to be nice. He didn't miss anything. And every time Mats played to Björn's forehand, he killed it.

With Mats Wilander eliminated, Jocke Nyström had a small breakthrough. For the second time in two weeks, he defeated Victor Pecci, after which he advanced all the way to the semifinals. Pecci had a slice backhand that he hit with precision and stubbornness against Jocke, who, in turn and even more stubbornly, returned the ball with deep topspin groundstrokes.

Since Borg and Nyström were in different halves of the draw, and therefore wouldn't get to play each other until a potential final, the two practiced together the entire week leading up to what was to become the last tournament win in Björn's career.

Nyström says, "Björn's tempo in practice was incredibly high even if you were just hitting. He had such focus. To go out and play a Chilean who just sliced the ball after that, it made things feel extremely slow. You got fired up from practicing with Björn. I was more nervous to talk to him, I was a quiet guy from the north, but he was always nice."

For Mats Wilander, the tournament proved two things he already knew. One was how awfully far he had to go before he'd be even close to Borg's level. The other was that Jocke was closer.

"Jocke was the one person who showed me that it's possible to beat the great players," says Mats Wilander. "Victor Pecci, he played in the 1979 French Open final and was a Top 10 player. He was a player you looked up to. I remember the match. Pecci kept slicing his shots, and Jocke hit topspins back, as if to say: 'Go ahead and slice the ball, I'll hit everything back.' Jocke was brutal. He was for me kind of like Miloslav Mecir was later in my career, a player I had a terribly hard time playing."

Around the same time, Onni Nordström came back to Jonte Sjögren with good news. He'd been digging for gold. Not at the Skånska concrete foundry, where he'd tried at first, since his cousin worked there. But Svenska Industribyggen AB—Siab for short—another construction giant, had taken Nordström up on his unorthodox sponsorship proposal. At the first meeting, Siab's CEO Håkan Birke had just muttered: "These kids aren't going to amount to anything." But Onni Nordström had planted a seed, talked about giving the kids some time, about investing in youth and the future. Three weeks later, he asked for a decision, and by then he'd started to bond with the company's marketing director, who loved the idea. Together they convinced the CEO.

Siab contributed a million Swedish kronor per year for two years, to pay for Coach Jonte Sjögren's salary plus four players' travel and accommodations for tournaments and training camps. The four were assembled like one of the music industry's boy bands—handpicked to fill certain roles in a quartet, namely, the Davis Cup team. Wilander and Nyström were the gifted single players. Anders Järryd and Hans Simonsson were to make up the Swedish doubles team.

Simonsson and Nyström were present at Siab's headquarters as representatives for the young, new, and promising tennis generation, when Onni Nordström conducted his final negotiations with the Siab CEO.

"Onni picked up the phone and pretended to call other sponsors while Håkan Birke listened. He wanted to make him believe that there was a first-come-first-served situation for who'd get to sponsor us," says Simonsson. "Jocke and I sat there like two school boys with our mouths open: 'Ah, this is how things get done in the business world.'"

There are always good reasons for wanting to leave Sweden in late fall. Nineteen eighty-one was no exception. The darkness swept in over cities and forests, leaving them in a quiet slumber. People pulled their jacket collars closer, and one morning late in October, a Soviet submarine ran aground in a military protection zone outside of Karlskrona.

The U-137 incident was an unpleasant reminder that the cold war between the Soviet Union and the United States also affected Sweden. This was the fall when American President Ronald Reagan gave the green light to the development of a neutron bomb and plunked down a total of 44 billion dollars in the Star Wars project, a sort of space umbrella that was going to protect the American people against Soviet ballistic nuclear weapons. The power struggle between the superpowers made hundreds of thousands of Europeans participate in peace demonstrations.

At this time, Team Siab was on the road, on its way to a country as far away from Europe as one could go, where people said, "g'day mate," lived one day at a time, and drank light-colored beer. With half of the total two-year marketing budget from Siab, the team boarded the plane for Australia.

"It was so amazing," recalls Anders Järryd. "The goal was to be based in and train in Australia, but there was also a tournament in Bangkok that was convenient to play on the way there. It went great, I made the semifinals, and Mats made the final, in a 75,000-dollar tournament."

Because Järryd and Wilander advanced much further in the tournament than anyone had expected, Sjögren had to rebook the entire team's reservations for a later flight to Australia.

"And this could only be done with cash, not check or card," says Sjögren, "so I had to withdraw the equivalent of 40,000 kronor and carry the cash walking through Bangkok's shadiest neighborhood to a small travel agency. And I'm a chicken in those kinds of circumstances. I was shaking, I was so nervous. I thought I was going to be robbed and that our whole trip would come to an end before we even reached our destination."

Jonte Sjögren had read the books by the legendary Australian coach Harry Hopman. And he'd gotten to know Australia's Davis Cup captain, Neale Fraser. Jonte's idea was that the young Swedish players should learn how to play on grass and how to volley because only when you mastered all parts of the game, on all surfaces, were you a complete tennis player. And where could you learn the grass game better than in Australia?

In the short, truncated shade, the temperature hovered above 85 degrees Fahrenheit. But that's not where you'd find Wille, Jocke, Ante, and Hasse. They were out on the tennis court, where the sun roasted the already brown and burned grass. They performed one of Jonte Sjögren's "drills," which he called his exercises, that were based on the Australian model. In Borg's days, when Björn decided the format of the practice sessions, it was almost always only match-like play, keeping score. That suited Borg, but perhaps not everyone else. Jonte Sjögren's policy was that at least half of the time on the court would be spent on predetermined exercises. He had a special volley exercise, another where the shots were to be hit in a certain order—long, short, forehand, backhand. His favorite drill was the one that consisted of four minutes of free play, without any line boundaries. In this drill, the guys would play every ball, even if it was way off the court, until, after four minutes, Sjögren blew his whistle and they were allowed to rest. The coach's favorite private joke was to occasionally let his watch tick to both five and six minutes before whistling.

"Everything was so much fun. We were in Australia, a new country, the sun was shining. We trained hard. Compared to Växjö, there was a huge difference. We were friends, we practiced, joked around, helped each other, and went out and partied when the time was right," says Mats Wilander.

Anders Järryd has similar memories:

"We woke up pretty early. Hasse was my roommate, our room was nice and neat. Then Mats and Jocke would come out from their room, which was always a disaster zone. And then we went to the courts. We had one practice session in the morning and one in the afternoon. We ran a lot and did a lot of body weight physical exercises out on the courts, push-ups, sit-ups, things like that. At the same time, we didn't live like monks, which I think was important. You need to have fun at that age. We'd party on Fridays and Saturdays. But on Monday, it was back to hard work. We were hot, we wanted to get ahead, and we encouraged each other. Jonte was hot, too. He got to test his wings, along with us. He was motivated, you could tell he believed in us and thought it was possible to bring up new top players. It was contagious for all of us."

As mentioned, the heat sizzled from the sky, as well. Järryd, with his energy-consuming style of play, ran himself completely ragged in the hot sun. Thomas Högstedt, a junior who'd flown in to participate in parts of the first training camp, hadn't put on sunscreen lotion—a product many people in Sweden were barely familiar with—and got so badly sunburnt that his entire face swelled up. He was taken to a doctor, who prescribed an ointment. A couple of days later, he again practiced out in the sun, now wearing long pants, a track jacket zippered all the way up, and a baseball cap.

The only one who didn't sweat was Mats Wilander.

"I could wring out the sweat from my shirt after practice," says Anders Järryd. "But Mats barely had a small spot under his armpits. He practiced hard but was always relaxed, unlike me. I was always tense. That takes energy, it tires you out. But Mats didn't waste any unnecessary energy on the court, and it always benefited him the day after and the day after that."

Before the training camp in Perth, the four young guys didn't know one another especially well, except for the friends Jocke and Mats. Although Hans Simonsson had traveled with both Mats and Jocke a few years earlier with the junior national team, he hadn't really made a close connection with either of them.

Simonsson says, "Neither one of them said anything. Especially Mats, he was quiet like a mouse and always sat in the very back of the bus to the left, right where the speaker was, where the coach's Bob Dylan cassettes could be best heard. He usually slept. He could sleep for ten hours straight. And because he never talked, you forgot that he was there."

Now that the walls between the players were torn down, they learned about one another's weaknesses and strengths. Jocke was the quiet sports fanatic. Hasse was a professional and had a ball touch that made everyone else jealous—almost as jealous as they were of his long, flowing curls and beautiful eyes, which always made the girls notice him first. Anders Järryd was the stickler with the hot temper. He traveled with two suitcases. In one, he carried all his clean clothes; in the other, all his dirty laundry. Because he folded his dirty laundry as meticulously as his clean clothes, he was the only one who could say which suitcase was which.

And then there was Mats:

"Mats still didn't say very much," recalls Anders Järryd. "He was an observer, he'd stay in the background and study how people behaved and what they said. He judged people, pondered the kind of characters they were, and then he'd come back and ask about them later. He put all the information away in his mind somewhere, in case he might have use for it in the future."

Although above all, they were a team. They mixed up the training in Perth with tournament play in both juniors and main draws. When one of them played a match, the others watched.

"We helped each other tremendously," says Joakim Nyström. "If a foreign player was good, we'd go and check him out: what does he do well, what do you need to do to beat him? It went on like that for several years. Between us, we talked a lot of strategy."

Suddenly, Sweden had what it had lacked in Mr. G's era: a big talent pool from all parts of society and, above all, a great deal of innovation. Instead of the lone wolf Borg, there was now a collective of young players who trained together. Between the solidarity and the sponsorships, it was as if the newly finished '70s had married the new decade in a perfect match.

In Australia, the Swedish kids had a strong sense that they were on their way to entering a new era. Not only in terms of themselves—they were boys becoming men, young talents on the way to becoming professional players—but also in terms of everything around them, in fact, society as a whole. Technical development was in focus. Push-button telephones replaced the old rotary phones in Swedish homes. The digital watch made its debut. That fall, an English band with the difficult-to-pronounce name Depeche Mode released its first single, *Just Can't Get Enough*, which was full of bubbly electronic sounds. The group Adolphson & Falk sang in Swedish about the emerging computer society in its hit song *Blinkar blå*. That's the kind of music Jocke listened to. It wasn't for Mats, who liked Bob Dylan and Ulf Lundell, a Swedish singer-songwriter of the same mold. Technology solved this disagreement for them. Each could lie in his own bed and listen to his own Sony Walkman. And then there was the new Saab provided by the Swedish Tennis Association, the one that Jocke Nyström drove—he'd gotten his driver's license back home in the days between the Stockholm Open and the Australia trip—which had central locks, power windows, and rearview mirrors that could be adjusted from the driver's seat.

The technical development also applied to the game. The wooden rackets had already been replaced by steel rackets, which now began to be replaced by models made of graphite and with a larger head. Mats found his favorite early on, the graphite racket F200 by Rossignol.

But Mats really didn't care much about the materials; he was most interested in the tactical aspects of the game. When Mats watched his Team Siab buddies play, he often felt inferior. Järryd was faster and had a better volley. Both Nyström and Simonsson had amazing ball touch. Wilander had something else: a pronounced interest in tennis strategy and the mental game. That's where he was most confident, in anticipating play and slowly outmaneuvering his opponents. In terms of the specific strokes, his confidence was not as strong. Therefore, he did what he used to do at home on the asphalt court in Torpsbruk—he became a copycat.

"When I played with my brothers and my dad, nobody tried to teach me anything. I just picked up a racket and tried to do what I've seen on TV. And when I played minitennis with my friends, we'd ask each other: 'Who are you?' And we'd say, 'I'm Connors' or 'I'm Nastase,' and then we'd play like them, too. Hit flat forehands like Connors or attack the net like Nastase. Not many people know this, but I continued to do the same thing when I got older, too, in fact my whole career. I tried to copy Peter McNamara's sliced backhand, or Nastase's serve, or Lendl's forehand, or even Edberg's serve many years later. . . . If you teach yourself the game in this way, you'll probably become a strategist and analyst, like me. That's where I got my passion for the game. I'm good at imitating, but I've never thought that my tennis is particularly sharp, really. I'm good at the game, but not at hitting shots. That's why I always searched for a better technique, and I always looked at other players."

In early spring 1982, the tennis protégés returned to European soil and continued to travel together. The players felt safe under Jonte Sjögren's leadership. He seemed to know people all around the world. Sjögren himself thanks Bergelin and Borg for having served as the door openers.

"Because we were Swedish, we were met with respect everywhere, even if we weren't famous," says John-Anders Sjögren. "I benefited from Bergelin's contacts. I was really much more reserved and confrontation-adverse than Bergelin. I couldn't have managed my job as well if I hadn't been able to follow in his footsteps."

Lennart Bergelin's English was much worse than Sjögren's, but he got results anyway, by patting people on the back and by being persuasive.

"I remember a trip to Hungary with the Davis Cup team in the '70s, says Sjögren. Labbe was going to fix something for Borg. In the evening, he found the Hungarian equipment manager and yelled: 'KLISTER! I want KLISTER [glue]!' The Hungarian didn't understand a thing, of course, but three minutes later Labbe had gotten his glue anyway."

After the training camp in Australia, the players had also matured, both as players and people, and their friendships had deepened. None were tighter than Nyström and Wilander.

"Jocke knows me better than anyone else, my wife isn't even close," says Mats. "Although Jocke knows me much better than I know him, because I didn't care as much, I was much more goal-oriented. I wasn't interested on a personal level, whether he was feeling good or bad, I didn't think that was my problem. I was a bit diva-ish in that way, not that I was mean or arrogant, but internally. I had a lot of self-confidence, both on the court and off. That's how it would even occur to me to wear clogs to a dinner banquet. I didn't care what people thought."

The effects of the tough training camp would soon be seen in the results on the court. In late February, Mats won a challenger tournament in Germany. The following week, he advanced all the way to the final in the

ATP tournament in Brussels, where Vitas Gerulaitis won by 2–1 in sets. That same week, Anders Järryd won two titles in an ATP tournament in Linz, Austria, in singles over José Higueras and in doubles together with Hasse Simonsson.

Still, the achievements made only moderate echoes on the sports pages. A place in the final in a medium-sized ATP tournament wasn't really much to write home about compared to Borg's six straight Wimbledon finals. If articles were written about tennis—and they were—it was still mostly about Borg. Journalists, experts, and tennis fans were still puzzled by Björn's decision to take a time-out from tennis. Borg announced that he was going to make a comeback on his home court in Monte Carlo in April. But it was still unclear if it was a full commitment to regain the tennis throne. The magazine *Hänt i veckan* interviewed Lennart Bergelin, who said: "I'll make Borg the world's number one again!"

The tennis fans needed promises like that. Björn had taken a four-month break from tournaments and had, unlike the rest of the world's elite players, refused to sign a contract with the International Tennis Federation committing to play at least ten Grand Prix tournaments in the year. Instead, Björn had made only one brief statement: "I'm tired of tournament tennis. Tired of the demands and obligations. Tired of the psychological pressure created because I always have to win."

But no one really believed his words. Labbe tried to convince him to play in the tournaments, and so did IMG. Rumors had it that Björn still wanted to play the major Grand Slam tournaments. McCormack made an attempt to get ITF to circumvent the rules and give Borg a wild card to the French Open, Wimbledon, and the U.S. Open but received the cold shoulder. Philippe Chatrier, the president of the International Tennis Federation, said: "To let Borg play Wimbledon without qualifying, to make an exception for one single player, no, that'd be too controversial. Especially if we made an exception for the great champion."

After Brussels followed Rome, where Mats reached the semifinals. After that, the plan had been to pack the tennis rackets and fly to Paris for the French Open, but a strike in Italy ruined the plan. Instead, Jonte, Mats, and Annette, his high school sweetheart from Växjö, drove together to Paris in a rented Renault 5. Or rather, Mats threw his Stiga bags on the floor in the back, laid himself down on top of them, and slept until they got to Paris. Jonte drove the entire way without a break.

They arrived at 7 a.m., and Jonte called the tournament organizers to arrange for a practice court. They responded: "Yes, that's fine, you can have the center court with Jimmy Connors this morning."

"It was so crazy," says Wilander. "He was my idol, I thought he had such a cool style with his flat shots and a powerful serve with his crooked style. And he was tough and a little dangerous."

Practice with Connors was simple. You warmed up for 45 minutes by hitting rockets back and forth to each other. Without a break, without placing the ball or aiming for the corners. Just 45 minutes all out with the ball in play the entire time.

Then, when you started to get tired, you played games.

By then, Connors, the soon-to-be thirty-year-old and world number two, and Mats, the seventeen-year-old, had barely exchanged a word. They'd just been hitting their shots.

"I managed to take the lead by a break, 4–2 or 3–1," Mats says. "As we were changing sides, when we passed each other by the umpire's chair, Connors hissed: 'You fucking cocksucker!' I turned to Jonte and asked: 'Did you hear what he said?' 'Yes,' said Jonte. 'Don't worry about it.' 'Don't worry about it? We practice together and he calls me 'cocksucker'!"

Mats didn't win any more games that morning. It was an awakening. The professional tennis tour was something entirely different from a Team Siab training camp. Here, all that mattered was winning. Here, all kinds of shenanigans were allowed.

The tournament began, and Mats Wilander defeated Alejandro Cortes from Colombia and Cassio Motta from Brazil. Then he played Fernando Luna, a tricky Spaniard whom Mats destroyed with an aggressive style of play, 6–3, 6–1, 6–0. The easy win provided self-confidence, but according to all reasonable estimates, even the ones made by Jonte Sjögren and Mats himself, Mats's tournament would come to an end in the next round. There, he was going to face Ivan Lendl, who was four years older than Mats, physically strong, equipped with a feared forehand, and the runner-up to Borg in the previous year's final. The Czech had reached the final in his last 18 tournaments, had lost only three of his last 94 matches, and was most people's favorite to win the entire tournament.

Mats lost the first set, won the second, and lost the third. He was consistent and stubborn, slowed the pace down, and made sure to keep the ball on Lendl's backhand side until suddenly surprising him with an attack to his forehand. With a score of 2–2 in sets, Mats knew he was approaching unfamiliar ground. He'd never played a five-set match before.

Beneath the blazing hot sun at Roland Garros, Mats took a 3–0 lead in the fifth set. On match point, Mats attacked Lendl's backhand, and the Czech sent his shot into the net.

Until the Lendl match, Mats had held his press conferences under an oak tree outside the arena, with the two or three Swedish journalists who covered the French Open. Because Borg didn't play, most of the newspapers had opted to keep their reporters at home. But now everyone flew down to Paris, where Mats became hot prey for the world press as well as the teenage girls. He posed for photographs by the Arc de Triomphe with Annette, before she flew back home to attend to her schoolwork. He had to cancel his own ticket for the same flight. At the press conference, Mats said: "When I became nervous in the last set, I decided not to show it to anyone. It's always best just to keep playing. Everyone thinks that Lendl was my toughest match, but I just get slow against Lendl, I don't get tired. Lendl can only push you from his forehand. Gerulaitis is tougher, he can put pressure on you from both his forehand and his backhand."

Gerulaitis was the player waiting for Mats in the quarterfinal. Swedish Radio decided to broadcast live with the commentators Mats Strandberg and Ove Bengtson. Annette was one of the listeners, on the patio of her family's town home in Växjö. But if the match against Lendl was a real nail-biter, the match against Gerulaitis became a rather pleasant affair. Mats outrallied yet another top name, another seeded player, by 3–1 in sets.

Back home, Sweden enjoyed a lovely early summer. People prepared for some big rock concerts and sports events: Simon & Garfunkel at Råsunda arena, Rolling Stones at Ullevi, and Floyd Patterson was in Stockholm to run the Stockholm Marathon along with Ingemar Johansson. Those who were interested could watch the final set of Wilander's match in a taped recording on late-night TV. For those who did, they saw a Wilander who methodically stayed at the baseline and waited for Gerulaitis to make mistakes, although that wasn't a true reflection of the match as a whole. In the first sets, Mats attacked the net and played a style of tennis that was aggressive and varied. Foreign tennis connoisseurs noted that Mats was already a better volleyer than Björn Borg had ever been. After his victory, Mats said: "I hate baseline rallies. Sometimes, though, I have to stay back there to win matches." Gerulaitis called Mats the "Ball-Wall from Sweden."

Looking back, Mats says:

"Up until around 1983, I was 95 percent sure that I wouldn't miss my shots, because I didn't take chances. I thought it was a mistake, not a good strategy, to hit the ball too close to the lines or too close to the net. That was probably the biggest difference between my game and other players' games. It was awfully boring to watch, but I was totally indifferent to what people thought."

Consequently, nobody expected entertaining tennis in the semifinal. At least not if by entertaining you meant a varied tennis game with net attacks and drop shots. Mats Wilander had certainly shown signs of having such qualities in his win over Gerulaitis, but in the semifinal against José-Luis Clerc from Argentina, it was clear that this was a different match. If Guillermo Vilas was the overall favorite to win the tournament now that Lendl had been eliminated, his countryman Clerc was the second favorite. They were both very consistent, methodical clay-court specialists who could hit groundstrokes from the baseline until the cows came home. But they didn't like each other. Clerc was a simple, talkative working-class guy, who didn't appreciate Vilas's snobbishness, his interest for poetry, or his businessman-like style. Clerc claimed that Vilas demanded to get paid twice as much as Clerc to play for Argentina in the Davis Cup.

As expected, the match didn't exactly sparkle. Methodically and consistently, Mats broke Clerc down. At match point, the score was 7–5, 6–2, 1–6, 6–5, with Wilander up 40–30 on Clerc's serve.

The point got going, Clerc hit a shot out of bounds, and the umpire proclaimed Mats the winner.

Every match, every tournament has its special moment that will stay in your memory forever. This was that moment at the French Open in 1982.

Back home in Sweden, Wilander's achievements had finally increased the interest in tennis, had made the sport hot again. Swedish television broadcast the semifinals live. Millions of Swedes celebrated when the umpire announced: "Game, set, and match, Wilandeaaar." The new kid had fought his way to a Grand Slam final.

It was just that Mats wasn't cheering. Instead, he walked up to the umpire and conferred for a while. Soon, the umpire announced: "At the request of Mats Wilander, the point will be replayed." The TV audience in Sweden wondered what in the world the boy was doing.

Everyone who has ever set foot on a tennis court, if only for a fun match with a neighbor during vacation, knows the many thoughts that will cross your mind when you see that your opponent's shot appears to be on its way to landing outside the lines: you wish for the ball to go out, you try to pull it with an invisible fish line, and when it bounces off the ground, you hope that it really was out, so you won't have to fib. . . . And what to do in that moment of doubt? Should we give ourselves the point or be sportsmanlike and give it to our opponent? And we go through an internal crisis, because we know the person we'd like to be, but can we be that person?

Mats requested that the match point be replayed, in the semifinals of the French Open.

Afterward, he said: "At first, I thought that Clerc's forehand landed outside of the line, but when I checked the mark, I saw that the ball had bounced off the outer edge of the line. When the umpire gave me the match, I wondered what the heck I should do. And then I remembered a similar situation in Italy last year and requested two balls."

He won the replayed match point and was through to the final. The way in which he acted transformed Mats Wilander from a talented kid who was well liked by the Swedish tennis audience to a global role model and example of the good in sports. But for Mats, what happened was nothing new. He'd experienced the same thing, and acted in the same way, just a year earlier. In the final of the European Junior Championships against the Yugoslav Slobodan Zivojinovic, Mats had had match point up 5–2 and 40–30 when Zivojinovic, just like Clerc, hit a shot that was called out. Mats offered "two balls," but the Yugoslav was adamant: if the ball was good, then he should be awarded the point. Zivojinovic went ahead to win the game and came as close as 5–4, before Mats could take home the title.

Mats Wilander possessed a calm and maturity similar to another Swede. Was it the same person in a new edition? Was Mats in fact a Björn in disguise, who'd started to hit a bit softer and, to protest the organizers' unwillingness to let him skip qualifying, had decided to play under an alias?

Mats was so young that it was difficult to believe he really could have eliminated three seeded players on his way to the final. If he went on to win the final, too, he'd have his own place in history as the youngest Grand Slam winner of all time. And he hadn't even won a regular Grand Prix tournament before. His road through the tournament was fascinating.

Only two people seemed annoyed by the hype around the young Swede: his opponent in the final, Guillermo Vilas, and Vilas's coach, Ion Tiriac.

Vilas, faithful to his poetic character, said: "A lot of people travel across the Atlantic Ocean today. You don't become unique by taking such a trip. The only unique guy is the one who went to America in 1492."

Tiriac ranted about "these preprogrammed Swedes who show up every fifth year." He continued: "Do you have some kind of laboratory for tennis machines in Sweden? Machines you put small heads on?"

The thought that Borg and Wilander had originated from the same production line, from some small factory hidden deep in the Swedish pine forest, did hold a certain logic. Maybe Sweden had uncovered a secret recipe. Take appropriate golden locks raw material, lure him away from the draining sport of ice hockey, put a racket in his hand, and fill him up with conditioning, stubbornness, and icy cool. Then roast him under the hot sun in Rome, ship him in a messy way to Paris, and voilà, there you have a finished world-class star.

Jocke Nyström was chilling in his boyhood room at home in Skellefteå. He'd followed his friend via radio and TV. Now he reached Mats on the phone in Paris.

"What are you doing?" asked Jocke.

"I'm practicing my speech for tomorrow. First, I'll have to congratulate Guillermo on his victory. In English."

"Congratulate? What do you mean?"

"Yeah, he's way too good for me." First of all, I'd like to congratulate Guillermo to the victory. . . . Does that work?"

Only a year and a half had passed since Mats and Jocke had calmed each other's fear of the dark during that stormy night with their host family in Florida. And it was just a month prior that Mats had played Vilas in Madrid. That match had been an easy victory for Vilas in two sets. Mats couldn't see how he'd have a better chance this time.

Today, analyzing things in hindsight, he is struck by how quickly he improved as a tennis player in the spring of 1982.

"The learning curve, the development we had in Team Siab those first two years really was unprecedented. During the two weeks in Paris alone, it was unbelievable how much I'd matured. That time alone feels like two months. I was seventeen years old, incredibly susceptible, and I soaked it all in like a sponge. I was improving even in the final against Vilas. I got better and better the longer the match went on. If the Mats who played the last set had played the Mats who started the match, I'd have beaten myself by 6–1. Before the match, I didn't even think about being able to beat Vilas. I got one game in the first set and was happy with that. But then he started to panic, while I played . . . just right. I didn't play a great match, but I played strategically correctly. One of my strengths was that I could sense when my opponent lost his technique. I could see if it was luck when he hit in a backhand winner, or if he'd be able to hit it again. I noticed how Vilas started to lose ground, he started to hit funny backhands with a side spin, he tensed up and started to argue with Tiriac during the changeovers."

After having lost the first set by 1–6, Mats began playing deep, high shots to throw Vilas off. It gave results, but the match became just as boring as many had feared. The ball passed the net 80 to 90 times in many of the points. At the Råsunda arena, Simon & Garfunkel had to postpone their concert 20 minutes before they took the stage, so that 40,000 concert-goers could finish listening to the radio broadcast.

The final was so monotonous to watch that you could engage in long discussions during play, without missing much of anything. Commentator Bud Collins said he thought "Wilander was going to walk up to the chair umpire and say that he didn't want to win after such boring play," a nod to the Swede's sportsmanlike gesture in the Clerc semifinal. The former great Fred Stolle complained: "And journalists like you would tell me and my generation buddies that we were boring if we played serve-and-volley!" After the match, there were sincere proposals suggesting that, as early as next season, a warning light would start flashing when the ball had passed over the net 30 times, forcing the players to end the point within five strokes.

Alas, the criticism didn't take away from the spoils of victory. Mats won after 4 hours and 43 minutes, the longest match he'd ever played. He became the youngest player ever to win a Grand Slam tournament. He was called "Superman" and "phenom." He was a young, handsome, polite representative for the new tennis generation, just when tennis needed one, in a time when the sport was dominated by big egos like Connors and McEnroe, who cursed and acted up, and Lendl, who was sullen and introverted.

Mats remembers the weeks in Paris in an almost exclusively bright light, of course. He remembers the life-changing wins over great players: Lendl,

Gerulaitis, Clerc, and Vilas. But still, just over 30 years later, there is another match he ranks as being more important.

"There's only one match in my entire career when I tried to play like Björn Borg, and that was against Luna in the third round. I tried to hit those semiflat forehands, just like Björn did in his match against Klaus Eberhard in Båstad. It worked well, it was my best match to date. I didn't play well at all in the first two matches in Paris, but the match against Luna gave me confidence. It was the first big step I took as a professional, and it was thanks to Björn.

"The only thing that wasn't a positive with Paris in 1982 was that Björn didn't play. I think everyone felt that way, the whole tournament felt a bit flat. I'd played against Björn just a year earlier, and he was so damn good. Had he played in 1982, I know that I'd barely have gotten a game. That's how good he was. On the other hand, that's why everybody felt they had a chance to win. Lendl, Vilas, Connors. . . . Everyone felt they had a chance. And I think that's why I won. The others choked, they tensed up, suffocated themselves and underperformed when they realized they suddenly had a chance to win because Björn wasn't there."

So, what was Björn Borg, the former tennis king, doing on this day June 6, 1982? Well, he celebrated his 26th birthday. He, along with his wife, Mariana, and Onni Nordström, who at this time not only helped Joakim Nyström, but was also described as "Borg's Swedish manager," landed in a helicopter in the garden outside Svaneholm Castle in Skåne, where a few other friends were waiting. Together, they walked into the castle for a very private event. A few hours later, the birthday boy with entourage re-appeared, jumped in the helicopter, and took off, allegedly for Copenhagen. The only information that trickled out to the media was that the TV broad-cast from Paris had been on, at least for a while.

Meanwhile, in Paris, Borg's international manager, Mark McCormack, enjoyed a victory dinner with his younger client, Mats Wilander. Mats's dad, Einar, and Jonte Sjögren participated in the celebrations, too. They toasted with champagne, and McCormack promised to make Mats a rich man. The contract they'd signed a year and a half ago was going to be renegotiated. Now, IMG was taking charge of young Wilander's career and finances.

One obvious part of this was, of course, for Mats to relocate to Monte Carlo. Only a day earlier, Mats had told the Swedish press that he planned to stay in Sweden at least ten more years. After the victory dinner, he'd changed his tune. Mats explained to *Expressen*'s reporter: "McCormack seems to have certain plans for me and my tennis game. When the plans are starting to take shape, it might be time for me to reconsider where I'll live."

Just a few years earlier, both the press and the general public had condemned Björn Borg's move from Sweden to the tax haven of Monaco, and the anger had been directed at Björn personally. He had to answer for his own decision. Now, Mats's move was seen as an obvious and reasonable measure for a newly minted millionaire at the age of seventeen. The decision didn't even seem to be viewed as Mats's own, but rather some sort of law of nature in the form of an American agency that couldn't be refused. *Expressen*'s headline read: "Is McCormack forcing Mats to move to Monaco?" The thinking seemed to be that it was reasonable for Mats not to let 80 to 90 percent of his fortune go to taxes, and that he'd follow in the footsteps of Borg, Ingemar Stenmark, and Ralf Edström and take up residence in Monte Carlo.

After all, it was 1982, and you should invest in yourself. That was the persistent message of a political campaign, first promoted by the employer organization, SAF, and then continued by the conservative Moderate Party. By strengthening the individual's position, society would get stronger. Even if the society in this case might be Monte Carlo.

Jonte Sjögren was proud. He and Mats's dad had formed a close connection and toasted to Mats and his victory. At the same time, Sjögren wasn't able to fully enjoy the champagne. He glanced across the table and saw how Mark McCormack leaned in and whispered something in Mats's ear. When the group broke up to go back to the hotel in the early morning hours, Jonte told a Swedish reporter: "I'd like everything to be like it was, with the Team Siab national team and my training and tournament travels with Mats, Jocke, Ante, and Hasse. But that probably won't happen after this."

No, things weren't going to be like they were, and if anyone was looking forward to that, it was Mats's Team Siab training buddies.

Joakim Nyström says, "We'd had that team for about eight months when Mats won the French Open. As a seventeen-year-old! That didn't exist, you didn't believe it was real. But I'd just turned nineteen, and I reached the fourth round in the same tournament, where I lost to Clerc. My best ranking had been around 50, but when Mats won the French Open, it was as if it hit home with me: 'I'm going to be good, too.'"

Anders Järryd had more confidence, too: "It brought a hell of a spark to the rest of us. 'If he can do it, so can we!' It was just like that. 'I beat him at times, therefore I can win a Grand Slam, too.'"

"Strictly technically speaking, we came up in the right era," says Nyström. "Our game with topspin and two-handed backhands could break down opponents. We often played the Spaniards, who hit sliced backhands. They could put topspin on their forehands, but we controlled play and were good at running. We didn't need to kill the ball, we could run and wait for the opponent to make a mistake."

Only a month after Mats's triumph in Paris, the entire Team Siab was in the U.S. But they were no longer a group of junior players at training camp. They were Sweden's Davis Cup team. The generation shift had gone lightning fast. Now there was no Kjell, no Ove, not even a Per Hjertqvist or Stefan Simonsson. The Swedish team that stepped out onto the blue surface at the Checkerdome, the gigantic indoor arena in St. Louis, included two twenty-year-olds and two teenagers.

It was Hasse Olsson's first season as Davis Cup captain. Since the players already knew one another inside and out and were already tactically advanced, Hasse Olsson could focus on his absolute strength, to spread good cheer and act as a nice father figure.

Anders Järryd was the team anchor; he played both the first singles and doubles. He lost to McEnroe in the first match. Mats Wilander then defeated Eliot Teltscher. On day 2, Järryd and Simonsson had nothing to answer John McEnroe and Peter Fleming, the world's number-one doubles team.

"Then Teltscher got hurt, and I played Brian Gottfried and won in three straight," says Anders Järryd. "Now Mats and McEnroe were going to play the decisive match, the reigning French Open champion against the Wimbledon runner-up. It became a superb battle."

It sure didn't look that way after McEnroe handily took the first two sets and started the third by breaking Wilander's serve. Here, some of the 16,000 spectators, who'd already seen three sets of tennis between Gottfried and Järryd, got up from their seats and began heading for home. But rather than quitting, Wilander gritted his teeth and fought his way back into the match. In the seventh game of the set, Mats saved four break points and followed that up by breaking the American's serve: 4–4.

BJÖRN BORG AND THE SUPER-SWEDES

A month earlier, Guillermo Vilas had seen Mats as a new version of Björn Borg, but now McEnroe saw something new, a player who challenged him in different ways. For one thing, Borg always stood several feet behind the baseline when returning the American's serves. Wilander kept his toes on the baseline, on both the first and second serve, and he attacked on his returns from far into the court.

Game after game rolled by. Mats held his serve, McEnroe held his. Mats with his graphite racket from Rossignol, McEnroe with his trusted wooden companion from Dunlop. Five–five became 6–6, 7–7, 8–8. As the match kept on going and didn't turn into the quick affair McEnroe had hoped for after two sets, the world's number one's blood began to boil.

Mats walked calmly back and forth between the baseline's right and left side, in true Borg fashion, ready to take on his next task. McEnroe, on the other hand, was fast approaching, at a furious speed, the stage where he believed the whole world was against him. He whined and complained about every single questionable call. For every shot that touched a line, a grimace distorted his face. He was twenty-three years old, but a child trapped in a man's body. His impulse control was gone, his head and entire body twitched. He moved as if he were walking on an electric blanket. When McEnroe served to win the game and the female line judge called him for a foot fault at 13–13, he lost it.

For an entire minute, he barked at her. The match was put on a lengthy hold. Hasse Olsson, his unruly dark bangs glued to his sweaty forehead, threw his hands out to his side. But no penalty was given. Olsson searched through his bag, found his tennis rule book, and held it out demonstratively for the umpire to see. He wasn't the only one who was upset. In the middle of the match, the reporter for the ESPN sports channel announced that the linesmen had held an emergency meeting and decided that they were ready to walk off the court if McEnroe didn't stop his verbal assaults, or was punished for them. The American commentators chuckled: "Well, then McEnroe can finally make all the calls himself, and that's really what he wants."

"McEnroe saw that I waved the rule book, of course, and that made him even angrier," says Hans Olsson. "At the next changeover, when he walked by my seat, he put his foot on my chest and kicked me so hard that both the chair and I fell backward. Not even that was sanctioned by the referee; I guess they thought it's fine to kick the opposing team's captain."

The players held serve for 23 straight games. McEnroe had break point three times, and Mats was able to escape all three times.

By now, the news about the match having transitioned from a walk in the park to a gut-wrenching struggle had reached the ticket holders who'd left their seats, and the gaps in the stands started to fill in again.

"It was fascinating to see Mats in that match," says Järryd. "McEnroe argued. The crowd was on the American's side. And it was brutally hot. I remember that we sat next to Peter Wallenberg, who was the president of the Swedish Tennis Association, in the box right behind the players. He was sweating bullets. He kept saying, 'I'm so thirsty, I'm so thirsty' the entire match, and his grown sons, Jacob and Peter Wallenberg Jr., had to run up and down the stairs each time to get water for their dad."

"Wallenberg got on my case, too," says Hans Olsson. "He thought I should express our dissatisfaction much more vigorously. He sat right behind my captain's chair and punched me in the back with his fists: 'Get up and protest, Olsson! Get up and protest!'"

After 32 games, Mats was able to break and win the third set, 18–16. The set had lasted 2 hours and 38 minutes.

After that, Mats only needed about half an hour to win the fourth set. He fell behind in the fifth set but managed to get caught up again, thanks to a series of masterful passing shots that hit the lines. In the end, it still wasn't enough. After 6 hours, 22 minutes, and 79 games, Mats's final shot landed in the net. McEnroe had won the longest Davis Cup match in history. He was so tired that he cried as he hung on the shoulders of his captain, Arthur Ashe, who a bit later said: "John has my permission to go out and get drunk tonight."

Mats had mixed feelings. He wanted to be disappointed, and he was, to some extent. He'd lost, and Sweden had been eliminated from the tournament. He really felt that McEnroe's ground strokes weren't that good, and he was convinced that the American would have been disqualified for unsportsmanlike conduct had it not been for his home-court advantage. But deep down, Mats also felt that he'd accomplished something special. He'd kept pace with the world's number-six player for more than six hours. It was conflicting emotions. Back in the locker room, he found a pair of scissors in his bag and told his teammates: "This doesn't work. Cut it off!"

Mats Wilander's curls fell to the floor in the locker room. Ante, Jocke, and Hasse didn't stop until Mats had a closely cropped crew cut. It was an overreaction, but also a sort of ritual that was needed to mark that something important had happened.

Anders Järryd reflects: "That match, that's when we had the opportunity to see how Mats measured up to McEnroe on a fast indoor surface. And he went the distance, on a court away from home. I think that was an important match for Mats, too. And that's when we knew that Mats had sort of surged ahead of the rest of us."

GOOD GUYS ALWAYS WIN

"I had a hell of a time against Stefan. I was annoyed because I was older and should win, and he was so damn good."
—MATS WILANDER

The first outdoor tournament of 1983 was just a short moped ride away from Mats's new home. From his condo on Boulevard de Larvotto it took no more than a couple of minutes to pop over to the Monte Carlo Country Club. Lendl and Vilas were the top seeds, Mats the fifth. But another player stole all of the spotlight. He arrived in a limousine: Björn Borg was going to play his last tournament.

In January, Björn had finally announced his decision to retire from tennis. But there would be one more tournament, in Monte Carlo. Borg was followed by journalists from morning to night. There was a longing, a thirst, to see the master in action one more time.

Björn Borg won convincingly over Clerc, No. 6 in the world, in the first round. It was a sensationally solid match following the former clay court king's absence, a result that begged for more. Henri Leconte, the twenty-year-old new French tennis hope, was next. Björn Borg still danced along the baseline, and when his passing shots went in, it looked like 1981 all over again. But the shots didn't go in often enough. Borg lost, 2–1 in sets. Despite the fact that 10,000 spectators rooted for Borg more than for the Frenchman, it was clear that the killer instinct and the stubbornness that had been Borg's trademarks were no longer there.

"A year and a half ago, I would've won this type of match, but not today," said Björn afterward, while explaining that the idea of practicing three or four hours every day was difficult to even think about. The desire was gone. He longed for sleeping in and everything else but tennis.

Had Borg defeated Leconte, he'd have played Mats in the third round. This didn't seem to mean anything to Borg: "Whom I lost to doesn't matter," he said, trying to avoid the subject.

The relationship between Borg and Wilander was nonexistent. Despite their similarities and common interests, they rarely spoke. In the media hype before the tournament, the reporters had pushed Mats to get closer to Björn for a photo opportunity. They both posed for a few seconds, and that was that. Mats would have liked to talk to Björn some more, but he was too shy to impose.

Wilander says: "I don't know what Björn thought of us youngsters back then, but I think he both appreciated us and didn't, the fact that we came up then. It was hard for him to play the Davis Cup. He had to carry the whole team by himself, while he also didn't have a good relationship with the journalists. In that way, our generation made it easier for him to quit. On the other hand, nobody was tempting him or nagging him to make a comeback anymore."

There was no need. Wilander whipped Björn Borg's conqueror Leconte by 7–5, 6–0. Two matches later, Mats had won the first title of the year. The changing of the guard was complete.

The spring season continued with tournaments within a comfortable distance from Monaco. Mats won in Lisbon and Aix-en-Provence and was undefeated in the World Team Cup in Düsseldorf. When he lost to Yannick Noah in the quarterfinals at Hamburg's clay court tournament, it was the end of a streak of 43 straight victories on clay.

While Borg might have lost his desire to grind it out and fight, the situation was the opposite for Mats. He was eighteen years old and driven by a curiosity for his own game and the world around him. Everything was new and exciting and worth focusing on. Every point, every stroke, every person and player.

And there were people that sparked his interest more than others. Yannick Noah was exactly the person Mats Wilander wanted to be. Or at least, he wanted to be close to Noah. The Frenchman was four years older, handsome, and cool with his dreadlocks. He played music, sang, was opinionated and verbal. But most of all, he had a charisma that could slay both women and men, a force that was almost impossible to resist. If Mats was the country boy who longed for the big city, Yannick Noah had already arrived, he had swagger, was a world citizen. He was a different kind of tennis player, too—larger than most, with strong legs that could lift him within reach of the most difficult of lobs, and long arms that could catch up with the most well-placed passing shots.

Two weeks after the loss in Hamburg, Mats had a chance to get his revenge against the Frenchman, on the same center court where his coming-out party had occurred a year earlier.

Henrik Sundström, McEnroe, and Higueras had all been defeated by Mats on his way to his second straight final in the French Open. Before his match with Noah, Mats had high expectations. They'd met four times and won two matches each. In the matches that Noah had won, Mats had felt fairly close.

But the Frenchman didn't play then like he was playing now.

As Mats explains it, "Noah hit high forehands to my backhand, and I went for the net. No one used to hit to my backhand, since it was my best stroke. And he also hit short, sliced balls in the middle of the court, a little to my backhand side. That was a shot he hadn't used at all in our previous meetings."

Wilander quickly realized that he couldn't pass the Frenchman.

"Those short shots up the middle, you couldn't hit a lob off them. And the high shots to my backhand that I had to return high over my shoulder, I couldn't generate any power off of them, even if it was actually my best side."

Few people uncovered these tactical nuances. Or thought about them. The crowd was spellbound by a fantastic final between the passionate hometown player and the methodical Wilander, whose passing shots made Noah dive like a panther at the net. Mats kept grinding, unable to figure out his opponent's unexpected style of play. Noah took the first two sets. In the third, Wilander was able to keep pace until they reached the tiebreak. Wilander, with his economical style of play, was prepared to keep going indefinitely in the hot sunshine, but for Noah things were not as bright. At the start of the tiebreak, he suffered from cramps, igniting Mats's hopes of turning the match around. But that wasn't to be. Noah found a last spark of inspired energy. On match point, Mats hit a forehand that sailed long. The court filled up with celebrating friends, relatives, and supporters of Yannick Noah, before the elapsed ball had even bounced twice.

Says Wilander: "As soon as the match was over, my disappointment over what had happened in the match disappeared. Everything turned into chaos on the court, and all you could do was go with it. People came running down from the stands, I heard how his dad fell right behind me. I shook Noah's hand as he jumped over the net. He didn't see me, I didn't exist for him or for anyone else. The crowd's hometown boy had just won, and I just sat there and watched the excitement. I thought it was so freaking cool, like watching a movie."

It was a movie in which Mats wanted to play a part, or at least have a small cameo role. It was obvious that Noah's people knew how to live.

As Wilander puts it, "Noah was a guy you wanted to connect with. I wanted to get to know him. I didn't dare ask Noah himself, but in the locker room I cozied up to one of his friends and asked where they were going that night. What else could I do? I didn't want to go and hang out with Jonte."

The champion and his people steered their steps toward the trendy club Le Duplex, next to the Arc de Triomphe. Mats Wilander went there, too. He sat by himself in the bar all night, had a few beers, and kept glancing over at Yannick Noah and his group of friends, hangers-on, and female models.

He had lost, but he was still enjoying the victory party. Among his many memories from Paris, that evening is one of Mats's most vivid.

In 1983, it was difficult for anyone to resist Mats Wilander, both as a player and a person. The titles kept coming in with regularity. When December arrived, Mats had won eight tournaments, including at home in Stockholm and Båstad. In Cincinnati, he beat both Lendl and McEnroe in straight sets. He was undefeated in the Davis Cup. During the same time period, he received tons of honorable mentions from player colleagues who, unprovoked, sang his praises. After their semifinal at the French, the defeated Higueras said: "It's a pleasure to play against Mats Wilander. He's such a gentleman and sportsman."

At Wimbledon, Mats won a first-round five-set match against John Fitzgerald, who, when finishing up his press conference afterward, said: "I have one thing to add: Our sport has fallen from grace a bit during the last few years. I really hope that Mats Wilander will be our next champion. With his honesty and his sportsmanlike behavior, he's the man who despite his youth can give tennis its magic back."

The lost final in Paris had given Mats a new insight: he had to learn more strokes. He'd been influenced by the many people who said his game was dull, and he also understood that he must find an antidote to Noah's tactics. Mats knew his tennis history, and he'd seen those short balls in the middle of the court that Noah had tortured him with before, but on television. That was precisely how Arthur Ashe beat Jimmy Connors in the 1975 Wimbledon final. When a player hits short, sliced balls that land in the middle of the court, it's impossible to get under the ball enough to hit the topspin shots that were the foundation of Mats Wilander's game.

Wilander says, "In the past, I'd just played around with a sliced backhand during practice, I'd try to hit it like McNamara. Now I realized it was a shot I had to master. A slice should have even more backspin, like Noah's or Pecci's, so I started to work on it in practice, not just for fun, but to expand my repertoire."

The status of the fourth Grand Slam tournament of the year had slowly risen, and it had become interesting for the top-ranked players. The Australian Open was even more important this year because the three earlier Grand Slams had been won, in turn, by Noah (Paris), McEnroe (Wimbledon), and Connors (the U.S. Open). Now, there was a prize check of $600,000 up for grabs for the player who was proclaimed the winner of the Grand Prix tour. An unofficial title of World Champion, decided by a three-man jury that was put in place by the International Tennis Federation, was also an enticing factor.

Mats Wilander's stunning development continued. On the fast grass at the Kooyong Stadium, he swept the court with Johan Kriek in three straight sets, then he beat McEnroe by 3–1 in the semifinal. The latter match had a profound implication: the ball pusher and clay court specialist Wilander could apparently also win over the world number-one on grass. This showed that not only was Mats a top player, but he was a player who, when he was still a teenager, could be part of the discussion about who was the world's best tennis player.

The final against Lendl was up next. There, the hard-hitting Czech had to accept that Mats Wilander's tennis mind outmaneuvered him. Mats won, 6–1, 6–4, 6–4, and took home his second major title. Wilander had now won more titles (nine) than anyone else during the year, and he was the only player who'd brought home tournament wins indoors as well as on clay, grass, and hard court. With that, Mats secured the hefty prize sum as Grand Prix winner. Voices were raised for the ITF jury, which included former tennis greats, to also award him the title World Champion of the Year. But after McEnroe defeated Mats in the Masters, the American was given that honor, despite the fact that Mats had beaten McEnroe three times earlier in the season.

While the tennis world was being dazzled by the kid from Småland, other Swedes, schooled in the same system, began to make their own impression on the tour. Järryd and Simonsson won the doubles title at the French Open. Other tournament winners that year were Jan Gunnarsson, Henrik Sundström, and Jocke Nyström. And among the juniors, something happened that had never happened before. One player won all four major tournaments. He, too, was Swedish. His name was Stefan Edberg.

Young Swedes were showing up everywhere. Despite the fact that Team Siab had officially been dismantled in the fall, in practical terms almost nothing had changed. Jonte Sjögren continued to serve as Wilander's and Nyström's personal coach, and he also assisted Hans Olsson at most Davis Cup matches. The players continued to act as a team.

"The Swedes' unity has to do with their culture," said the American Tim Mayotte. "Whenever I play a Swede, I usually see the other players in the stands, supporting him. They already have a psychological advantage there."

Wilander was the youngest of all the new Swedish talents, but the leader of the pack. He could inspire his peers and pull them along in a different way than Borg, perhaps because he wasn't an extremist. Borg's contemporaries never had anything bad to say about him. Björn was a good guy, but when they compared themselves to him on the court, they couldn't see themselves. They couldn't relate to how hard he trained, and they couldn't see themselves in his uncompromising focus. If that's what it took to become the best, it wasn't worth it.

With Mats Wilander, things were different. In order for Björn Borg to succeed, tennis had to be everything. With Mats, the opposite was true: tennis must not be everything. He wasn't fanatical about his training, but Jonte Sjögren tricked him into working hard by coming up with fun exercises. Mats didn't keep track of the hours he slept. He'd be happy to hang out in the bars until the wee hours of the morning if it felt right. He was more human than Borg. It made Mats easier to like, if not as beloved and admired as Borg.

"Mats, you're a life connoisseur," said Jonte Sjögren to Mats once. Perhaps he referred to Mats's need to suddenly go to a concert instead of practicing, or to the fact that Mats could show up at a Davis Cup reception wearing the team jacket and clogs.

Jonte's words were some of the most beautiful Mats had ever heard: "a life connoisseur." He thought: *If a grown man who knows me says that about me, then I must be doing something right.*

Hasse Olsson strolled around in the Australian sun with a cloud hovering above his head. Sweden had made its first Davis Cup final since 1975, and the many great results by Swedish players had quickly made his team selection more difficult. Up until very recently, it had been a given that Anders Järryd, with his explosive style of play and quest for short points, would complement Mats Wilander in the singles matches against Australia. But then the phlegmatic clay court specialist Nyström had gone and won his first title on grass, and after a victory over the opposing team's number-one player, Pat Cash, no less.

"That was very impressive, at least to me," recalls Hasse Olsson. "It was so damn difficult. When the guy beats Cash on grass . . . shouldn't I let him play? Järryd was good, too, but it would be very tough to play two long singles matches in the sun, plus the doubles, especially considering Järryd's style of play."

Anders Järryd had enough energy to crack one or two Australians, but his power could be misguided, too. He had a short fuse and easily became angry and frazzled. During Team Siab's first trip, he'd suffered an acute attack of cramps after a match in the Bangkok heat. So Hasse Olsson gave Jocke Nyström the singles spot. Thus, Sweden came with a team made up of the newly crowned Australian Open winner, a recent winner of the ATP tournament in Sydney, and the winning doubles team from Paris. But Jocke was nervous.

As was Hans Olsson. He'd held a number of coaching jobs within the Swedish Tennis Association system, and a couple of years earlier, he'd ended up as a member of the Davis Cup Committee, which, among other things, was responsible for appointing the Davis Cup captain. When Jonte Sjögren became Team Siab's coach, there was no obvious candidate for the Davis Cup captain position. Olsson said: "I'll take it," whereby he gave himself perhaps the most prestigious job in Swedish tennis. He'd been a good player, Top 10 in Sweden, but he felt pretty small as he walked into the arena the day of the final. The Kooyong Stadium was a tennis Mecca, and Australia's team captain, Neale Fraser, was one of the sport's greats. He'd been ranked number one in the world in 1959 and 1960, had won Wimbledon once and the U.S. Open twice, had been knighted by the Queen, and had served as captain for the Australian tennis national team since 1970.

Olsson remembers, "And here I was, in my first season as captain and with a semifinal spot at the King's Cup tournament in Sweden as my biggest achievement. I didn't have much to offer. It was a big deal for all of us to be there."

The Swedish live broadcasts started at two in the morning the day after Christmas Day.

For everyone who managed to stay awake, it turned out to be worth the effort. Australia was exotic in so many ways. The bright sun from the opposite side of the world made the TV picture almost blinding for eyes that had adjusted to the dark Swedish winter nights. The sounds from the crowd were different, and the graphics in the Australian production were of the modern type.

Mats started things off by defeating Cash, an ultraaggressive grass court specialist who wore a bandana around his straggly hair and a diamond in one ear, a grumpy and angry teenager. At tournaments other than the Davis Cup, he'd often find himself booed by his own home crowd.

In match number two, Jocke fell flat against Fitzgerald.

"It was just too big for me. I was too nervous," recalls Jocke.

"I think I should've played. Even if I had lost, it would've given me chance to get a feel for the court," says Järryd.

Järryd and Simonsson played way below their normal capacity in the doubles match and lost, so on the last day of play, both Wilander and Nyström had to win their matches. The Swedish newspapers were critical of Olsson's selection of Nyström, as they begged for a miracle turnaround:

"So, Jocke—can you do what 'Miracle-Birger' did?" asked *Expressen* in its frontpage headline.

But it wasn't to be.

Järryd says, "Mats won his matches, as usual. If I had a choice of one player in the entire history of tennis to have on my Davis Cup team, I'd choose Mats. He's so cool in the critical moments. He's the one you'd want next to you if your house caught fire."

If he absolutely had to, Mats Wilander could live with losing to other Swedish players, but he hated losing to a younger player. In March 1984, he did just that. In the final at Milan's big indoor tournament, Mats faced Stefan Edberg, who was closing in on the world elite players at record pace.

They barely knew each other. Only a few months before, Edberg had played on the junior circuit.

Wilander says, "I always felt that all the pressure was on the older player, regardless of the circumstances. I had a hell of a time against Stefan. I was annoyed because I was older and should win, and he was so damn good."

Edberg demolished Wilander with his high-bouncing serves, which Wilander never could get a handle on. The final score was 6–4, 6–2.

One month later, Mats faced yet another Swede in another final. Henrik Sundström won in Monte Carlo. Born in the same year as Mats, Sundström had come to the ATP tour via minor leagues in the US and tournaments in Asia, and now he was quickly climbing in the world rankings.

Wilander saved his best for the Davis Cup matches in the fall. Against Czechoslovakia, he gave Sweden the lead with an easy win against Tomas Smid. In the next match, the superstar Lendl had Henrik Sundström up against the ropes by winning the first two sets. Then, the Swede changed his strategy and turned the match around. Sundström's game plan was to attack the ball with power and extreme topspin.

"Sundström had the most beautiful one-handed backhand I'd ever seen," says Wilander. "He played a big game. He was better than me, at least on clay and at least from the backcourt."

BJÖRN BORG AND THE SUPER-SWEDES

The year ended with Wilander winning his third Grand Slam by defeating Kevin Curren in Melbourne. Consequently, he was Sweden's obvious choice for team anchor in the 1984 Davis Cup final against the USA, which was to be played at the Scandinavium in Göteborg during the last days of the year. But this had also been the year when the other Swedes had almost caught up with Mats. The Swedish players who began practicing at the Scandinavium before the final were ranked Nos. 4 (Wilander), 6 (Järryd), and 7 (Sundström) in the world. Jocke Nyström was ranked No. 8 but realized he wasn't going to make the cut, so he chose to go on vacation with his wife, Susanne, and their young daughter. Stefan Edberg was selected as Järryd's doubles partner.

Sweden was no longer one man's team, like in the Borg era. The only problem now was that the USA Davis Cup captain, Arthur Ashe, had brought the world's two best singles players, John McEnroe and Jimmy Connors, and the world's sharpest doubles team, McEnroe and Peter Fleming, who'd won all of the 14 Davis Cup matches they'd played, to the match at the Scandinavium.

While the finishing of the floor continued, guards in brown uniforms assembled the gigantic Davis Cup trophy. Truckload after truckload of Santa-red tennis clay was rolled out inside the hockey arena. "It's cowardly to put clay indoors," complained McEnroe. He had his best season ever behind him and had lost only two matches all year. One of the losses had come on clay. Jimmy Connors, the world's number-two player, saw a chance to fill his prize cabinet with a Davis Cup trophy and had abandoned his longstanding boycott of the US national team.

The close-knit Swedish team was fired up. Sundström and Edberg were new to the squad, but they fit in well. The reserve players, the brothers Hans and Stefan Simonsson, acted as sparring partners. Hans's task in practice was to slice his backhand and attack the net like McEnroe. Stefan's was to hit flat, Connors-like, groundstrokes. The practice sessions were focused. The team hunkered down, clenched their fists, and promised one another to bring their very best. They didn't need to try very hard to pick up on signs that their opponents' team spirit wasn't as strong.

"Once, when we practiced right after the Americans, I sat down in the chair that Connors had used a minute earlier," says Mats Wilander. "When

I looked down on the ground between my feet, I saw that Connors had scribbled 'Fuck you, Arthur' in the clay. It was rather absurd."

The two American singles players and their captain had such radically different personas. The blue-collar Connors could never stand Ashe's intellectual attitude, and the bitter atmosphere from the 1975 Wimbledon final was far from healed. McEnroe and Connors hardly talked to each other. They never had. McEnroe and Ashe usually held a mutual respect for each other, which made them avoid open conflicts. Still, Ashe's role as team captain was a red flag for the authority-hating world number-one player.

Mats Wilander quietly prepared for his first singles match, against Connors. As he sat in the locker room, pinning sponsors' advertising logos to his match shirt, Anders Järryd sat next to him:

Järryd describes Wilander's prep process: "When he was done, Mats pulled out shirt number two, his extra shirt, and was about to put the logos on that, too. But then he suddenly stopped abruptly. *Nah, there's no need for another shirt. This won't take more than three sets.* Then he walked out and beat the number-two player in the world by 6–1, 6–3, 6–3. He had such an incredible self-confidence."

Connors freely spread both his shots and his bad temper around during the match. He cursed, dropped F-bombs, called the umpire a fag, and finished things off by walking up to the umpire's chair and shaking it.

"I thought there's no way I'd lose to Connors. Not on clay, it doesn't happen," says Mats. "Also, he'd just changed his racket, which was rather strange, since he'd just won the U.S. Open. So, I was quite confident that day."

Mats Wilander is a bundle of contradictions. On the one hand, he had, and still has, a deeply rooted confidence in himself and in his way of playing tennis. That was the side of him that always impressed his opponents and teammates—his way of never backing down from challenges, of trusting himself at critical moments. On the other hand, he was easily impressed by other players' talent and technique and was able to see, and correct, his own weaknesses. That's also why he can say so positively that "Henrik Sundström was much better than me on clay" or "Anders Järryd was much better than me indoors."

Mats was simply smart enough to realize there was always more to learn. Should he get too impressed with the world around him, all he needed to do was call his parents at home, something Mats did after almost every match in his career.

The conversation almost always followed the same format:

"My mom would answer and I'd say: 'Hi mom, it's Mats, can I speak with dad?' 'How the hell did you beat him? That's so damn good, Mats!' said dad. And I'd say: 'But he's only 25th in the world, and I'm 3rd . . .' 'Yes, but I saw him play the other day and he had a hell of a good volley!' said dad. 'Yes, but we played on clay,' I'd say. 'Well yeah, but it's fantastic . . .' It'd go on like that. . . . And it meant a lot to me to have a dad who was always and without exception so impressed by my accomplishments."

For the Davis Cup final's second match, it was Henrik Sundström's turn to step out onto the indoor clay. He drove McEnroe insane by never missing a shot; everything came back. In the end, all McEnroe could do was curse the calls and the stupid court surface the Swedes had put down. Sundström won in three straight sets, 13–11, 6–4, 6–3.

The next day, playing before 13,000 loud fans, Järryd and Edberg kept their nerves in check and won the doubles match by 3–1 in sets, against a sullen and angry McEnroe and an obviously shaken Fleming. The 6'5" doubles specialist, who'd won four previous Davis Cup titles, bid farewell to the tournament with a double fault and his first loss.

It was a magnificent Swedish triumph, the second in the Davis Cup. Furthermore, it was a victory for the Swedish collective over an unruly and divided American team of superstars. The Swedes celebrated their victory, while the Americans drowned their sorrows. On the third day, the match between Wilander and McEnroe was supposed to start things off. It could have been a great match between two of the world's top players, a potential replay of their epic battle in St. Louis, and a springboard into the next tennis year. Now it became something else. During the introduction at the net before the match, McEnroe hissed at Mats through his teeth: "Hey kid, I hope you're just as hungover as I am." "It's cool, I am," whispered Mats in response.

Considering the circumstances, the match was well played. McEnroe won, but nobody really cared aside from the statisticians. One of the greatest triumphs in sports by one of the most well-liked teams was already a fact. The temperament of the two teams was also obvious. It had traveled straight through the television sets and into the living rooms of Swedes, Americans, and tennis fans across the world. The Swedes were the good guys, sportsmanlike; the Americans were . . . the opposite. This became major news in the US, and the USTA felt compelled to take action. In the tough competition with other televised sports, tennis couldn't afford to waste valuable exposure by letting the players behave like spoiled brats. Even if McEnroe's behavior was far from the worst ever seen from him on a tennis court, he was suspended from the Davis Cup for all practical purposes. Or rather, his captain was prohibited from selecting him to the team. McEnroe wouldn't play for Team USA again until 1987.

Wilander said, "It was a great victory for us. At the same time, it diminished a bit in value the more we heard about how things had been on their team. McEnroe and Connors refused to play against each other in practice, and Fleming only played doubles. As a result, their fourth man, Jimmy Arias, had to hit with both of them. He spent eight hours a day at the Scandinavium arena and would lie down in the locker room to wait for Connors or McEnroe to show up."

But that was the Americans' problem. In the Swedish tennis sky, there were no clouds, only the emergence of new stars.

A LONE WOLF WITH HIS OWN TACTICS

**"Stefan had such a beautiful backhand volley,
it cut like a knife. I noticed it and said to him:
'Stop playing your two-handed backhand.'"**
—PERCY ROSBERG

As usual, Stefan Edberg sat in the back of the classroom. As usual, he didn't raise his hand. As usual, he tried to bring as little attention to himself as possible. He didn't meet his teacher's look but fixated his eyes on the lines in his notebook on the desk in front of him. The feeling was so familiar, how he counted the seconds from when his teacher would ask a question and when she would call on someone in the class to answer it. The seconds were always so long while the question still hung in the air, he always just wanted someone else's name to be called so he could stop being nervous, and then: "Stefan, would you come up here to the blackboard and show us?"

He just didn't want to. He could feel himself beginning to sweat.

As a matter of fact, Stefan liked school. He didn't have a difficult time learning, and he had friends. It was just that he didn't like the attention. From an early age, he lived by the same motto he'd follow as an adult: "Not saying anything at all is better than saying too much." The best part about school was recess. When the bell rang, Stefan and his friends would run out

Björn Borg was still just a 17-year-old when he joined the pro circuit, making him the youngest player since Ken Rosewall and Lew Hoad toured for Australia in 1952. His coach Lennart Bergelin, right, became almost like a second father to Björn when they travelled and practiced together. Here they are pictured at a party before the start of the World Championship of Tennis tourney in Dallas, May 9, 1974.

Wimbledon used to be a place where men and women of the upper classes politely applauded the efforts of sportsmen and sportswomen. All that changed in 1974 with Borg, who drew hordes of teenage girls to the courts. Borg routinely had to exit hotels via windows and backdoors to escape fans, and escort by police and security guards became a necessity.

Björn Borg did not have high hopes for the French Open in 1975. He arrived in Paris just a couple of hours before playing his first game in the tournament and was down 0–4 in the first set. Two weeks later, he defeated Guillermo Vilas in the final to win his first Grand Slam title.

One month after his 20th birthday, Borg won his first Wimbledon title in 1976. The protocol demanded a dance with the winner of the ladies' title, Chris Evert, at the Wimbledon ball.

Jimmy Connors and Björn Borg shake hands after the U.S. Open final in 1976. Connors won, 6-4, 3-6, 7-6, 6-4. Borg went on to play another three U.S. Open finals but never won the title.

Björn Borg pictured at the U.S. Open at Forest Hills, N.Y., on September 2, 1977. Borg's looks, his game, and his enigmatic personality turned him into the world's most recognizable athlete alongside Muhammad Ali.

Borg posing with the Wimbledon trophy for the third straight year, 1978. In consecutive finals, he defeated Jimmy Connors.

Björn Borg with Mariana Simionescu in Monaco, December 21, 1979. The couple met in 1976, married in Bucharest, Romania, in the spring of 1980, and remained together until they divorced in 1984.

Rune and Margareta Borg, parents of Björn, together with Marie Simionescu, mother of Mariana, at the country club in Monaco on July 26, 1980.

Björn Borg after winning the Gentlemen's Singles final at Wimbledon 1980. In one of the greatest matches in tennis history, Borg defeated John McEnroe to gain his fifth consecutive win at Wimbledon.

John McEnroe shakes hands with Björn Borg after defeating Borg to win the Men's title at the U.S. Open in New York on September 14, 1981. Borg had just lost in the U.S. Open final for the fourth time. Moments later, Borg picked up his rackets, walked into the tunnel leading from the court, and retired from the sport. McEnroe lifted his trophy with the runner-up nowhere in sight.

After his playing career was over, Borg ventured into the fashion industry. Here, at a gala held at Roland Garros in Paris, September 5, 1983, he walks down the runway with two models to introduce his sportswear line. Björn Borg earned a percentage on the sales of the sportswear, underwear, bags, and accessories until 2016.

John McEnroe emerged as the winner of this Davis Cup match, played against Mats Wilander (above) in the St. Louis Checkerdome, on July 11, 1982. The American prevailed 9-7, 6-2, 15-17, 3-6, 8-6, after a record 6 hours, 39 minutes and 79 games. Wilander had to wait two years for his revenge on McEnroe in Davis Cup play. McEnroe and Wilander were to meet 13 times in ATP matches, McEnroe winning seven of them.

Mats Wilander burst onto the scene in 1982 winning the French Open, thanks, in large pa to patience and steady groundstrokes, such this trademark two-handed backhand. His w of returning almost every shot frustrated Jo McEnroe during the Davis Cup quarterfinals St. Louis, Missouri, in July the same year.

The eight best tennis players in the world gathered to play the Nabisco Grand Prix Masters in New York, December 1986. Seated, from left: Stefan Edberg, Boris Becker, Mats Wilander, and Ivan Lendl. Standing, from left: Miloslav Mecir, Andres Gomez, Henri Leconte, and Joakim Nyström.

Mats Wilander had a jump start to his tennis year in 1988. Here he celebrates with his wife, Sonya, in Melbourne after he defeated Australia's Pat Cash to win the Australian Open singles final, January 24, 1988.

On September 11, 1988, Mats Wilander defeated Ivan Lendl in the U.S. Open final, reaching the No. 1 spot on the world's tennis rankings.

Finding a way to beat Lendl was Wilander's object in training for many years, and after becoming No. 1, Wilander's motivation wavered. He fell through the rankings but remained active until 1996.

The 1988 U.S. Open final lasted five sets, but ultimately Wilander held the winner's trophy.

Mats Wilander was Sweden's Davis Cup captain between 2002 and 2010. Here, he coaches Jonas Björkman in a match against India in 2005.

Mats Wilander and Björn Borg did not have much of a relationship during their active years. More recently, they have met and played together several times on the Senior Tour or at exhibition matches. Here they are in Ostrava, Czech Republic, November 5, 2010.

Stefan Edberg lived in London and made Centre Court at Wimbledon feel like his second home. In 1988, Edberg won the title against Boris Becker after the game was delayed overnight because of heavy rain.

Stefan Edberg celebrating his 1988 Wimbledon title with girlfriend Annette Olsen. The couple married in 1992 and moved back to Sweden from London in 2000.

Stefan Edberg's attack tennis was usually not best suited for slow clay tennis. In 1989, he came agonizingly close to beating Michael Chang in the French Open final, but the American prevailed, winning 6–1, 3–6, 4–6, 6–4, 6–2.

In 1991, Edberg won in straight sets against Michael Chang, Javier Sanchez, Ivan Lendl, and Jim Courier when he cruised to his first U.S. Open title.

In 1992, the ending was the same, but Edberg's road to a consecutive U.S. Open championship was far longer and bumpier. Before lifting the trophy, Edberg had to play 24 sets of tennis, including a quarterfinal against Lendl (documented above) and a 5 hour, 26-minute semifinal against Chang.

Edberg's volley, arguably the finest in tennis, paved the way for his eventual 1992 U.S. Open Championship title.

By winning the U.S. Open in 1992, Edberg returned to the top of the rankings. In total, he spent 72 weeks as World No. 1.

Stefan Edberg announced early on that the 1996 season would be his last. The year turned into a sort of a farewell tour, which Edberg admits affected his focus. Here, he blows a kiss to the crowd at Roland Garros in Paris, after being eliminated by Switzerland's Marc Rosset in the fourth round.

to the playground, where they played field hockey, soccer, or other sports. The same was true for afternoons and weekends: go inside to eat with dad Bengt, mom Barbro, and younger brother Jan, then go back outside and play sports with his buddies.

The Edberg family lived in one of Västervik's few rental communities. Today, says Stefan, it would almost be considered "a ghetto." Then, during the '70s, everything was shiny and new, the apartments were filled with newly arrived families with young children. The goal nets on the community soccer field were intact.

In 1973, a summer of Borg fever, Stefan's mom Barbro noticed an ad in the newspaper promoting "A Day of Tennis." She sent her seven-year-old son away to the Westervik Tennis Club and, a few days later, Stefan's dad brought home a tennis racket, which became Stefan's companion during the entire summer break. He attended tennis school and played on the club's clay court, he hit against the garage wall outside his home, and he learned the elements of Borg-style tennis: forehand and a two-handed backhand.

When Stefan was ten, he quit soccer; when he was eleven, he noticed that he was better than all of his friends the same age. He won his first tournament in his hometown Västervik, "The Pearl of the East Coast." It became clear to the local tennis club that it had discovered an exceptional talent. It was also clear that his tennis style was completely different from that of Björn Borg: Stefan wanted the points to be short, not long, grinding rallies from the baseline. He attacked the net to end the point as quickly as possible.

In high school, Stefan crossed paths with Percy Rosberg. Rosberg had noticed Edberg's dexterity and technique and wanted to help the young, talented player. The issue was the 175 miles distance between Stockholm and Västervik, and the fact that Bengt Edberg's policeman salary was the family's sole source of income and wouldn't cover an excessive amount of traveling. Bengt inquired with the principal at Stefan's school to see if Stefan could get some extra time off. He then raised money from local businesses, and eventually a solution was identified: Stefan would take the train to Stockholm one day a week for a full day of training with Percy at the SALK hall.

"Stefan was quieter than Björn," says Percy Rosberg. "When he came here to train, he was very shy and unassuming. The other coaches and players, we'd all sit at the same table for meals, but he sat by himself at his own table. I'd say, 'come and sit with us!' and he would, but he just didn't want to impose. He was humble and very willing to learn."

Percy Rosberg is a man with an open personality. He has a word for everyone and answers all questions about tennis technique from anyone who asks, in a pleasant Stockholm dialect that's spiced with parables and '50s slang. He spreads warmth, but one can also envision how it could all be very intimidating for a shy boy from Västervik.

Stefan Edberg was already schooled well when he came to Percy. He hit most of his strokes correctly, and his lean athlete's body allowed him to move around easily and quickly. "It's a funny serve you have there," said Percy. "You should keep it. But it won't be kind to your back, kid."

There was one thing that Percy wanted to change, however.

"Stefan had such a beautiful backhand volley, it cut like a knife. I noticed it and said to him: 'Stop playing your two-handed backhand. Hit it with one hand, just like you hit your volley. Go back to the baseline and try again.'"

Ten years earlier, Percy had given Björn Borg the opposite advice—telling him instead to *keep* his two-handed grip on the backhand—and the effect was just as great this time.

"I showed Stefan: 'Reach out with both arms, press your shoulder blades together! That'll give you a natural motion, your arm is made to reach out, a two-handed backhand isn't natural!'"

Stefan remembers that he followed the advice without questioning it.

"I was fifteen years old then and had already won the European Junior Championships. It was actually foolish to learn a new stroke so late. It's not something that's normally recommended. But Percy was encouraging, and I was willing. So, I kept working at it, and it's pretty incredible, really, that my backhand became as good as it did."

In practice, Percy soon noticed that behind Stefan's introverted front there was a dogged stubbornness that came in handy both in tournaments and on the practice court.

"Stefan came to us and played his first tournaments here, and I've seen kids that are so nervous that they almost jump behind the curtains behind the baseline. But Stefan played, and although he had some problems with his backhand at first, he never went back to the two-handed grip. He'd made up his mind to learn the new stroke.

"On the other hand, his forehand was shaky. He shoveled the ball over, like a damn snow shoveler, but that's how he wanted it. It wasn't much of a stroke, but because it was softly hit, he had time to get up to the net and finish the point there."

Stefan continued to commute to Percy in Stockholm. Just like Borg, Stefan wanted to keep score and play games, instead of grinding out his strokes. After five minutes, he'd tell Percy: "I'm warmed up. Let's play a match now." Every week, he was given homework to show his coach in Västervik. He also did a lot of groin exercises and rope jumping, something Percy never did with Björn. Percy wanted Stefan to have strong groins so he could get down low with his feet wide apart at the net when hitting his beautiful volleys. With his commuting to Stockholm, Stefan doubled his workout volume from four hours per week to eight.

"And then everything happened quickly. After I graduated from ninth grade, I decided to give tennis everything I had, and I started to play in satellite tournaments. And as early as 1983, I won all the junior Grand Slam tournaments. I remember my first match against McEnroe, an exhibition. I watched the scoreboard and saw my name next to his. It felt completely unreal, I was so young."

And that's how he was known among both tennis coaches and other players—"that promising junior"—when he found himself standing face-to-face with Mats Wilander in the final in Milan, the match that would be so irritating to Mats, because "an older player should always beat a younger one."

During these first months on the men's tour, Stefan had Percy Rosberg by his side. Percy was pretty sure that Mats was most uncomfortable when he played an opponent with a varied game, so he instructed Stefan to alternate between soft and hard shots, short and long, to prevent Mats from finding his groove.

The plan worked perfectly, and a big reason was Stefan's serves. The crowd, and his opponent, noted that his second serve was almost better than his first serve.

At the press conference afterward, Wilander spoke at length, like the seasoned top player he'd become: "When I was coming up, Björn Borg told me I could become one of the best players in the world because I used my mind when I play. With his serve, Edberg can play without thinking. If he plays like he did against me today, few players in the world can beat him."

Stefan was sitting next to Mats. The result from the just-finished match had brought him from 53 in the world rankings to 17. Throughout the press conference, he brought his hand to his forehead to push aside the bangs that kept getting in his eyes. He tried to control his emotions, not sound too happy after having outperformed a countryman. But when he was asked whether he knew how much money he'd just made, he let out a chuckle: "Yes, that I know: $68,000."

Stefan Edberg was greeted with open arms by the world's tennis connoisseurs. Finally, here was a Swedish serve-and-volley player among all the baseline grinders. The close-knit collaboration with Percy was coming to an end. Rosberg had agreed to travel with Stefan for a year, but he was struck by the same insight he'd had with Björn: being a traveling tennis coach wasn't for him.

"A few months passed, and I started missing my family too much," says Percy. I liked to study other players, Edberg hated to watch others play. He wanted to browse record stores for hours, and that wasn't for me. Being a coach can be like a damn babysitting job. Stefan met Tony Pickard, who took over. I was fine with that. I'd already done all the work with Stefan; he was ready. He already had all his strokes. There was just one thing for Tony to work on, and that was his mind."

Yes, there was this matter of Stefan's temperament. Stefan had a tendency to let every small mistake get into his head and linger there like a parasite, which affected all the strokes in Stefan's toolbox. Both on and off the court, Stefan won points by being nicer and more courteous than any other player. All the journalists' questions, smart and dumb, were answered in the same correct and articulated language. Sometimes it almost sounded as if he were reading aloud from a book.

But on the court, he suffered from anxiety. While McEnroe turned his anger outward and let it punish anyone who happened to be in the vicinity, Stefan turned his negative emotions inward.

Stefan could play brilliantly a series of points, a game, or an entire set. When his game flowed, he could obliterate anyone. But many of his matches also contained slumps that could last equally long. The valleys were almost always triggered by his own mistakes. It looked as if his neck muscles had stopped working and his chin fell down, as if he were about to break down crying at any moment.

The Englishman Tony Pickard, who worked as an agent for the racket manufacturer Wilson, had seen Stefan play in the Junior European Championships, when he became Europe's best fourteen-year-old and was still hitting his two-handed backhand. Pickard had been impressed by the Swede's physique and had memorized his name. They met again in Bournemouth in 1983, and Tony invited Stefan to his home in Nottingham for a few days of training. They kept in touch, and after the 1984 French Open, where Stefan lost to Anders Järryd in the second round, Stefan contacted Tony again. A collaboration was initiated. They conducted most of the training at the Queen's Club in London. The club let Pickard and Edberg use courts free of charge.

Tony Pickard has a benevolent appearance. He is always well groomed and well dressed. He chooses his words carefully, speaks in a calm voice, and likes to engage in quiet British understatements. He has a fondness for order and planning. It was obvious that Stefan and Tony, or just "Pickard," like Stefan liked to say, were a good fit for each other. It also seemed to be perfectly in order that, when it was time for Stefan to find a place to be a better starting point, both logistically and fiscally, for his tennis life than Västervik, aside from Monaco, he moved to Kensington in London. In London, Stefan could have the anonymity he desired. Also, the politeness of the British way of life made him feel right at home. London was a place where Stefan's gentlemanly manners were appreciated.

Percy might have been right when he said that Stefan was a finished product as a tennis player, but Pickard worked him hard. Of the four players who regularly made it to the semifinals in the major tournaments—McEnroe, Lendl, Connors, Wilander—only McEnroe had a diverging style of play. The others, and most of the players behind them in the world rankings, were baseline players who relied on their groundstrokes. Notwithstanding Edberg's elegant backhand, the sum of his groundstrokes was not enough to win rallies against those players. That wasn't what Stefan wished for, either, and together, Stefan and Tony developed an even more aggressive style of play. They invested enormous amounts of time in Stefan's volley game, to make his volley the very best it could be. That's the only way he'd be able to handle the ever-emerging wave of baseline sluggers.

Edberg and Pickard quickly received proof that the training had provided results. In January 1985, Stefan won the U.S. Indoor Championships in Memphis, defeating players like Brad Gilbert, Jimmy Connors, and Yannick Noah.

Meanwhile, Mats Wilander sat in a hotel room in Philadelphia and pondered his life. He'd just lost to Greg Holmes, an American whom Mats should've beaten handily. But Holmes had a particular style of play—he hit both his forehand and his backhand with a two-handed grip—and Wilander never could find his rhythm. He lost in two straight sets. For the first time in his life, Mats Wilander found tennis boring.

"After the Davis Cup final in 1984, I felt: *Isn't this enough now?* I'd already proven something. I'd won three Grand Slam tournaments, on both clay and grass, we'd defeated Team USA in the Davis Cup. What more could people ask of me? And when I started to think like that, the pressure went away. And when the pressure wasn't there, I didn't play well, so I had a crappy start to 1985."

To further complicate matters, a racket detail turned into a big deal. Mats's new Rossignol frames were painted green rather than the previous grayish blue. Mats was sure the change in color had made the racket stiffer. The factory said that was impossible, but Mats was convinced.

"I had a short backhand swing. The stiffer the racket, and the shorter your swing, the harder it is to add power to your shot. My serve and forehand had improved, but I'd lost my backhand. On the backhand side, I just pushed the ball. My entire game had been built on setting myself up to hit my backhand, either down the line or crosscourt, that's what all the points should lead up to, that's what my opponents feared. And now I couldn't hit it anymore."

During this same time, Mats had made some new friends on the tennis circuit and was looking for new experiences. Together with his friend Mel Purcell, Mats went to Memphis to see Eric Clapton—"this was before Clapton quit drugs, so he was probably both high and stoned onstage." He'd also begun to occasionally hang out with McEnroe.

"I think it had to do with the Davis Cup match in Göteborg, that we had the same kind of attitude when we'd been out celebrating and were hungover," Wilander says. "In a way that tied us together. I had lost to Greg Holmes and called John up. 'What are you doing?' 'I'm in my hotel room, come over!' he said."

McEnroe was about to play his first match in the same tournament from which Mats had just been eliminated. He was sitting in his big suite playing a guitar he'd connected to a huge amplifier he'd brought with him. The left-handed McEnroe played with a right grip, but now he was sitting with a traditionally strung guitar facing the wrong direction, listening to music and playing along.

Wilander says: "He could play both ways, had doubled up on learning all the chords. So, we sat and talked and played for a while, until he said: 'I have to get going now, but stay if you want.' So, while he left to play, and win, against Peter McNamara, I stayed in his suite and played the guitar. I felt so incredibly cool."

During the early spring, Mats reached the final in both Brussels and Monte Carlo, but he also lost unexpectedly several times to low-ranked players. An American reporter asked what was wrong with his game. Mats responded: "Nothing's wrong. I don't want to be obsessed with being number one in the world. I don't want to be like Borg. I'd rather take my time and have some fun on the way."

The first Davis Cup match of the year was an away match against Chile. It was exactly ten years after the protests in Båstad, when Sweden had played the same opponent. Not much had changed in Chile over the past decade. The same man, Pinochet, was in power, supported by his military junta. What had changed was the political climate in Sweden, and in the world. This time around, there was no debate whatsoever on whether or not Sweden should send its tennis ambassadors to Chile. The social commitment wasn't enough for all corners of the world, and in 1985, it was Africa that was in focus. The whole world had been touched by the horrific famine in the Horn of Africa. In every news broadcast, images were shown of starving children with swollen bellies. Nobody reacted more strongly than the Irish artist Bob Geldof, who drew from all his contacts in the music industry to organize the largest-scale charity concert the world had ever seen, a gala that took place on July 13, simultaneously in London and Philadelphia. Every participating pop and rock artist performed for free to raise money and create public opinion to help the victims of the drought. Phil Collins was flown on a Concorde across the Atlantic to be able to perform in both locations.

The famine disaster engaged the public, and so did the political state of affairs in South Africa. The regime was under increasing international pressure to abandon the apartheid policy. Sweden was one of the driving countries, with its long history of supporting the ANC.

Sweden brought its strongest team to Santiago: Wilander, Edberg, Järryd, and Sundström. Upon their arrival, they checked in to the Hilton, went for a dip in the pool, and then sat down for a meal in the dining room, under a large carriage wheel that had been converted into a magnificent ceiling lamp. While they were having their meal, the lamp started swaying. The captain Hasse Olsson and coach Jonte Sjögren looked at each other, at the players, and then they heard the sound of broken glass as the panorama windows facing the swimming pool shattered. Panic broke out all over Santiago. People screamed, people ran, and despite the staff's appeals for people to stay indoors, to stay underneath a door frame, almost everyone ran out into the gardens. They saw walls cracking and waves in the pool.

"It was terribly uncomfortable, of course. The earthquake lasted for more than an hour, and the aftershocks continued through the night. The players reacted very differently, but I think everyone probably had trouble sleeping," says Hans Olsson.

The day after was strange. The Swedes left for practice and passed through parts of the city that looked like war zones. When the aftershocks started up again midway through the practice, Wilander had had enough. He and Jonte wanted to go home. Few of the team's members thought it made sense to play tennis when Chile had just suffered a natural disaster. But the Chilean organizers put pressure on the Swedish team to not go back to Europe. Perhaps they could go to Rio de Janeiro for a few days and return when things had quieted down? Neither Sjögren nor Wilander was especially open to negotiations. In the end, the whole team went home. When the effects of the earthquake had been tallied, 177 deaths were reported, and around one million people were left homeless.

When the match was finally played six weeks later, Sjögren, Wilander, and Järryd opted not to go. Instead, Sweden was represented by Janne Gunnarsson and Thomas Högstedt and won rather handily. In the evening after the victory, the Chilean hosts invited the Swedish team to a soccer match. The match was played at Chile's National Stadium in Santiago, the same arena the Pinochet regime had used as a concentration camp and execution grounds during the military coup in 1973. The social science and geography teacher Hans Olsson from Uppsala was given a seat in the VIP box, with two generals seated on either side of him.

"If people in Sweden had known how we were received, it would surely have sparked a debate," says Hans Olsson. "All of a sudden, the spotlights were being pointed at our seats. From the loudspeakers blared a long tirade in Spanish that I didn't understand, but the message was clear—the regime was using us to showcase the good relations it had with democratic European states in general, and Sweden in particular. It didn't feel right.

"I was well aware that the Swedish national soccer team's coach, 'Åby' Ericson, had gotten himself in trouble when he made a comment about the soccer World Championships in Argentine, talking about how everything was so beautiful and nice. But when you're a guest, you're not supposed to see any of the bad. We met the junta leaders' wives and children, there were banquets, the organizers took such good care of us. It's easy to be fooled. At the same time, those experiences on the Davis Cup trips became great lessons for the players. Instead of me telling them, they got to witness the situation in Chile, and the poverty in India, with their own eyes."

A few months later, the French Open final. Wilander against Lendl. Wilander had lost four of their five most recent matches, so the odds were clearly against him.

"I lost the first set big, which made me start to think, *Okay, well, but I'm not going to lose this way.* I had won the French Open one year, reached the final, the semifinal, and now here I was in the final again. I had nothing to prove and thought, *I'm going to attack.*"

As his backhand still didn't work like Mats wanted, he had to come up with an alternative. And once again he became a copycat: he began hitting soft balls up the middle and ballooning forehands. It was the exact style of play Noah had used to baffle Wilander in 1983. And Mats copied Edberg's serve.

"I tried to hit a kick serve, just like Stefan, then rush up to the net. And five minutes into the second set, I knew that Lendl wasn't going to have a chance. I played incredibly consistent, maybe because I wasn't afraid to lose, I wasn't nervous at all. That match is, in a way, the most important match of my career, because that's when I realized there was more to my game than just staying behind the baseline."

The score in the last three sets: 6–4, 6–2, 6–2. Wilander the winner was back.

Meanwhile, the other Swedes also began to advance further in the major tournaments. At Wimbledon, Anders Järryd reached the semifinals, where he was eliminated by the young Boris Becker, who went on to win the tournament. Edberg reached the round of 16 at both Wimbledon and the U.S. Open.

Joakim Nyström reached the quarterfinals at Flushing Meadows, as did Järryd, who, in the hot sun, won the first set against Mats Wilander and was on his way to one of his biggest career wins. Then Järryd paid the price for his energy-consuming style of play and his intense doubles play schedule. Mats was up 5–0 in the third set when Järryd collapsed from heat stroke, was taken into the locker room, and placed on a mattress with his body covered in ice packs. Järryd became news on American television. Dramatic footage of his collapse was accompanied by the headline WHEN YOU CAN'T STAND THE HEAT.

For some time in that same heat, it looked as if Mats Wilander would successfully take down McEnroe in the semifinals, but he finally succumbed after five tough sets. But when Mats remembers the 1985 U.S. Open today, it's not his semifinal match that comes to mind, but an event that happened after his win over Greg Holmes in the fourth round:

"I was walking off the court when someone called out my name. I was getting ready to sign an autograph for the guy when he said, 'This girl wants to meet you, too,' and he pushed this girl toward me. It was easy to see that she couldn't care less about me, but my eyes had grown big as saucers. I knew vaguely who the guy was, his name was Marlon Stoltzman. He was a modeling agent, and his dad owned Adidas in South Africa. I thought they were a couple, but I still couldn't stop staring at her. I'd never met a model before in my life. Then they asked if we could go out for dinner, and I gave them the address to my hotel."

The girl was Sonya Mulholland, a South African who had just started her modeling career in New York. She accompanied Stoltzman to the dinner that night. Mats, who wasn't sure about the nature and circumstances of the date, brought Jocke Nyström, Hasse Simonsson, and the Danish player Michael Mortensen to Bill's Gay Nineties, a piano bar on 54th Street with a history dating back to the Prohibition era. After that evening, Mats and Sonya continued to spend time together for the duration of his stay in New York. Three days after he had landed back in Europe, he'd ended his relationship with Annette.

"There was chaos inside of me. I was sad to break up with Annette and happy to have met Sonya. But the weeks and months that followed were pretty confusing."

Mats was in love and had a new spark in his personal life, but it didn't immediately show in his performance on the tennis courts. If anything, it had a negative effect, as the object of his affection was in New York while Mats was traveling the rest of the world. To burn off some of the excess energy, Mats explored the bars in Geneva, in Barcelona, and in Malmö, where the Davis Cup team quickly disposed of Australia on clay. A new player named Michael Pernfors had joined the team as a training partner to the given foursome Wilander, Edberg, Järryd, and Nyström. Pernfors was the latest in a number of Swedes who'd appeared out of nowhere and suddenly played on a world-class level. Pernfors was in his first year as a professional. He'd won the NCAA Men's Tennis Championship two years in a row, but that hadn't given him a lot of attention.

"We're the same age, but we hadn't seen each other since we were thirteen. I didn't even know he still played tennis," says Mats.

It was easy to rekindle their friendship. Pernfors and Wilander plugged in Mats's electric guitar in his hotel room—Mats now followed McEnroe's lead and toured with a guitar and an amplifier in his luggage—and opened up the balcony door to the pedestrian walkways of Malmö, then jammed into the wee hours. The last evening of the Davis Cup match, both teams went out together and partied with friends and girlfriends.

After the Davis Cup, the tennis tour took Stefan Edberg to Basel, where he beat Yannick Noah in the final. Mats went to Tokyo, where he lost his final against Lendl. The Tokyo tournament coincided with a photo shoot for Sonya in the Japanese capital, and that week, they officially became a couple. Mats then went home and lost in the first round at the Stockholm Open. Edberg lost to Anders Järryd in the semifinal.

It was a vagabond life, but Australia and the Kooyong Stadium had become almost like a second home to the Swedish players, who were well-liked by the Australian crowds. They were also successful. Wilander and Edberg advanced through the tournament on either side of the draw. After two weeks of play, a historic occurrence was a fact—for the first time ever, there'd be an all-Swedish final in a Grand Slam tournament.

"The final was played on a Monday, because rain had wreaked havoc in the schedule. All the other players had left, we were the only ones still there," recalls Stefan.

The remaining tennis experts and coaches looked at the two Swedes' preparations with skepticism. The night before the final, they had dinner together, at the same place where they'd taken their meals all week. In the morning, they were seen in the hotel's breakfast room together, and when it was time to warm up, they hit with each other. Were they rivals or best buddies?

Stefan explains, "Normally, you'd put your name on a list for the center court, since that's where everyone wants to practice. But now there were no alternatives, so it had to be Mats and me. It didn't bother me, we knew each other so well."

It bothered Mats more:

"I don't know anyone who likes to hit with Stefan. He wants to get up to the net and finish the point at all times, so there's never a rhythm. And I also thought it was anticlimactic to play Stefan, since he was a friend. Why couldn't I get to play someone I really wanted to beat, like Lendl or Cash?"

The warmup was interrupted by a heavy rainstorm. And there they were, sitting in the locker room, Mats and Jonte Sjögren, Stefan and Tony Pickard. They chatted, were quiet, pondered.

"I was so sure the match wouldn't be played, and I was fine with that," Mats says. "I didn't feel like playing. My girlfriend had left and I was so in love, I just wanted to go to New York and be with Sonya."

The Australian Open's heightened status had made more players seek out the tournament, which was considered the happiest, most fun-loving tournament on the tour. The players on the court didn't necessarily exude this mood. At the time, occasional debates would flare up about the boring personalities of modern tennis players. Spectators and journalists who'd been around for a while would tell juicy stories about Nastase, the young Connors, Gerulaitis . . . The gallery of characters of that era had appeared much more lively and outgoing. But there were those who thought that suggesting players to show more "personality" was really to ask for more jerks, and that the game of today was as entertaining as ever.

The semifinal match between Stefan Edberg and Ivan Lendl had proven both sides right.

The match had been an amazing battle on the center court. Under the bright sunshine, the Czech and the Swede had the crowd spellbound in a five-setter that showcased both a hardcore baseline game and a spectacular aggressive attack-tennis. When Edberg hit a forehand passing shot to close out the match, he'd won by the score 6–7, 7–5, 6–1, 4–6, 9–7. The crowd gave a standing ovation to both players for their performance. But neither of the two players gave very much back in terms of sharing their feelings. It's hard to know how much Stefan Edberg's game was actually affected by his surly disposition, since he did in fact manage to turn the match around and win. But the fact remained: the semifinal was played between two individuals who were identically dressed in a white Adidas shirt with a blue pattern, where one of them seemed morose (Lendl) and the other sad (Edberg). You could see why the tennis world would be so enthusiastic about the young Wimbledon winner Boris Becker and could've hugged him to death. He played each shot with his beating heart on his sleeve. When Edberg missed an occasional shot against Lendl, it looked as if his world were about to crumble. When he hit a winner, he looked mostly embarrassed. He reached match point by hitting an amazing forehand return on a tough serve, which he followed up with an even better backhand passing shot. He then clenched his fist in a victory gesture that lasted all of a millisecond. After that, his usual sullen disposition returned.

Perhaps it was just that he was so totally focused on carrying out his task. Stefan was raised not to act like someone he wasn't, to always be honest with himself, and to remain true to who he was. If he didn't feel like living it up on the court, he wasn't going to do that. After match point, he thanked Lendl and the umpire, swung his tennis bag up over his shoulder, and was gone from the arena 45 seconds after the last shot of the match had landed inside the lines. The 8,000 cheering spectators didn't even get a hand wave.

Now, sitting in the locker room taking cover from the rain, Stefan Edberg was just as focused. He knew he was standing on the threshold of winning his first major title, and a little rain wasn't going to disturb him. When the referee came in and said, "The rain has stopped, the match will begin in an hour and a half," Edberg thought, *Finally!* Mats thought, *Oh no, not already!*

Stefan recalls: "With Mats, I knew he was a formidable opponent, but I also knew that if I played well, I'd probably win. I was the one who dictated what happened on the court, he was more cautious. I knew I had the weapons to outmaneuver him. And even if we were friendly, we were competitors on the world elite level, and we each ran our own race. With our matches, there was the extra prestige of being the best player in Sweden. That had been the foundation since the Juniors: to be the best in Sweden as an eleven-year-old, the best in Sweden as a twelve-year-old, and then suddenly you're the best player in Europe. But it's ingrained in you that you want to be the best in your country."

Soon, Stefan had proven that he was just that, at this time.

"It was like a repeat of Milan in 1984," says Mats. "He started getting his kick serves in, and his annoying style of play, the balls bounced so damn high on the grass. . . . I soon felt this wasn't going to work out for me."

His intuition was true. Stefan won by 6–4, 6–3, 6–3 in a lopsided final that was over in an hour and a half. Edberg had won his first major title, and three of the year's Grand Slam tournaments had been won by teenagers: Wilander, Becker, and Edberg.

Wilander's win at the French Open, his place in the semifinals at the U.S. Open, and the Davis Cup triumph still made this tennis year, which had contained so much doubt, a good year. When he finally arrived in New York to be with his new love interest, he felt like the coolest man in the world. He stayed with Sonya in her apartment on 22nd Street, and during the day, while she was at work, Mats searched for practice partners in New York. He found them at local tennis clubs.

"I played at a place called the University Place; they had a tent on the third floor, above a bowling alley, right in the middle of the city. It was an amazing time."

It was around this time that Mats received a call from Jocke Nyström, who sounded cryptic.

Mats remembers:

"He told me that my ex-girlfriend had found a new boyfriend. *Okay, good for Annette*, I thought. And then he said that her new boyfriend played tennis. I guessed a bunch of different names, like old tennis acquaintances from Växjö, until I finally asked: 'Is it Stefan?' And it was, of course. Naturally, I was surprised, but at the same time it seemed logical. I knew that Annette had always thought that Stefan was such a nice and decent guy."

When the relationship between Stefan and Annette became official, the Swedish players' international colleagues received it almost with a sense of resignation. Not only did they eat, train, and travel together. Now the

Swedes also exchanged girlfriends with each other! Wasn't there anything that could threaten their team spirit?

For Annette and Stefan, who'd always been protective of their privacy, it was a delicate situation.

"It was different," says Stefan Edberg today. "But sometimes in life you end up in those kinds of situations, and then you'll have to try to handle it as well as you can. It's really not something I want to talk about."

Anders Järryd says:

"At first, there was some talk amongst us, of course. I'm sure it was a bit uncomfortable for all three of them. But it quickly passed. Neither Stefan nor Mats made a big deal out of it, and it quickly turned out that it was good for everyone. We were young; it wasn't surprising that people broke up and started dating someone else."

Mats Wilander calls 1986 "a crappy year." Everyone in Sweden would agree. On the last day in February, Olof Palme, the prime minister, was shot to death on a Stockholm street. In April, a nuclear disaster occurred at the Chernobyl nuclear power station in the former Soviet Union. The murder of Palme is described as the moment when Sweden lost its innocence, and the rest of the year had the country's population suffer through the mismanaged hunt for Palme's killer. Meanwhile, reports kept coming in about deficiencies in the world's nuclear power plants and higher levels of radioactive contamination in the berries and mushrooms in the Swedish forests.

But Mats Wilander is, of course, referring to his tennis game. It can sound coy coming from a player who won the doubles tournament at Wimbledon with his best buddy Jocke Nyström and spent the entire year in the second, third, or fourth spot in the world rankings. What he refers to is the fact that he didn't go far in singles in any one of the Grand Slam tournaments, and he only managed to win two Grand Prix titles.

This was also a year when the world's tennis experts wondered whether Wilander would ever make a sincere effort to reach the number-one spot or in fact be content to hang around just behind the very best.

The latter was true. Mats didn't think it was that bad to be almost the best in the world, and, after all, there was so much to explore and discover. That fall, he took a two-month break from tournaments.

As Mats explains, "Tennis wasn't that important. I was getting to know New York and a new life. It wasn't an obvious choice for me to move there. What would my parents say? And how would it affect me financially? After all, I'd be going from a 0 percent tax rate in Monaco to 40 percent in New York. But I was in love and ready to go all in."

Stefan Edberg had also won two titles when he returned home to the Stockholm Open that fall. He was upset about his mediocre results at both Wimbledon and the French Open and focused on training hard.

But if Wilander and Edberg, the two giants, had now hit a slump, there was an abundance of other Swedes lifting trophies to the sky. Swedish tennis talents kept coming as if from a cornucopia; young Swedish players seemed to take the step from talent to finished top player with the same ease with which they tiptoed along a baseline. Nyström, Järryd, and Sundström brought home new titles. Jonas B. Svensson from Kungsbacka, Kent Carlsson from Eskilstuna, and Ulf Stenlund from Hedemora won their first titles. And Mikael Pernfors from Höllviken advanced all the way to the Paris final, with his superb drop shots and lobs.

Indeed, the world was witnessing a Swedish tennis miracle. The success was met with admiration, and a certain fatigue. Everyone—possibly with the exception of Pernfors, who was a product of American collegiate tennis and who wore his hair in short hedgehog style—was blond, polite, correct . . . And a bit bland.

At Wimbledon, a reporter from the *Chicago Tribune* complained about the Swedes who swarmed around the grass courts, that they all looked alike. "If Sweden has something that you really want, then the best time for stealing it is the Wimbledon weeks. All the men are away playing tennis. They all look like ten guys in the same outfit. If they had a banquet for the Swedes and some joker moved the place cards between the salad and the coffee, not even their relatives would notice."

At home, the pride naturally knew no limits. It was as if the development were entirely natural; just look at other sports. Because clearly wasn't what we saw an entire sports miracle? How could it be that Swedish athletes were so extremely successful?

A few days before Mats Wilander and Stefan Edberg were to meet in the 1986 Stockholm Open final, as the world's No. 3 and 4 players, respectively, Swedish television broadcast a long program with the modest title "Made in Sweden." Here, the viewers were introduced to the biggest Swedish sports stars of the '80s in short portraits. The program offered insights into what had formed them as children and adolescents and what had made them into world-class athletes.

Mats Wilander was one of the featured athletes. He mentioned how tennis in Sweden was a sport that could be played by kids from working or middle-class upbringings alike, unlike in countries such as America or Germany. The program continued with Swedish sport heroes from other fields; cross-country skiers, soccer players, motocross riders all spoke about how virtues such as modesty and stubbornness had helped them become world-class athletes. The show ended with the most stubborn of them all, slalom legend Ingemar Stenmark, and then, legendary sports commentator Sven Petersson summed it up, in a fatherly voice: "The sports movement is strong, but it has no interest in power. It is primarily concerned with the youth, with training and development. It seeks to preserve certain traditions that are disappearing: responsibility, humility, fair play. The Swedish sports movement, it's unique in the world."

It was against this backdrop that Stefan Edberg and Mats Wilander were introduced at the Kungliga Tennis Hall. What had been completely overlooked was that both had fled the Swedish forests and river rapids for the pulse in London and New York. The world and its values had blazed ahead into the '80s, but the Swedish sports ideal had barely changed since the '50s and '60s.

The crowd in the Kungliga Tennis Hall Stomped their feet as they tried to inspire a great matchup between champions, but it was soon clear that talent and elegance would defeat the classic Swedish virtues, stubbornness, and willingness to run. Wilander won only four games in three sets. After the match, Edberg contemplated whether he had made any mistakes but couldn't think of a single one: "I played my best match ever on my home court, so it feels wonderful and almost unbelievable."

The reporter Jan Svanlund from Swedish sports television asked Stefan if he had matured. If he'd now stopped hanging his head when things didn't go his way? "Since I played so well today, there was no reason to."

The ceremonies on the court didn't go any further when they were interrupted by Jocke Nyström, the musician Totte Wallin, the Davis Cup captain Hasse Olsson, and an additional dozen or so friends, who marched out onto the court with a stretcher and a sign with the words MATS'S BACHELOR PARTY. Wilander was laid down on the stretcher and carried into the press conference room, where he was forced to converse with reporters dressed in a straitjacket before being transported away to celebrations out on the town.

Mats was going to marry Sonya in the days between Christmas and New Year's in her home village in South Africa. This was a decision he'd had to defend in the press—South Africa was subject to both sports and financial sanctions. The wedding also meant that Mats wouldn't play in the Davis Cup final against Australia in late December. With the surplus of tennis talent Hasse Olsson had at his disposal, perhaps there was no harm done, but it was still disappointing to many of the Swedes who planned to go to Melbourne and root on the team, faces painted yellow and blue.

These were happy times in the Swedish labor market, as unemployment was nonexistent. Recent graduates could find permanent employment in factories and in retail, save up money for a few months, resign from the job, buy a plane ticket with five stopovers around the world, make a stop in Australia, pick oranges on a fruit farm to pad their travel funds, cheer on the Swedish tennis players in Melbourne, and then fly back home and walk into their former boss's office and sign another employment agreement. This all provided a fantastic here-and-now atmosphere for both the fans and the players, who were carried by the beer-fueled cheering sections in the stands.

This time, they would cheer on Stefan Edberg and Mikael Pernfors. The latter wore a torn sheet around his forehead that made him look almost as tough as his opponent, Pat Cash; however, this only carried Pernfors to an honorable five-set loss in the fourth match. For the second time, Sweden had lost a Davis Cup final at the Kooyong Stadium.

In New York, Mats Wilander was trying to settle into everyday life after his wedding. Mats was involved in the ATP players' organization and had gotten to know Matt Doyle, an Irish-American who was in the process of finishing off his professional career. After an ATP meeting, Doyle and Mats went out to a bar.

"Doyle is Irish and I'm me, so we began ordering beers," recalls Mats.

After a while, Doyle spoke up:

"Mats, listen to me. You have one of the world's best backhands, right? And you have one of the world's best forehands. You don't believe that yourself, but you do. You never miss on the forehand side. It's just that you're lacking power. If you start to do strength training with me, you'll add 10 percent to your serve. And then you'll add 10 percent to your forehand, and to your backhand, a little bit here, a little bit there. . . . What do you say?"

Mats looked Matt Doyle straight in the eyes. Committing to becoming the world's number-one player meant to never break down, to never lose to lower-ranked players, to always be focused. After two messy years when his motivation had wavered, Mats knew that his life was entering a new phase. For two years, Mats had hung around at the absolute top of the world rankings, without being as uncompromisingly dedicated as the other athletes portrayed in the TV documentary. Could he become like Ingemar Stenmark?

He raised his beer mug in a toast.

"Okay. Let's do it."

WHEN SMÅLAND RULED THE WORLD

"How can a guy who's always been a classic baseline player change his game so radically?"
—JOHN McENROE

The first outdoor match of the season always seemed to cause a certain degree of doubt in Mats Wilander. You were supposed to pick up where you left off the previous fall, and it could feel unfamiliar with the breeze and the sunshine, and balls that bounced differently from indoors. In addition, the "King of Clay" had not won a single title on his favorite surface in almost two years, not since he crushed Lendl at the French Open in 1985.

Now, just before his first match at the Monte Carlo Country Club, there was still a great harmony between his body and mind, and any nervousness was gone with the wind. When Mats warmed up in a match against Janne Gunnarsson, warm breezes came in from the Ligurian Sea. Mats's racket sang when he hit the ball, and his timing was perfect.

An hour or so later, the two friends lingered at the net. Gunnarsson had won just five games, and Mats had advanced in the tournament.

"It had only been a week or two since I'd started the strength training with Matt Doyle," Mats says. "The effect obviously wasn't there yet, but the training had created such a huge spark for me. My motivation was back, I felt so damn strong, I just wanted to crush any obstacle in my way!"

In a press conference a few days later, Mats surprised all the reporters who'd gotten accustomed to his laid-back attitude about life as a tennis pro, by announcing that he was now fully committed to becoming the world's top-ranked player.

Starting this spring, Matt Doyle was going to join Mats, Jonte Sjögren, and Jocke Nyström, who often practiced and played with Mats, on the tennis tour. Starting now, they'd complement the technique training by Sjögren out on the court with tough weight training by Doyle in the gym.

"Jonte was the one who gave structure to my day, plus he was incredibly good at technique and form," Mats says. "Tactically he was good, too, but that was sort of my strength anyway. I thought I already knew how to play. But the most important thing was that he cared so much about me, both as a person and as a player. He was much more nervous than I was. Sonya always said, 'I can't sit next to him because he kicks so much and throws snus around.' But for me, it was amazing to have someone that cared so much. I knew I had my dad at home, and Jonte in the stands. That was the best part of catching up with Jonte after matches. He was happier than I was that I had won. We did a lot together, but our relationship wasn't as tight as Borg and Bergelin's. Jonte gave me the space to be an adventurer, play golf, go to concerts, or play music. He understood that I needed that."

The preparations for the French Open included exhibition matches in Barcelona. Mats was going to play Lendl and arrived on a delayed flight the day of the match. Mats didn't have a bad relationship with the Czech, but not a good one, either. Few did. Ivan Lendl wasn't the warm and cozy type. He trained extremely hard according to a structured schedule and liked to talk about it. He'd recently announced that cycling was his new form of cross-training. His sense of humor made few people laugh, and his obsession with order affected his opponents, too. If a towel happened to hang just slightly crooked next to the court, he could interrupt play and ask a ball boy to fix it. All of these were minor details, of course, and wouldn't have annoyed anyone if it weren't for the fact that Lendl was also the best player in the world.

When Mats stepped off the plane at the Barcelona airport, it turned out his luggage hadn't made it there with him. Rackets, shoes, clothes . . . everything was lost, and he had to go out and buy both clothes and equipment. When the match started, Lendl was well aware of what had happened to Mats but didn't at all take it into consideration. Instead of allowing the crowd to experience an amicable event between two of the world's greatest tennis players, Lendl took the opportunity to let Mats have it. With borrowed equipment, Mats had no chance, and Lendl won, 6–0, 6–0. Even in tournaments, it's considered almost unsportsmanlike to "bagel" an opponent. Often, the superior player will gift a game or two, like Björn Borg had done in his only match against Mats six years earlier.

Ivan Lendl didn't think he'd done anything wrong. The following morning, the phone rang in Mats's hotel room. A deep voice said in an Eastern European accent: "Hi Mats, it's Ivan. Do you want to practice today?"

There was no way that was going to happen. Mats was both angry and surprised. When the story reached McEnroe, who wasn't one of Lendl's strongest supporters himself, he decided to do something about it. When the tennis stars landed in Rome for the next tournament, the draw turned out so that Joakim Nyström would play Lendl in the third round. McEnroe called the Swedes and suggested a meeting at a restaurant.

"Lendl had told the press that I'd never be able to beat him," says Joakim Nyström. "He boasted in the newspapers about having brought his bicycle so he could get in some extra training before the French Open. And Lendl was known for always punishing himself with tough training after losses. So here I was with McEnroe and 'Wille,' I was drinking water and they were drinking beer, and they pumped me up, planned the strategy, encouraged me. I won in three sets the next day, my only victory ever against Lendl. Afterward, Mats and John were happier than I was in the locker room. They were ecstatic, high-fiving, and McEnroe gathered us in a circle: 'Guys, you know what Lendl is going to do now? He's going to sit down on his damn bike and pedal all the way to Paris!'"

Mats won the tournament in Rome, but he lost to Lendl in the French Open final.

The first point in Wimbledon's rulebook regarding players' clothing and equipment reads: "Competitors must be dressed in suitable tennis attire that is almost entirely white and this applies from the point at which the player enters the court surround." Point two: "White does not include off-white or cream."

In an additional eight points, the Wimbledon organizers emphasize, among other things, that "a single trim of color around the neckline and around the cuff of the sleeve is acceptable but must be no wider than one centimeter (10mm)," and that undergarments are also subject to the white clothing code. Add to this rules on how to stand and walk in the arena and how to greet the royal family, and it's easy to understand that a young John

McEnroe couldn't resist the temptation to walk in wearing a bright blue shirt and say, "Oh, I guess I must have forgotten your silly rules." Most of the players giggle and shake their heads at the arrangements, but know that these are the rules and traditions that make Wimbledon the greatest of them all. Stefan Edberg was one of them.

Stefan had started out the year 1987 just as strongly as Mats Wilander, with tournament wins in Memphis, Rotterdam, and Tokyo. Now he was seeded fourth at Wimbledon and was heavily courted by reporters, not least the British. In the absence of a domestic title contender, the English had adopted Stefan—he lived in Kensington, he was coached by an Englishman, and he behaved like an old school gentleman. And Stefan wasn't as involved with the Swedish guys.

"The old Team Siab was a pretty close-knit group," says Stefan Edberg. "When we played the Davis Cup, all of us blended well, and we had a good time. But I wasn't really the same type, and I'd chosen my own path with an English coach. People change over time, and if you want to be part of the elite, you have to first and foremost look out for your own interests. Back then, tennis was evolving more toward one-man teams. Becker had his team, Cash had his, and I had mine."

Mats Wilander:

"Nobody had anything against Stefan, but he was his own guy to a great extent. Many of us were clay court players who played the same tournaments, while he chose different surfaces. And he also had an English coach, who sometimes tried to steer Stefan away from us. Maybe because he was trying to manage Stefan's moods; he could be a little mopey at times."

For Stefan, Tony Pickard meant security. He both planned and administered the training and also kept TV and the newspapers in check.

"Everybody pushed and pulled. There were very few people close to me, and I let Tony act as a filter as much as possible. I participated in the media events that were expected and required of me, then I left. I kept it to a minimum. There was no talk about being media-trained or selling yourself. I didn't want to be seen, and I was pretty introverted. I could open up to the people closest to me, but I kept the curtains drawn in public life."

However, unlike with Percy Rosberg, with Tony, Stefan had developed some common interests and a coexistence that resembled that of a father and son. They went out to eat and talked about things outside of tennis. Stefan remembers discussions about business and investments, Tony remembers that they recommended movies and music to each other. If they'd lived in their home countries, they would probably have been interested in what happened in society, but like for so many others, life on the tennis tour became a bubble, and neither of them kept up with what was happening at home. On election day, when Margaret Thatcher was reelected as prime minister, Tony Pickard happened to be home in England, where he saw Edberg lose to Pat Cash at the Queen's tournament.

The secret behind Edberg's volley was his legs. While McEnroe, the game's other volley artist, stood upright and flicked his wrist to steer the ball in the direction he wanted, Edberg used to say that he played his volleys with his legs. His strong and explosive thighs and calves were the foundation for his feared, high-bouncing kick serve. His legs allowed him to cover the distance between the baseline and the net quicker than anyone else. He moved like a ninja warrior. His opponents saw him serve, let him out of their sight for a brief moment to return the ball, and when they refocused their gaze, he was suddenly up at the net. How did that happen?

It was these movements that Tony and Stefan kept practicing so diligently—get up to the net, move back, up to the net, right, left, back, knees bent almost perpendicular, feet gliding forward like a fencer's.

When Stefan Edberg played his best, things looked so easy. One, two, three shots, and the point was won. It saved energy, unlike Mats Wilander's style of tennis, which seemed to build on gradually getting under the opponent's skin and then slowly and methodically breaking him down.

When everything clicked for Edberg, he could "bagel" almost any top player in the world.

In Wimbledon's first round against Stefan Eriksson from Enköping, who was the same age as Wilander, Edberg was ahead 6–0, 6–0, 5–0. The crowd started to whisper. Was he really going to do it? Was he that mean?

Yes, he was. Despite his image, Edberg had a killer instinct that was too strong to allow him to give up a game in tournament play out of compassion. Especially at Wimbledon. He won one of the championship's shortest matches ever.

It was matches like the one against Eriksson that caused some analysts to say the same thing Wilander had said after his loss to Edberg in Milan three years earlier: "Stefan can play without thinking." Edberg became angry, almost hurt, when he heard that kind of talk. As if he didn't think? As if his game came to him for free, just by pushing a button? The only thing he would agree with is that it seemed harder to play like Wilander.

Today, Stefan says:

"I just think it's more fun to play aggressive, be a bit creative. Tennis for me is to outmaneuver your opponent. You'd rather have your opponent deep down in one corner, and then put away a short ball in the other corner, so that he is 15 meters from the ball. Then you've succeeded. I wanted to win the point as quickly as possible, while expending as little energy as possible, and having my opponent as far away from the ball as possible. To me, that's so much more fun than just bounce the ball back and wait for the opponent to miss."

This was something that Mats Wilander heard time and again, that he was a wall at the baseline, that he just got the ball back, that it was so boring.

Wilander didn't take to this opinion too kindly, "Got the ball back? It's a little different if it's a twelve-year-old who gets the ball back or if it's an adult player who's one of the best players in the world. Even if I hit the same shot ten times in a row, for me each shot was incredibly important. Every single spot where the ball landed was thoroughly thought-out. My absolute strength was that, from the time I played in the Junior Swedish Championships and through 1988, I was totally focused on each shot I hit. Each and *every* shot.

"I've always believed that I play more aggressively than a player like Edberg or McEnroe. I think they play a tennis of chance, win or lose. I think that's a negative attitude, which stems from the fact that you're not good enough from the baseline. My game was built on hitting shots that prevented my opponent from hitting his best shots. To rush up to the net like that is like holding up a dartboard and giving your opponent an arrow. If he makes his shot, I won't be able to hit the ball. If you give your opponent a half meter on each side to hit, then you give your opponent an opportunity."

Stefan Edberg's analysis of the same scenario is completely different. He believes that everything is built on probability.

"Tennis is like chess; you must determine your moves and calculate the probability. If I move toward the net with a forehand down the line, then I know that the guy on the other side of the net will be pressured for time, and it's going to be very difficult for him to hit cross-court. I'll ask myself how many times out of ten he'll be able to hit a good cross. Maybe twice or three times. Therefore, I'll cover a down-the-line shot ten times out of ten, and I'll congratulate him the few times he's successful with the cross. And I'll still win seven or eight points out of ten with that play. That's kind of how you have to look at it. There are so many tennis players, but perhaps not everyone learns about strategy and probability."

Two Swedish stars, each raised in a village in Småland, were about to conquer the tennis world. They had a common goal to become the best player in the world. However, their plans for how to achieve their goal were completely different.

On the short and dry Wimbledon grass, Mats advanced to the quarterfinal round, where Pat Cash would prove too difficult. Stefan defeated Anders Järryd in his quarterfinal match but lost to Ivan Lendl in the semifinals. At the U.S. Open, the two Swedes met in a semifinal match, which Wilander won. In the final, Lendl was too good, just like he'd been in Paris.

Both Mats and Stefan realized that they had to train with even more purpose, and even harder. Stefan, who topped the doubles ranking in 1986, decided to stop playing doubles in the Grand Slam tournaments. When he lost to Mats in the semifinals at the U.S. Open, there had been signs that he was worn out.

Mats was going to get even stronger. And he was going to find a way to beat Ivan Lendl. Mats hadn't beaten him since the 1985 French Open final. At their latest meeting at the Masters in New York, the crowd had booed the world number two, Wilander, as Lendl swept him off the court in two straight sets.

"After that, we started to train with a clear purpose to beat Lendl," says Jonte Sjögren. "The problem with Mats's backhand was that he'd started having difficulties keeping the length. It wasn't very noticeable against many opponents, but Lendl would attack immediately on a short ball. Therefore, the sliced backhand was a good alternative, and we worked on it extremely hard for some time."

In combination with Doyle's strength training, the changes to Mats's game were going to turn Mats Wilander into a tennis machine. Not the ball-pushing robot Ion Tiriac had seen in 1982, but an efficient, well-oiled winning machine with a strong engine.

At the Australian Open, Mats Wilander made it to the final, where he faced the home country favorite Pat Cash. As Mats trailed, 4–5, in the fifth set, in a match that lasted over four hours, he showed a new side of his tennis game. Twice in a row he'd follow up his hard serve by rushing up to the net and putting away a volley that was completely unreturnable by Cash. His colleagues on the tour could barely believe their eyes. "How can a guy who's always been a classic baseline player change his game so radically?" asked McEnroe. "His serve is amazing," said Andreas Maurer. "He covers the court incredibly well. He plays the important points unbelievably well, and the most amazing thing of all is that he can now be superaggressive." Wilander says:

"I was a bit lucky that I didn't have to play Lendl in that tournament, because I wasn't ready for him, I couldn't hold onto my new game that well yet. But I felt incredibly strong, and I kept up the tough strength training."

In 1988, Mats was more committed to his tennis than ever, and, parallel to his game, he also stepped up his involvement with the ATP players' organization. At the same time, he lived what from the outside looked like a jet-set lifestyle—he partied with Keith Richards, jammed with John Hall from Hall & Oates, and played guitar or tennis with John McEnroe.

At the French Open, Mats was put through the wringer. In the third round, he managed to come back from 2–5 in the decisive set; in the quarterfinal, Emilio Sánchez had three set points to a 2–0 lead, but Wilander weathered the storm. In one of the other quarterfinals, Jonas Svensson won in three straight sets against Ivan Lendl, and with that victory he spared Mats from facing the Czech anytime in the near future. Instead, after a tough five-setter against Andre Agassi, Mats would face Henri Leconte in the final.

Leconte was the home-court player, but Wilander's box in the stands was the most jam-packed. Mats's life in New York was starting to show in his guests of honor. "A lot of strange characters started to hang around Mats," as Jonte puts it. Just as the final was about to begin and everyone had taken their seats, a blond man showed up and began pushing his way through the crowd.

"It's full here, you're in the wrong place," said Birgitta Sjögren, Jonte's wife.

"But I'm Sting," said Sting, who'd just received a platinum disc for his album *Nothing Like the Sun*.

"That's okay, Britta," said Sonya hurriedly. "You can sit here, Sting."

Soon, Mats Wilander would take home his second straight Grand Slam title, making him two-for-two for the year. Late in the June night, Mats traded his winner's statuette from the prize ceremony at Roland Garros for Sting's platinum album.

Boris Becker positioned his feet in the right place for the first serve of the match. The way he dug his shoes into position, it looked as if he were getting a tripod ready. He swiveled his thick legs to the right position, swayed back and forth twice, and then, boom! It was as if a spring shot up through Becker's body and he jumped, feet together, and from the highest position possible, he crushed the tennis ball down toward the opponent's service box with all his might.

Eight years after they'd watched the Wimbledon final between Borg and McEnroe together in Västervik, now Becker and Edberg had arrived here themselves. They'd followed each other through their tennis careers, had become both antagonists and good colleagues. They had a lot in common but were also different. Becker was a large man, big and strong. He exuded will and energy on the tennis court, and he rarely left it without stains on his clothes. He'd learned the basics of tennis at the Blau-Weiss Tennis Club in Leimen, Germany, at a facility designed by his father, an architect. After his breakthrough victory as a seventeen-year-old at Wimbledon in 1985, he became a national hero constantly chased by paparazzi and gossip reporters at home in Germany. Edberg and Wilander could share the weight of being Sweden's tennis hero, while Becker stood alone, in a country with a much larger population. It was a sometimes inhuman task for a twenty-year-old.

Now here came that serve toward Stefan, and he really hated it. To play against Becker was the hardest challenge Stefan knew. Stefan wanted to play for and challenge each point, but often against Becker he could only do that every other game, in his own service games. Becker was a difficult opponent strictly based on his tennis game, and it was mentally tough to know that in several games "Boom-Boom," which was his nickname, would blast home his serves without losing a single point.

The London summer was cool and damp. Boris was wearing a slipover over his tennis shirt, Stefan his usual, specially designed shirt from Adidas with the initials "SE" printed in graffiti style on Miró-inspired paint splatter.

It was a mystery how he'd been able to squeeze that shirt past Wimbledon's dress code rules. Maybe because this year, the colors on his shirt weren't the usual red, green, and yellow, but Wimbledon's own colors, green and purple.

Stefan had made it to his first Wimbledon final by playing brilliant grass court tennis. The performance that both Tony and Stefan had found most energizing was Stefan's semifinal victory over Miloslav Mecir, who had eliminated Wilander in the previous round. Mecir was a nightmare opponent for Mats. Despite feeling stronger than ever, he was so impressed by the Czech's touch and feel for the ball that he was practically beaten in advance. Stefan had also trailed Mecir by 0–2 in sets but had been able to get out of trouble and turn things around.

"My attitude wasn't negative now, was it, Pickard?" asked Stefan with a smile when his coach joined him in the locker room after the match.

"I'd always believed I had a chance to win Wimbledon. Everyone said that the tournament and the surface would suit me, and I agreed. This time, I was a bit of an underdog, since Boris had already won there twice. But I had a good feeling after my comeback against Mecir."

The final had only been going on for a few minutes when rain started to fall, as feared. Edberg had begun brilliantly by breaking Becker's serve, but before the match was paused, he'd lost his own serve.

Stefan stayed in his own apartment during the tournament. The car ride home could take anywhere from 25 minutes to an hour and a half, depending on traffic. Pickard drove. In the car, Stefan couldn't stop thinking about how he'd lost his service game to Becker. Instead of 3–1, it was 2–2, and the match was back at square one. But he decided to laugh it off. It was what it was, and it'd be like they were starting a new match over.

When play resumed, Stefan didn't have the same nice touch he'd had in the first games. Boris kept plunging forward and won the first set. The German directed play in the second set, as well, but Edberg managed to hang on and force a tiebreak.

Stefan explains, "Matches can often turn after a successful game or a great shot. Suddenly, one of the players has flow and self-confidence, and things just roll on from there. It can be really small things that have a major impact on the play and the match. Now I'd had a bit of a tough time, but the tiebreak became my turning point. I've always liked to play tiebreaks. There's room to take some chances and I imagine that it's a good fit for my aggressive style of tennis, where I take the initiative."

Stefan won the tiebreak, and, in the third set, he showed off just that tactical attack tennis that he liked the best. He won the set, 6–4. Later, both when he played to get to match point and during the match point itself, he stood so close to the net that it looked as if he wanted to climb over on Becker's side. Edberg served, he was ahead 40–30 and 5–2, and followed up with a move to the net, as always. His first volley was nice but a little short, he got his racket on Becker's next shot, too, but wasn't able to put any pressure on the German. The third volley, a mishit off the frame, went straight up in the air and landed on the T between the service boxes. Edberg stood by the net like a gunslinger in a duel in a western movie, his opponent ten or twelve feet away from him. Becker smacked the ball, it's going straight toward Edberg's solar plexus, and then . . . It was caught by the net tape. Edberg fell backward as if he'd been knocked down. He glanced up toward the stands. He saw his dad applaud with a smile from ear to ear, he saw Annette who hadn't stopped biting her nails even if the match was over, and he saw Tony Pickard pull his trench coat waistband tighter and clench his arms in a victory gesture.

Players from Småland had now won all of the Grand Slam tournaments in 1988, and by year-end, both Wilander and Edberg had the chance to reach the top spot in the world rankings. Mats continued his rigid training routine and the relentless grinding work on his sliced backhand. It was clockwork. His old passing shots, the feared backhand, came out occasionally but vanished just as quickly. All his new training was focused on beating Ivan Lendl. At the U.S. Open, he'd have the chance, or the risk, to play him again, but for that to happen, Mats would have to reach the final.

The U.S. Open was something special. Borg had never won it, despite reaching four finals. Mats had lost in the final to Lendl the previous year. It was beginning to become a truth that the tennis Swedes couldn't handle the atmosphere in New York. The tournament wasn't as fun-loving as the

Australian Open, not as sexy as the French, not as picturesque and elegant as Wimbledon. New York was wild and loud, and if you didn't like it, you should just stay home. To find any form of inner peace in this environment, you had to embrace the chaos, learn to appreciate the screaming trinket vendors, and accept that the crowd watched the Jumbotron more than the court.

Mats felt that he could appreciate it all now. Although he and Sonya had relocated from Manhattan to Greenwich, Connecticut, New York was still close to being his hometown.

In the first round, Mats again faced Greg Holmes. This time, he won easily. Mats noticed a small man in the crowd who looked overjoyed every time Mats won a point. Mats had no clue who he was, but he kept glancing over at the man throughout the match and picked up on his energy. Mats decided to do the same thing the entire tournament—find a person in the crowd, someone who could infect him with their enthusiasm, someone for whom Mats could take that extra step.

In the second round, Mats was forced to an unnecessary five-setter by Kevin Curren, but after that, his way to the final became easier. There, on the other side of the net stood, as expected, Ivan Lendl. Everything was at stake: the U.S. Open title, the right to call yourself World Champion, and most important of all, the world number-one ranking.

For a long time, Ivan Lendl had been considered too weak to win a major title. Of his first seven Grand Slam finals, he won only one. Now, in 1988, these statistics were just a memory, and Lendl's psyche had long since caught up to his skills. Ivan Lendl had topped the world rankings for over three years, and Flushing Meadows was his living room. Lendl, who lived in the same area of Greenwich as Wilander, had won the last three U.S. Open tournaments and was about to play his seventh straight final. Rather than being mentally weak, he now seemed to be a man with an iron psyche.

Mats Wilander was confident in his basic strategy—to approach the net on Lendl's backhand. But he also knew that strategy is organic, it can change during a match and you have to be able to improvise. Strategy is to do things at the right time, and strategy is also to dare play to your opponent's strengths.

The match lasted almost five hours and became the longest Grand Slam final ever played. Wilander sliced his backhand and kept slicing his backhand, stubbornly and consistently. He went for the net, he put away volleys.

The only thing he didn't do was hit topspin backhands. Mats sweated and labored, just like Lendl. The crowd didn't have time to watch the large video screen; a gladiatorial game was taking place on the tennis court right in front of them.

Finally, Mats was one point away from fulfilling his dreams. And he was nervous. He didn't let on, but he was so nervous he was shaking.

"I was very confident in terms of deciding to play in a certain way. I believe that's the difference between those who win Grand Slam tournaments and those who don't. Once I'd decided, I was committed 100 percent. I didn't want to hit a forehand, I was too nervous for that. I didn't want to hit a short ball up the middle. I had to test him: 'Can you hit past me?' So, I went all in on a serve to his backhand. I didn't need to hit a super serve, but as strong as possible, and then come in as close as possible to the net. Once you've committed, you have to follow through with absolute conviction. I think that's the difference between players like Stefan, Björn, and myself compared to Nyström, for example, who was more talented but didn't win as much."

Lendl's backhand return went into the net: 6–4, 4–6, 6–3, 5–7, 6–4. Mats Wilander had reached the summit, he was the new world number one, and he screamed with joy. The court quickly filled up with press photographers. In the chaos, Mats spotted his dad in aviator glasses and a light blue shirt. He'd somehow made it down to the court and was standing in the midst of all the telephoto lenses with his small Instamatic camera lifted above his head. He was snapping photo after photo, with the same speed as the press photographers.

"It's one of my fondest memories," Wilander says. "My dad wasn't always around, but he was there when I won in Paris in 1982 and when I won the U.S. Open. There were at least 50 photographers on the court, there'd be an endless number of photos of me, and we could have bought whichever ones we wanted. But he wanted his own memories."

A long party in the New York night followed. Parents, girlfriends, wives, coaches, friends, hangers-on . . . The champagne was plentiful, Mats and Jonte hugged, and Keith Richards and Birgitta Sjögren sang "For He's a Jolly Good Fellow" together. The only person who didn't look entirely happy was Matt Doyle, the strength coach. He said: "Fucking Wimbledon. We should have won all four."

"I didn't understand where he was coming from," Wilander says. "This was my biggest win, I had won on all surfaces, won in Cincinnati and Key Biscayne, too. That is, five of the six biggest tournaments. All I wanted to do was go out and celebrate and party. I went almost straight from the bar to morning TV shows, Letterman, radio interviews . . . I was completely drained. The following week, I had a clay court tournament in Palermo. I went there because of the big guarantee-money, but I was still totally exhausted. I won the tournament anyway, because I was so strong. I beat Kent Carlsson in the final, and I attacked the net the entire match, a really stupid strategy. But I couldn't lose."

A CRACK IN THE FACADE

**"There was no way I was going to play that match.
I lived in America and could just escape there."**
—MATS WILANDER

During the '80s, to play the Davis Cup final had become as much of a recurring tradition for Swedish tennis players as celebrating Christmas. The loss to Australia in 1983 and the win over the US in 1984 were followed by another triumph the following year against West Germany.

In 1986, Australia became too difficult on its home court, and in 1987, Sweden won one of history's easiest Davis Cup finals ever, against India in Göteborg. The Swedish players would have won that final on any surface, and with ping-pong rackets as tools. The India team still comprised the same brothers Amritraj who led India to the 1974 Davis Cup final. They knew they were going to Göteborg only to act as extras to the Swedish stars. Still, to secure the victory lock, stock, and barrel, the Swedes again took on the tedious task of putting in a clay court at the Scandinavium arena.

Now it was 1988, the year was almost over, and the red clay had once again been spread out onto Scandinavium's floor. It was time for a new party—Sweden was the world's dominant tennis nation and would play in its sixth straight Davis Cup final, against West Germany. The captain Hasse Olsson said he counted on the victory being secured after two days of play.

Sweden had a rock-solid team. Mats Wilander was ranked number one following his three Grand Slam titles, Stefan Edberg was the reigning

Wimbledon champion, and Anders Järryd was considered the world's best doubles player. Should one of them sprain his ankle or come down with a cold, the rising clay court star, Kent Carlsson, ranked No. 6, was ready to jump in. Mikael Pernfors was part of the team, too, in the role of sparring partner. In 1988, he'd won his two first ATP titles, and he was currently ranked No. 19. The Davis Cup final was going to be the heroes' homecoming, a king's tour, and a rare opportunity for the Swedish people to get a close-up look of their favorite sons.

In the first match, Mats Wilander played Carl-Uwe Steeb, a twenty-one-year-old lefty ranked No. 74. The first set gave the spectators more drama than they'd wished for. Expecting to see Wilander toy with his opponent on his favorite surface, they instead saw a young German who put up a good fight. Wilander finally took the first set, 10–8. The second set ended according to plan, 6–1 Wilander.

But Mats felt insecure:

"I couldn't hit a topspin backhand for my life. I had gotten so used to the sliced backhand I'd been working on, and hitting the slice I used a completely different angle of the racket. I remember Jocke Nyström used to tell me in practice: 'How are you hitting, Mats? You've got to hit like this!' But I couldn't. I did pretty well with shots down the line, decent if I took the ball early. But cross court was impossible, and I wasn't able to drive the ball. Against Steeb, all I did was run and push the ball back in play. Although I had match point, it wasn't enough."

Steeb won the final three sets and took his career's biggest win in front of stunned Swedish tennis fans, who were drowned out by the loud German supporters who'd come to cheer on their countrymen in Göteborg. Before going home that evening, the crowd also saw a focused Boris Becker win over Stefan Edberg in three straight sets. The fans were stunned as they made their way home from the Scandinavium arena that evening, and so were the players, who now had to try to recharge their batteries.

On Saturday, the pattern from Wilander's match repeated itself. Järryd and Edberg won the two first sets in the doubles match comfortably, but Boris Becker and his unexperienced partner, Eric Jelen, turned the match around and won. The Davis Cup final was indeed over after two days, but with the wrong winner.

Becker and Jelen hugged, the beer flowed, and loud German fans celebrated while Järryd and Edberg sat silently on the Swedish side of the umpire's chair. Pernfors and Wilander stared with empty eyes, as hollow-eyed as the porcelain leopard that sat behind the Swedish bench. A porcelain leopard? Yes, an observant person would have been able to see signs early on that the Swedish players' concentration wasn't 100 percent focused on the task at hand.

The leopard had come home with Wilander and Pernfors from an evening out at a nightclub earlier in the week.

"We'd swiped it from there . . . or actually bought it," says Wilander. "We made a deal with the bar staff, we thought it would be a good mascot. That's kind of who we were back then. We were cool, we were young, happy, and we partied a lot. We must've thought it was a fun thing."

On Sunday, the crowd returned to the Scandinavium, since they'd already paid good money for their tickets. With the final already decided, Stefan Edberg won his match in two straight sets.

"It wasn't necessarily fun; we had a good team on paper and had been the favorites. At least I did my duty that day. But after that, things didn't really go well," says Stefan Edberg.

The other players gave the Scandinavium crowd the worst possible Christmas gift. Suddenly nobody wanted to play. Wilander, Kent Carlsson, and Järryd all came running to Hans Olsson with fresh doctor's notes from the team physician Bengt Åberg.

Anders Järryd winces at the memory:

"In hindsight, it was a fiasco. The youngest player would normally play the last match if it was meaningless, so we thought Kent should play, but he didn't want to, he had an injury. And the rest of us definitely didn't want to play. Sure, we'd been out the night before, but it wasn't just that. It was our egoistical brains speaking, and that was just damn stupid. If neither Kent nor Mats wanted to play, then I wasn't going to play, either. It became a matter of principle."

Mats Wilander says he didn't care. The others could resolve it however they wanted, but he wasn't going to go out and play a meaningless match.

"Everyone was over it. We'd been beaten. Why the hell were we going to play that match? Sure, a lot of people thought that Kent should play, but at the same time, you could see how his grueling style of play took years off his career every time he stepped out onto the court. His knees hurt. As for me, I suffered from shin splints and definitely didn't want to play. Sure, I'm a bit embarrassed by it now in hindsight. If the match hadn't been over, for sure

I would've played. But I was number one in the world, imagine how I felt about losing to Steeb! There was no way I was going to play that match. I lived in America and could just escape there. I didn't care. It was the same as always: I didn't give a shit what people thought. That was often a strength, but maybe not in this case."

Hans Olsson found himself in a dilemma he'd never experienced before and for which he wasn't prepared. Since 1982, his amicable personality had made sure that Swedish tennis players thought playing on the Davis Cup team was the ultimate fun. He was a good-natured uncle type, who made sure that everyone felt good. He wasn't one to use force, partly because it wasn't him and partly because it had never been necessary. In the Davis Cup team, codetermination and equality ruled. It was a very Swedish-type leadership, a leadership that around this time was manifested by Jan Carlzon, CEO of SAS and "SAS-Janne" with the Swedish people. He'd guided the Scandinavian airline out of a crisis and turned it into one of the world's most successful airlines, and he'd summarized his theories on leadership in the book *Moments of Truth*, which became a global success. He wrote about flat organizations, managers who delegated, and the importance of putting the customer first. The one thing that a flat organization requires is employees who are ready to assume responsibility themselves. Now here was Hasse Olsson, who'd often received praise for his fingertip touch in selecting the team, with a bunch of world-class tennis stars who refused to collaborate and didn't even for a second think about the customers sitting in the stands.

The manager took one for the team.

First, the Scandinavium's speaker announced that Mats Wilander, Kent Carlsson, and Anders Järryd, as well as the German Boris Becker, were all injured. He went on to say that the announced match between Wilander and Becker would now be replaced by an exhibition match between the Swedish backup player Mikael Pernfors and Germany's fourth man Patrick Kühnen. For the crowd, this was like having made reservations at a five-star restaurant only to be served a plastic-wrapped cheese sandwich. Thousands of spectators erupted in boos and whistles.

Someone handed Hans Olsson a microphone. He could barely open his mouth before the boos drowned out his voice. For two minutes, he stood there, alone, receiving the whistling from the cheated crowd, while at the same time trying to justify his decision. He assured the crowd that the players were indeed injured and pleaded with the fans to remember all the joy and pride the tennis stars had provided earlier in their careers.

The situation was painful for all involved.

Joakim Nyström was present in his role of sparring partner to the team. Today he says:

"These things happen, it happened to me once when I was coaching the Austrian Davis Cup team in 2012. You have to decide, two must play. As a manager you just point, or you demand that the players resolve it on their own. But Hasse was so kind, and he didn't do that. And, in a way, that became his downfall."

The players' images were stained, but like Wilander, they soon left Sweden to play new matches, new tournaments. Hasse Olsson, who'd led the tennis national team to three Davis Cup victories and six finals, and who'd received the TT News Agency's prestigious Coach of the Year award in 1985, was left in the homeland in the midst of the wave of criticism washing over him.

Even today, he claims he did the right thing, that he had no choice.

"There were doctor's notes saying they shouldn't play. How could I argue with that? If I had forced someone to play, whose injury had gotten worse and forced him to miss six months, then I'd receive even more criticism. The doctor's notes existed for a reason. I couldn't have acted differently. I followed the same principles I had when I was a school teacher, codetermination and agreement. We all have a responsibility. If you don't want to play or are injured, then that is a decision that the individual has to make.

"But being booed at the Scandinavium is my saddest memory as a coach. At the same time, I was the captain, so I guess it was right that I had to take responsibility and speak to the crowd."

To the press, Olsson explained that he had no plans to resign. Yet not long after the match, it was clear that his contract wouldn't be renewed at the end of the year. When Sweden lost the next year's Davis Cup final, again to Germany, John-Anders Sjögren was in the captain's seat.

Mats Wilander flew back home to America. Fate had it that he didn't make his scheduled flight's departure from London to New York. As a result, he wasn't on board the flight that exploded over Lockerbie, Scotland, in a terrorist attack that killed 270 people. Not until he landed at JFK and was met by the chaos there, the distraught people, the security guards did he learn what had happened.

"Sonya, my mom, and others had no idea what flight I'd taken. I booked my own flights, so I had to call my friends and family and tell them I was safe."

Life, and tennis, would go on. But what had really happened to Mats's tennis? Losses to Dan Goldie and Carl-Uwe Steeb? Could painful shin splints be the entire explanation?

In 1988, when Mats was at his best, one of his American tennis colleagues said: "The biggest weapon in today's tennis isn't Agassi's forehand, it's Mats Wilander's brain." The quote has been credited to both Brad Gilbert and Jay Berger. Mats himself believes it was Paul Annacone who said it first. Regardless, it summarizes Mats Wilander's tennis game well and is a good indication of how his opponents viewed him. But as early as fall 1988, it became obvious, especially to Mats himself, that his brain had begun thinking of other things.

"I couldn't tell anymore whether I played intelligently and tactically. I had suddenly lost that intensity, that total focus, which had made me have a purpose with each and every shot before. Now when I hit a shot, I didn't really know why I chose one stroke over the other. I still trained hard, physically I had no problems, I could run and I could battle, but the matches became more and more like tough practices."

Mats Wilander had counted on being one of the best players in the world longer. In 1987, when he decided to make a real and serious commitment to reach the number-one spot, he thought reaching the goal was two or three years into the future. When the reward came less than a year after his tough training began, he became indecisive.

"Occasionally, the intensity and killer instinct came back. Like it did against Nicklas Kulti at the Stockholm Open in the fall of 1988. He destroyed me in the first set and was ahead by 3–0 in the second. He was 18 years old, and I was the world's number one. I'd been at the Café Opera the night before and thought: *This isn't good.* That gave me a spark, and I managed to turn things around. But I still lost in the next round."

Mats took certain measures, attempted to make some changes. He broke off his collaboration with Matt Doyle ("I could no longer work with a person who complained that I didn't win Wimbledon when I'd just won three

Grand Slam tournaments"). Instead, he hired Joe Breedlove, who'd been Martina Navratilova's strength coach. Mats also threw away his Rossignol rackets and changed to Prince, hoping he'd get more power on his shots.

When the next tennis season started with the Australian Open, Mats's opponent was Ramesh Krishnan, a player with an exquisite ball touch who still usually came up short against the very best players.

Mats explains, "I really didn't like playing against Krishnan, he had a sickening style of play. He showed up at the wrong time in my career, with his low, sliced shots in the middle of the court, and it killed my spark. He beat me, and I'd had it with tennis."

The next morning, Mats, Sonya, and a friend left Melbourne. They rented a car and drove straight out into the wilderness toward Ayers Rock, a distance of more than 1,200 miles. For Mats, this was a perfect break from tennis, a chance to focus on other things. Also, it was a behavior that was made possible because the Swedish reporters didn't pay much attention to him.

"The very best thing about Stefan Edberg becoming a world-class player was that I didn't have to speak with the press after my losses. It was very rare that reporters had any questions after I'd lost, because Stefan had usually won and they'd rather speak with him. I never had to sit there and come up with explanations. And there were so many Swedes. Do you know how many Swedes played in the Australian Open that year, 1989? Fifteen! That's totally unheard of today. But it meant that nobody asked a lot of questions about what I was going to do.

Instead, Mats collected new experiences. Like staying overnight and buying meat and beer in William Creek, a village with a population of seven. Like suffering vertigo on Ayers Rock. Like seeing kangaroos jumping out right in front of the jeep.

Mats was waiting for his passion for tennis to return and continued to practice hard physically. But the list of anonymous players who easily advanced in tournaments at his expense continued to grow: Mikael Pernfors, Horst Skoff, Alex Antonitsch, Alberto Mancini . . . In early spring, he was beaten by the Italian Francesco Cancellotti, who after his victory commented: "The Wilander I beat today isn't the world's number-two player anymore. I didn't do anything to beat him, he just doesn't fight anymore. It looks like it doesn't matter whether he wins or loses. To see Wilander like this on the court isn't good for the sport."

Mats Wilander had always been a problem solver. On the tennis court, he was driven by the challenge to crack the code of the opponent across the net. Outside the court, it was the same. He'd sit in his hotel room and ponder Rubik's cube, he bought book after book of detective stories, whodunits, à la the board game Clue: "Officer Mustard, with his dagger, in the library." He'd read and solve the riddles on his flights.

Now, he found it boring to play when he was ahead, because there was no problem that needed solving. And then, when he let his focus go and allowed his opponent to catch up, there was obviously a problem to be solved, but by then his inspiration and energy had run out.

At Wimbledon, Mats showed some of his old game and temperament. He reached the quarterfinals and had McEnroe on the ropes but lost his grip.

In September, Mats's dad Einar was diagnosed with cancer. If Mats had had a difficult time focusing on his tennis before, after the diagnosis it became almost impossible.

The loss in the Davis Cup final to West Germany in 1988 damaged Swedish tennis. Perhaps not the loss itself, but it revealed diva behavior from the players, showed the weaknesses in Hans Olsson's leadership, and exposed cracks within the tennis association.

The only person who escaped unscathed from the debacle at the Scandinavium arena was Stefan Edberg. True to himself and to his principles, he hadn't caused any scenes. He'd been as disappointed as everyone else, but he'd played his meaningless match and won. Now he could prepare for 1989 without any skeletons in his closet.

At the same Australian Open where Wilander lost to Krishnan, it seemed at first as if Edberg might achieve greatness, but a back injury stopped him from playing the semifinal.

Instead, a healthy Stefan Edberg would show off his entire register in Paris later that spring. Aggressive serve-and-volley tennis often doesn't reap rewards on the slow clay, but it rarely looks as beautiful as it does there. Perhaps it is because the slower tempo gives the eye a chance to catch the grace and elegance in a net attack better than on a fast indoor surface or closely trimmed grass. Or perhaps it's the possibility of sliding to the ball that makes the volley game look smoother than elsewhere. Stefan Edberg was in excellent shape.

BJÖRN BORG AND THE SUPER-SWEDES

In the final, Stefan faced the surprise of the tournament, Michael Chang. Chang was a seventeen-year-old American with Chinese parents and a style of his own. He was a small, lightning-fast, and incredibly tenacious player, who always punished players whose game wasn't sharp enough. Pete Sampras, Andrei Chesnokov, and Ivan Lendl had all suffered that fate. In his match against Lendl, Chang confused the Czech by hitting underhand serves on important points.

Stefan knew what to expect; he'd already played Chang three times and lost their most recent match.

"For the crowd, it was an ideal matchup," says Edberg. "One player who attacks and one who runs, lobs, hits passing shots, and never quits. And hardly ever misses. To beat Michael Chang, you had to set your mind to accepting that it would take time. I'd have to outmaneuver him with patience and thinking. I didn't have the game of players like Becker and Sampras, who could just beat him up.

As the match begun, Edberg looked clumsy. He had a hard time finding his timing and sweet spot and lost the first set, 1–6. In the second set, he settled down on the court. Some fantastic points provided the final's best tennis, in which Stefan attacked behind his sliced backhands and Chang's ability to run down at least one more shot than expected on each point forced Stefan to find even more acute angles on his volleys. Stefan won the second set, 6–3, and went on to take the third by 6–4. When Edberg started out the fourth set by breaking the American junior's serve, he looked solid, aggressive, and confident. But just like Stefan already knew, Chang never quit, he never stopped running. Chang broke back and began to reap the benefits, even while Stefan kept attacking. In the third game, Chang trailed 15–40 in his own serve and saved a total of four break points. At 3–3, he came back from 0–40, thanks to unforced errors by Edberg. Then, Chang saved two more break points on his way to a 4–3 lead, and yet another break point in his next service game. Finally, Edberg hit a volley that found the net, and the fourth set went to Chang after Edberg missed ten chances to break the American's serve.

In the first game of the decisive set, Edberg was finally able to break the American's serve, but he couldn't maintain his advantage. Chang stepped into the court almost to the service box for his returns and returned Stefan's serves so fast that the Swede couldn't make it up to the net in time. Chang won the set by 6–2 and took home his career's only Grand Slam title.

Rarely has a runner-up looked as frustrated as Stefan did. The trophy should have been his. When Stefan reviewed the match stats, he noted that he converted only 6 out of 25 break points.

"Actually, I still wasn't overly disappointed after the match," says Stefan today. "I thought I'd done well on the clay, and I expected that the future would hold more French Open finals for me. Now that didn't happen, and that's why it's the one loss that, in hindsight, I regret the most. If I could replay one match in my career, that's the one. It'd actually be enough to replay one game, or even one single shot. That's how close I was."

The frustration for Stefan Edberg in the majors continued. At Wimbledon, Edberg and Becker again faced off in the final, but the drama from the year before was gone. Becker won in three quick sets in a match in which Edberg never seemed fully present. At the U.S. Open, Stefan lost in the quarterfinal to an inspired thirty-seven-year-old Jimmy Connors. When the Australian Open rolled around, Stefan skated elegantly through the tournament all the way up until he had to retire from the final against Ivan Lendl due to a pulled abdominal muscle.

Stefan Edberg had reached the final in the four most recent Grand Slam tournaments, but he'd come up short in all four. He needed to find his flow.

Following the Australian Open, Stefan had a decent spring and was, for the first time, seeded No. 1 at the French Open, where he lost immediately to Sergi Bruguera. It was a tough loss, but on the positive side, it gave Stefan plenty of time to prepare for Wimbledon.

Edberg says, "Wimbledon was still always number one. After Borg's victories, after my own title . . . it was always the most important tournament with the oldest traditions."

It was also a tournament where Stefan, who built his game and his life outside the court on familiar routines and habits, felt the most secure. The injuries that had plagued him—his back and abdominal area—affected his serve somewhat, but other things were in his favor. He could stay in his own home and, as the experienced Wimbledon player he'd become, he knew how he wanted things around his matches and workouts. He always used the same locker in the locker room, the same shower, the chair on the same side of the umpire during changeovers.

As soon as these arrangements were in place, it was as if his physical conditioning and big game automatically followed. Edberg's draw looked tough on paper, but he destroyed Chang in the round of 16, then made the process short with Christian Bergström in the quarterfinal. In the semifinals, Lendl waited. This year the Czech, who'd turned thirty, had been clear about his plans. His entire annual planning was aimed at filling the only gap (Wimbledon) in his otherwise fantastic track record. Lendl had skipped Paris to have more time to fine-tune his tools on grass. He'd changed rackets, and, in the warm-up tournament at Queens, he defeated both McEnroe and Becker on grass for the first time on his would-be road to fulfilling his goal. Now he was two matches away from finally winning Wimbledon.

He barely made it out onto the court before he was forced to leave it. Edberg pulverized him, 6–1, 7–6, 6–3. As a result, it was time for something that had never happened before: the same pair of players appearing in the final for the third straight year.

As Edberg explains, "Becker and I had played each other a lot, and our careers had been progressing in parallel since we were juniors. I became known as the world's best junior, he won Wimbledon, I won the Australian Open. . . . I think we both glanced over our shoulder to see what the other was doing, and we both strove to become number one. He was fiery and I was calm. It was a rivalry that was good both for tennis and for us as players."

Early in the match, Stefan Edberg played masterfully. He floated up to the net, his wrist a shock absorber for Becker's tough passing shot attempts.

"The way I played then, it felt as if the match would be over after an hour and a half," Edberg said. "Then things changed. I began playing worse, and Boris won the third and fourth sets. But before the fifth, I was very focused and decided I'd look at it as a new match."

Stefan took the initiative but lost his serve to fall behind 1–3 after suddenly making two bad double faults.

"It was a breezy day, and it didn't take much for things to go wrong," he recalls. "I remember I got really annoyed with myself. But again, matches can turn on a single mistake. Boris hit an easy forehand volley out and I could break back. That reenergized me."

To win the match, one more service break was required for either player. Edberg was the one who capitalized. With his natural and easy backhand, which had so enamored Percy Rosberg and which Stefan, 25 years later, believes is sharper than Roger Federer's, he outplayed Becker. First, he whipped in an unplayable service return. Then, under stress and with Becker at the net, Edberg chose the loveliest of strokes, a completely unexpected backhand lob that sailed high above Becker's head and landed well inside the baseline. In the final game, Edberg served with new balls. On the last serve of the tournament, Becker misfired his shot off the frame of his racket. It sailed high and lopsided. Stefan danced along with it, his hands already halfway up in the air as he watched it land in the doubles alley. He was a two-time Wimbledon champion.

In August, Stefan won against Michael Chang again, this time in the quarterfinal in Cincinnati. Consequently, he reached the number-one spot in the world rankings for the first time. He would remain there until year-end. Stefan Edberg had played twelve finals in the year and won seven. And he'd done it with elegance, efficiency, fighting spirit, and sportsmanship.

Still, when the news agency United Press International selected Stefan as Athlete of the Year, a title that had previously been awarded stars like Muhammad Ali, Sebastian Coe, and Diego Maradona, Sweden was caught by surprise.

The news reports at home had been dominated by Nelson Mandela's release from prison, Germany's reunion, the start of the TV4 channel, and the fact that Christer Pettersson received 300,000 kronor in damages—matching what Christian Bergström earned for his place in the Wimbledon quarterfinals—for his arrest in the connection with Olof Palme's murder. The sports fans had new heroes, including the players on the national hand-ball team, who won the *Jerring Award,* elected by listeners to Swedish Radio's sports programs. Edberg had received *Svenska Dagbladet's Bragdmedaljen* award for best sports achievement of the year, but that was in a domestic context. For Edberg to be the best in the world? Even for proud Swedes, he was a bit too bland, too vanilla, to be considered a superstar athlete. At the same time, there were signs that the interest in tennis had started to wane. Perhaps Sweden had begun taking the triumphs for granted? Maybe it wasn't as much fun when Stefan Edberg was all alone among the world's best. Joakim Nyström suffered from knee issues and had more or less fin-ished his career, as had Henrik Sundström. Anders Järryd focused more and more on playing doubles. Jonas Svensson had had a good season, but still not good enough to finish the year among the world's Top 10, which was the harsh standard by which Swedish tennis players were now being measured.

And the Davis Cup team had been eliminated from the tournament in the first round.

BJÖRN BORG AND THE SUPER-SWEDES

Only two years after his phenomenal 1988, Mats Wilander had plummeted to number 41 in the world rankings.

"That whole year I struggled with my dad's cancer," says Mats. "My dad passed away in May 1990. I had some good results, but I played without intensity. I was a completely different person. I did beat Becker at the 1990 Australian Open, where I played in a hat with a skull pattern. It was terribly symbolic, although I didn't realize it at the time. All those phone calls back home to my dad. . . . To have a dad who's so impressed by your achievements, that hole, you can never fill it, I learned that later. I realized I'd been playing for him. There was no way for me to regain the same motivation I had before."

Mats had squeezed the most out of his talent. Early on, he was seen as a baseline player, who just hit the ball back and mostly bored his opponents to death. But at his peak in 1988, he'd developed into one of the most all-around players the tennis tour had ever seen. He still didn't possess any spectacular winning weapons, but he also didn't have one particular weakness. His career counts seven Grand Slam titles. That's as many as John McEnroe, who is considered one of the most brilliant geniuses who ever set foot on a tennis court. Mats could quit tennis with a good conscience.

In November 1990, Mats won his last tournament, in Itaparica, Brazil. In the final, he defeated Marcelo Filippini from Uruguay. Then he took a time-out.

He explains, "I didn't play between the summer of 1991 and the summer of 1993. Instead of tennis, I'd decided to play a lot of music. A truck came to our house in Greenwich and dumped a bunch of concrete beams in our yard. Together with my buddies, I built a music studio. John Oates spent a lot of time there and helped me out, he played some tennis and we'd become friends. My thoughts were in the music studio back then, not on the tennis court. Evenings and nights, we rehearsed and recorded songs. During the day we played golf."

Mats Wilander wrote music and embarked on a tour playing outdoor venues in Sweden in the summer. With a serious, Dylan-inspired voice, he sang boyhood rhymes about his doubts on life and love. He played with Ulf Lundell's guitarist, Janne Bark, had an affair with one of the backup girls, returned to America, and began playing some tennis again.

"It might sound funny now, in hindsight, but I thought I was serious about my music, it was a big deal to me," he says. "And when you're the number one in the world at tennis, doors open that make it possible for you to go out on tour with professional musicians. Why would I say no to that? It's the same thing with the poems I read on *Good Morning Sweden* in 1985. I knew the host of the program, Fredrik Belfrage, we used to play charity golf together. He'd heard that I wrote poems and asked if I wanted to read them on TV. Why not? I don't care a lot about what people think. I think I'm the only one who was on the show three times when Filip Hammar and Fredrik Wikingsson did *Sweden's Funniest Moments*. You have to give a little.

He played a bit of tennis again in 1993 and started to climb slowly from his ranking around the 500 spot. He played throughout 1994 but was far removed from the results with which he'd spoiled the public. In 1995, things were going better, until Mats and his doubles partner, Karel Nováček, were caught in a doping control at the French Open when traces of cocaine were found in their urine samples. They were suspended for a month, while concurrently initiating a complex appeals process to clear their names.

"The urine samples had been sitting completely out in the open in the room where we were sitting, and there were a lot people running around," says Wilander. "When we spoke with our attorneys, they reviewed exactly and in detail how the testing had been conducted and encouraged us to appeal. But of course, Karel and I knew what we'd done. We got caught, and you learn not to do stupid things at the wrong time. When you make mistakes, you regret it like crazy, but I also don't want my mistakes undone. They're a part of life. Some people supported me, they were the ones who knew me best, who knew that 'this is Mats, he takes chances.' That's the part of me who's an adventurer, the lover of life."

In hindsight, Mats has mixed feelings about the bumpy conclusion of his career. His last really good year was 1988, but he kept his career going until 1996. He played his last Davis Cup match in 1995.

Mats says, "Really, I was in the process of quitting every week during those years. I played almost exclusively in North America. In the summer of 1995, a buddy and I jumped into my 1967 Buick, put Bob Dylan's "Oh Mercy" on the stereo, and drove all the way to Montreal. I beat Edberg, [Wayne] Ferreira, and [Yevgeny] Kafelnikov but lost to Agassi in the semis. So, I could still get good results. After Montreal, we drove to New Haven, where I reached the semifinals again, then to the U.S. Open. . . . I think I was up to 41 in the rankings at best. In fact, that was a bigger achievement than becoming the world's number one, if you consider how little I trained and how the game had changed during those years. But those were some messy years. I played rock and roll, I fought with my wife, we broke up, got back together . . ."

After a loss to the Brazilian Fernando Meligeni in Pinehurst, North Carolina, Mats had finally had enough.

"I realized that if I can't take more than three games from Meligeni, then it's time to quit. I had a wife and two kids, and it became harder and harder to roam around like that. I could've quit earlier, but on the other hand—the memories from the car rides in the Buick are as nice as the memories from when I was at the top of my career."

While Mats Wilander played rock star in 1991, Stefan Edberg played tennis and finished yet another year as the world's number one. He started his season well and finished it brilliantly. At Wimbledon, he racked up wins with efficient play until the second set in his semifinal against the German Michael Stich, where his streak ended. Without Edberg losing his serve a single time, the German won the match by a score of 4–6, 7–6, 7–6, 7–6.

Edberg explains the oddity of the match, "I guess everyone's career will include a strange match, it's just too bad it had to happen at Wimbledon for me. Otherwise, Becker and I'd have played our fourth straight Wimbledon final. This was Stich's year, and he won his only Grand Slam title after he went on to defeat Boris. It was the same thing with Chang at the French Open in 1989, it was his only win, too. I crossed paths with them that very year. But my confidence was still strong. At the U.S. Open, everything came together, it was all so incredibly easy."

In the final at Flushing Meadows, the arena in which Edberg hadn't won before, he outperformed the hard-hitting home player Jim Courier, 6–2, 6–4, 6–0. "I know it's a great day when I see Stefan floating above the court like that," said Tony Pickard.

After the final, the world's top tennis player noted: "It's the best match I've ever played. Everything worked like a dream."

Or, like the journalist Alison Muscatine once wrote in the *Washington Post*: "There is nothing more beautiful or more breathtaking than Stefan Edberg's tennis game when he is on. Every stroke is poetic, every movement lyrical."

ARTIST IN A HAIRSHIRT

"Your body language is so bad. It affects your game. You won't win any matches if you look like that out on the court."
—TONY PICKARD

In 1991, Stefan Edberg's game had such appeal and seemed so superior that tennis experts were convinced nobody would manage to knock him off the tennis throne anytime soon. "We'll need to get used to Edberg as the number-one player; he'll probably remain on top for a long time," predicted Arthur Ashe in the *New York Times*, when it was clear that Stefan would accomplish what only Connors, Borg, McEnroe, and Lendl had done since the ranking system was introduced: be the best in the world two years in a row.

Meanwhile, no tennis player was as misunderstood as Edberg. People still said he wasn't a fighter. The fact that he'd won two Wimbledon titles after coming back from difficult deficits didn't change anything in that respect. Nor did the knowledge that Stefan's climb to the number-one spot in the world rankings in 1990 and 1991 was preceded by a back injury, or that a Swedish audience of millions had watched on television as he'd secured Sweden's advancing in the Davis Cup by coming back from a 0–2 deficit in sets and winning the fifth set by 9–7 against the tough opponent Miloslav Mecir.

Edberg was a role model in other areas. He won the ATP's award for best conduct and highest level of professionalism and integrity on the tour so many years that the award was renamed—and is still called—the Stefan Edberg Sportsmanship Award. But the stubborn notion remained. Edberg wasn't a fighter. This was obvious from his demeanor on the court. It was a known fact because he was timid and reserved. Those aren't signs of a fighter.

It was said that Edberg survived on talent. And in 1992, talent matched up poorly to raw strength.

At the Australian Open, Edberg lost to Jim Courier in the final. As a result, he also lost his number-one ranking. The inclination that the Swede would have a hard time regaining the top spot was reinforced when Courier, wearing a baseball cap and with his warrior instincts, also won in Paris in June. Courier was a player cut from a different cloth from Stefan. He made his living taking hits. He stood feet wide apart on the court and kept the ball in play with his weak backhand, convinced that he could run around it at any time to blast a hard inside-out forehand, clench an arrogant fist toward his opponent, and get a mental advantage over his opponent. Courier had been drilled at Nick Bollettieri's Tennis Academy, where players learned to play close to the baseline and take balls early. That made life hell for serve-and-volley players, who could barely make it halfway to the net before their opponent's shot swished past them.

If Courier was Bollettieri's most successful protégé in terms of major titles around this time, Andre Agassi was the greatest talent. Agassi had previously had difficulties winning the major finals, but at Wimbledon in 1992, he played an almost fairy tale–like tennis from the baseline and never gave Becker in the quarterfinal, McEnroe in the semifinal, or Ivanisevic in the final a chance to win. As a result, everyone now believed that Agassi was ready, along with his countrymen Courier, Sampras, and Chang, to make the major tennis titles an all-American affair for the foreseeable future. The new-generation American tennis players hit harder than anyone else. And they were tougher, filled with tons of fighting spirit.

Stefan had lost to the "serve robot" Ivanisevic in Wimbledon's quarterfinals and hadn't even looked disappointed. It was as if he'd accepted the state of affairs. Shortly thereafter, he carried the Swedish flag at the Olympic Games in Barcelona; he was still Sweden's biggest sports star. But just a few days later, he left the Olympic Village after having been eliminated early. There were signs that his greatest achievements were behind him. He was already one of the oldest players among the world's best, although he was only twenty-six.

After Wimbledon and the Olympics, he faced renewed criticism for slumping his shoulders and hanging his head when things were tough. He didn't argue but said: "If I win the U.S. Open, it'll save my year."

That statement breathed a defiant hope and indicated that Edberg still believed he was good enough to compete with the new Americans, that he could peak anytime. But that was the crux of the matter—Edberg had to "peak," find that big game that enabled him to dictate the pace in matches. And even if he did, there was a big chance that, sooner or later, he'd find himself in trouble against one of the hard-hitting young players, and fold mentally. That's how quickly the perception had changed of a player who, the year before, had seemed nearly unbeatable.

Edberg prepared in the same way as the year before. To get away from everything he didn't like about New York City—the noise, the traffic, the stench of garbage and hot dogs—he settled into a house out on Long Island, from where he could easily drive his rental car to Flushing Meadows. The home was in Edberg's taste: modern and well equipped, but not over the top. Just a nice, appropriate place where he could be left alone.

The first week, his coach Tony Pickard stayed with him there. He remembers that the lousy year was in the back of his player's mind.

Pickard says, "Once we got there, we decided to focus on the things that weren't working. We increased practice time, and I talked to him about his attitude. What I constantly kept telling him was: 'Your body language is so bad. It affects your game. You won't win any matches if you look like that out on the court.'"

Those slumping shoulders and the surly grimaces he made every time he missed a shot, which made it look as if Stefan had been forced out on the court against his will, that all had to go.

"My response was always the same," says Stefan. "That I was too focused to walk around and look happy when I'd missed a shot. That I looked sad because I was sad, because I thought I should've made the shot, because those were my true feelings, because I didn't engage in things like fist clenching. That just felt unnatural. But that summer I agreed, Tony had a point."

But it wasn't just Stefan's body language that was lacking.

"The fact that I played worse during large parts of 1992 had to do with my serve. I'd had quite a few back injuries and so I had to change my serve, and it lost some of the impact it had up to 1990. I couldn't hit my kick serve as well, I couldn't generate the same torque as before. If you lose 10 percent of your serve, that's huge. If you take away a weapon like that, of course it makes a difference."

Tony Pickard didn't agree then, and he doesn't agree more than 20 years later:

"Stefan thought that his serve didn't bite like before, but this is typical for tennis players, they're anxious souls. There was nothing wrong with his serve, it was still one of the best. He'd changed his grip on the volley, too, which I suddenly discovered as I was watching a video clip. 'I want to get more pace on the volley,' he said. 'But all you do is push it into the net. Change it back,' I said."

Sometimes tennis isn't more complicated than that.

Stefan's results were good in the warm-up tournaments, and he felt that his peak might still be on its way. Once the U.S. Open started, Annette arrived, and Pickard moved out of the house and to Manhattan. The tennis elite that had gathered in New York late that summer included the usual suspects, but the appearance of many had evolved. Ten months earlier, Nirvana's "Smells Like Teen Spririt" had established grunge as a concept. There were distorted guitars, lyrics about frustration and angst, and a more bohemian style with checkered flannel shirts, long hair, and clunky boots. Tennis had always had its fill of frustration and angst, and now the clothing style became looser, the shirts more shapeless, and the headbands replaced by baseball caps.

However, Stefan Edberg still dressed in the classic style—tight shorts and a white shirt. He entered the tournament at lunchtime on Wednesday September 1, 1992, in the cool sunshine at the Louis Armstrong Stadium. At the players' entrance, the garbage cans of yesterday reeked. There was already action in the stands. The people in the stands talked, laughed, nibbled on sandwiches and snacks. Someone yelled for a hot dog, the vendor opened his tray, and the fumes traveled with the lively breezes out over the court, making Stefan grimace. A jumbo jet took off into the sky from La Guardia Airport, the black smoke coloring the sky, the noise deafening the air.

As always, the U.S. Open was a different animal from Wimbledon. The U.S. Open was the tournament where the forty-year-old Connors and thirty-three-year-old McEnroe still personified the very idea of what a tennis player should be: someone who spit, screamed, and fought with their heart on their sleeve, who shared everything with the crowd, match after match, year after year. Edberg had never been like that. He was the reigning champ, but there was still something confused and lost about his demeanor as he made it through his first match in three straight sets, against the Brazilian Luiz Mattar.

"The court felt so big, I'd forgotten how big it is here, I felt insecure," he admitted in his press conference afterward, where he also noted that he didn't see any Swedish reporters. In the '80s, the relationship between the Swedish newspaper reporters and the tennis stars had been so close that the reporters could have acted as ball boys during the players' practices, or played a game of their own on the court next to the Davis Cup stars. As recently as four years earlier, Swedish reporters would fill half of the press room as they followed Mats Wilander's victories. Now it seemed that era was long gone and tennis was no longer first priority for the Swedish scribes.

In their absence, the room was dominated by American journalists who wanted to hear Stefan's opinion on Courier, Sampras, Agassi, Connors, McEnroe, and Chang. And they wanted Stefan to share his thoughts on New York. They worked hard to get the tough statements and had a difficult time hiding their feelings when they failed. Edberg had nothing to say. He didn't want to be in the spotlight, he wanted to operate undercover, follow his old routines.

In the evenings, Stefan and Annette would eat a pasta dinner, then go to bed early, wake up early, take a quick walk, have breakfast—juice, milk and cereal, ham sandwiches—read the newspaper. Stefan looked for reports on his own matches, but they rarely extended beyond a few lines.

The tennis articles were about other things, like New York's mayor David Dinkins's hope for a nostalgic dream final between Connors and McEnroe. Or that Henry Kissinger, OJ Simpson, and Barbara Streisand had been in the stands for Agassi's evening match, where Streisand had taken the opportunity to discuss politics; she was going to support Bill Clinton in the presidential election later in the fall, because the country needed something new, and because the homeless in New York were a disgrace for all. The singer and actress also addressed questions about the rumors circulating that she was in a love relationship with the 28-years-younger Agassi. "He's very intelligent, very sensitive, very developed, much more than his linear years," she said. "He's a very special human being. He plays like a Zen master." Could a Zen master be the future of tennis? Agassi could certainly entertain the crowd, and he was in great shape, just like Courier and Sampras.

When the first two rounds had been completed, first impressions held true, wrote the *New York Times*. The tournament had all the ingredients to be the culmination of a fantastic American tennis year.

Out on the practice court, Pickard continued to encourage Stefan. "The new guys hit hard, but you're still a better tennis player."

The 1992 U.S. Open was the tournament when epochs converged, when extremely successful and long careers overlapped. Of the Open Tennis Era's ten biggest names from the early '70s to the millennium, only two were missing: Björn Borg and Mats Wilander. Lendl would play Connors on the American's 40th birthday, as early as in the second round, which was a replay of two straight finals a decade earlier between two of the sport's greatest players. The match schedule was so packed with high-profile matches that Boris Becker was banished to a distant outside court without real bleachers, where the frustrated world's No. 7 player lost the first set and spewed his disgust with the court, his conditioning, his lost status, and the shots that didn't land where he wanted. "This makes me sick!" he screamed after missing a forehand.

Almost all the stars had issues. The record crowds witnessed Sampras get in trouble in two straight matches. They saw Courier lose sets in all three of his first matches and saw Chang survive long battles, thanks to his fitness. Only Agassi seemed undeterred by earthly matters. He was never close to losing a set.

The atmosphere at the evening matches was completely different from that of the day sessions. The nights with their sold-out crowds were tense and magical. On Saturday, McEnroe performed magic with his racket like back in the good old days, in the dark and under the lights. Every one of his strokes was met by silenced captivation, every won game by deafening ovations; the meeting of the city's own son and the crowd was passionate. And McEnroe said he was ready for the next duel, ready to take on Courier in the round of 16. The 20,000 people in the stands were ready to carry him to a miracle.

But they couldn't do it. The old champ had no chance against the new world No. 1 as he kept blasting his forehand strokes past the thirty-three-year-old, who after the match confirmed that his singles career was over. "Is McEnroe's game obsolete?" a reporter asked Courier after the match. Courier didn't dare to respond.

In light of all this, Stefan Edberg was able to advance through the draw without anyone taking much notice. As for Stefan himself, he thought his game felt good, but a real test waited in the fourth round: the Dutchman Richard Krajicek. They'd played each other twice before, and both times the hard-hitting Krajicek had proven too much for Stefan. Even so, he told himself that now, in a major tournament, some factors were to his advantage. Like, the match might go to five sets, and he was the experienced one.

And for a while, it looked like Edberg's journey to the quarterfinal would be an easy one. But as he was about to finish out the match, he suddenly lost his serve and his game. Krajicek went on to win five straight games, evening the score at 2–2. There was to be a fifth set, a fifth hour of tennis. Earlier in the year, it was in these moments that Stefan had faltered. He hadn't had the stamina or hadn't been able to stage a comeback, or even showed that he wanted to. Now this pattern looked to repeat itself. In the decisive set, the Dutchman immediately broke Stefan's serve and grabbed a 3–1 lead. Krajicek's serve missiles were unreturnable. Edberg was on his way out of the tournament against just the type of player he disliked playing so much, those who never gave you a chance to play for the point.

But then Stefan won two points and clenched his fist in a gesture that showed he was still going to give it his all. In an instant, the Swedish world No. 2 had won the support of 20,000 fans, who were ready to give it their all, too, to help him turn the match around. The young Dutchman looked confused.

At 30-all and a lead of 3–2, Krajicek was in position to hit an easy shot, a high volley he only needed to put away, but he missed it. Stefan had been gifted a free break point. Krajicek blasted a missile serve way out to Edberg's backhand side. Edberg virtually jumped after the ball, reaching out with his racket and body as far as possible, and made a reflex save. A soft, high return that got caught in the wind, it took a funny arch and sailed over his opponent—who turned around, convinced that the ball was going out—and finally landed four inches inside the baseline. The crowd screamed. Stefan was back in the match.

A few games later, the arena went dead silent again. Edberg was one point away from losing his serve to 4–5, which would have given Krajicek the chance to serve home the match. Edberg breathed in. And missed his first serve. He hit a soft second serve. Krajicek slapped a good and clean hit with his forehand, an outright winner down the line—alas, half an inch out. Stefan breathed out, was able to hold his serve, and then broke Krajicek's serve, carried by sheer momentum. Suddenly he'd won and was through to the quarterfinal. The crowd cheered one of the world's most elegant players, who had now also fought and battled and shown his emotions. He'd played with a pounding heart on his sleeve.

At the press conference, Stefan said: "When you push yourself for four hours, you always feel much better the next day, even if you're a bit drained. You feel that you really hit the ball well. I'm sure that's how I'll feel tomorrow. You need these victories, because it's not at all like practicing for four hours. This was equal to 20–30 hours of training."

Meanwhile, the quarterfinals in the upper half were being decided. Sampras crushed Volkov, but all eyes were on the upcoming evening match between Courier and Agassi. When the two players, each wearing a baseball cap, came out on the court, the atmosphere was like that of a heavyweight boxing match. Most fans rooted for Agassi, but Courier was better at focusing. He clenched his fist at his opponent after winning important points and won the match in four sets. The new world No. 1 looked increasingly like the final winner.

For Stefan, Lendl awaited in the quarterfinal. Just a few weeks earlier, Stefan had been staying and training with Ivan at his huge residence in Connecticut. At Flushing Meadows, they continued to practice together. Unlike Wilander, Connors, McEnroe, and a lot of other players on the tour, Stefan didn't mind spending time with Lendl, who'd just become an American citizen.

"I'm a person who has a hard time really disliking others," says Stefan. You must allow for personality differences, so I had no problem with Ivan. "I trained with him a bit, because he's such a professional. You have to take Ivan for what he is. He has lots of good sides and some that aren't so good. He stands up for what's right and wrong, it's a lot of black and white with him."

Both were friends of order, dependent on order. Stefan needs routines to function; he washes his cup as soon as he's finished his coffee. At Lendl's house, rackets hung in straight lines in a separate room, where his tennis shoes were also stored in tidy rows.

Edberg said, "I only saw advantages to training with Lendl, because he hit the ball so hard. As a result, it didn't seem as if others did. He usually wanted to practice early in the morning, and I preferred to practice on center court. That worked out well, because early in the day, the center court was usually available."

But now it was about competitive match play. Stefan knew that the key to the outcome of the match lay within himself. The only thing that distracted from his relative optimism was that his quarterfinal was scheduled for the evening session. Stefan didn't find that ideal in any way. He knew that his kick serves had a better bite in the daytime heat than in the evening cool, and that the rowdy environment during evening matches had the potential of unsettling him. Playing under the lights made it more difficult to see the ball at net. It made the volley game—his signum—more difficult.

Starting things out, Stefan played his best tennis of the year. The first and second set were quick. Edberg lost the third set but took command of the fourth, and with the help of a couple of exquisite backhand passing shots, he earned himself four match points. On the first two, all Stefan needed to do was place easy forehands in a nearly abandoned half of the court, but both shots ended up in the net. With two aces, Lendl turned things around and forced a fifth set.

A quick glance at Stefan Edberg's face was enough to see that he was close to falling into that sour, grumpy mood that Tony Pickard wanted him to stay away from at all costs. It was close to eleven at night; Edberg was tired and had just wasted the opportunity for a good night's sleep. Instead, he now had to labor through another five-setter.

For Ivan Lendl, the situation was quite the opposite. Until now, the crowd had been on Stefan's side, but the four saved match points from Lendl showed a man about to escape from the Swede's grip, a fighting underdog the crowd wanted to support. As the players walked to their seats to catch their breath before the final set, the crowd gave Lendl a standing ovation, chanting his name.

In the fifth set, Stefan matched Lendl game for game, but the general feeling was that he was on his way to losing the match. Then came the rain.

"All we could do was pack it in and call it a day," Stefan says. "I was annoyed with having missed an opportunity, but I also thought that continuing in the daylight, with new conditions, could favor me. When we drove home in the dark, I thought of my missed chances—and began laughing. I thought to myself: *It is what it is. This is my match.* I slept well that night."

In the bright morning sunshine, the players picked up from where they'd left off. They were tired, but Edberg looked stoked. He spurred himself on, clenched his fist, jumped around between points.

The CBS commentator noted the Swede's mood. "It's been talked about so much and for so long how Stefan hangs his head when things are tough, that he looks like a sad puppy. But this is a different Stefan, now he's showing that he's mature, not just an elegant fair-weather player.

With the score 2–2 in the final set's tiebreak, Stefan got a lucky net cord. He stopped where he was, chuckled, bent down, and kissed the net. On match point, a stiff and immobile Lendl managed only to get the frame of his racket on a deep shot from Edberg, and the ball ricocheted into the stands. Edberg skipped over the net and patted Lendl's back in a friendly embrace. He got a massage, took a hot shower, and went home to prepare for the next day's match against Michael Chang, which promised to be even tougher.

Once again, Stefan went to bed early, woke up early, arrived at the court early. The semifinal started just after 11 a.m. It wasn't over until 5:30 p.m. Each point with Chang tended to be long.

Chang was often described as a fanatic. He was deeply religious, and several players were annoyed that he thanked God after his wins. Actually, they were probably more annoyed with the fact that he ran down every single ball, even the ones that looked impossible. If Edberg hit a mediocre overhead, Chang was there, took the ball on the rise, and steered it past Stefan. Chang always punished those who weren't sufficiently sharp. This will make anyone nervous, the kind of opponent who forces you to play flawlessly.

And Stefan didn't play flawlessly. He missed a series of easy shots and lost the first set. He couldn't seem to hold his serve but managed to break Chang's serve just as often and so was able to take both the second and third sets by the smallest of margins. In the fifth set, Chang went up, 3–0. Chang was Stefan's junior by eight years and had played fewer hours of tennis on his road to the semifinal. When the match reached its fifth hour, there weren't many signs that pointed to the reigning title holder.

It was already after 11 p.m. in Sweden. The match was available to households that had TV3, a cable channel, but most tennis enthusiasts had to rely on Swedish Radio, which had finally sent a reporter to New York who would provide a short summary report on the P3 radio station. When Gunnar Brink, the reporter from Swedish Radio's sports desk, went on air following the news, he reported that Stefan was trailing, 0–3 and 15–30 and probably would be eliminated from the tournament shortly.

Just as Chang was getting ready to finish things off, Edberg turned to his last weapon, the only one he knew: his volley. Two spectacular volleys helped him stay in the match, and suddenly, when he most needed it, he began serving aces out of reach for Chang. That was enough to turn the match around. On TV3, John-Anders Sjögren commented that he'd never seen Stefan serve better. The 20 double faults Stefan hit in the first half of the match were all but forgotten.

Stefan Edberg had reached his second straight U.S. Open final. There was only one problem.

He was dead tired.

Pickard tried to convince him that the fatigue was nothing to worry about: "When you win, you feel nothing. If you've made it through this kind of battle and won, all the fatigue will be gone."

But the fact remained: Stefan had played five-set matches in the round of 16, the quarterfinal, and the semifinal. He'd trailed a break in the fifth set against all his opponents. He'd played more tennis on the road to a Grand Slam final than any other player since the early '50s.

He says, "I could tell when I woke up in the morning of the final. I barely made it out of bed. And the morning walk, with some easy jogging thrown in, was almost impossible. Every single joint and muscle in my body ached. That I was going to play a final around 4 that afternoon seemed like a bad joke."

He didn't even want to think about the fact that his opponent was going to be Pete Sampras, who'd beaten Courier easily despite suffering from acute stomach ailments late in the match.

After his morning walk, Stefan read the *New York Times*, which on its front page that morning ran a story about a young man who'd been camping out in the Alaskan wilderness, got lost, couldn't find any food, and finally laid himself down with a tape recorder he'd carried with him and recorded his thoughts about his inevitable and imminent death. Stefan himself was going to venture out in the wilderness, too; millions of viewers were going to see him die an inescapable tennis death against one of the greatest prodigies he'd ever met, a player who had a serve that would surely just whiz past him.

He describes his warm-up that day: "I was hitting the ball terribly and I hurt everywhere. I felt like this wasn't going to work. But somehow your body and your brain get ready for the match anyway; there is a clock that tells your body it's time."

As the match started out, Stefan wasn't even close to touching Sampras's serve.

"I told myself: *You played for five hours yesterday, don't expect too much today. Just try to have some fun and do what you can.* I also thought about Sampras's situation. He was full of self-confidence. But when you've won as many matches as he had, you've almost forgotten how it feels to lose. All it takes is that little things begin to go wrong for everything to go wrong."

In the second set, Edberg's body began to awaken, and the Swede managed to even the match. The third set became key. Sampras served for the set but faltered, and when Edberg went on to win the tiebreak, Sampras's spirit was broken. Just over half an hour later, Stefan converted on match point, jumped over the net, embraced his opponent, jogged up to the seats, hugged Annette, and received a hug from Pickard.

It was a great victory. Not the prettiest, but the greatest in Stefan's career. The journalist Bernie Lincicome of the *Chicago Tribune* told it best the next day, under the headline A ROBOT JOINS THE HUMAN RACE: "Stefan Edberg looks better with callouses. He not only won his second straight U.S. Open tennis championship Sunday, but gained lasting definition as well. He has been the blankest of recent male champions, as impeccable as porcelain, as incendiary as chalk. And now he is one of us, capable of butchering the easy volley, perfectly able to throw one double fault on top of another. In one tough, seemingly endless tennis tournament, Edberg has shown us more about himself than he could, or would, ever tell, a survivor who can take a punch, go the distance, and overcome his own inadequacies, something that had not come up before."

It is clear in hindsight that no tennis tournament, either before or after, has had a comparable player lineup. In many ways, the 1992 U.S. Open was the tournament of the century, and Stefan Edberg won it. No one could ever again accuse him of lacking a fighter's heart.

Stefan's victory came days before Sweden was hit with a financial crisis that culminated with Sweden's central bank, *Riksbanken*, raising the prime rate by a shocking 500 percent. The effects from the rate rise forced throngs of Swedes out of their homes and produced new economic policies. The old pension system was scrapped and replaced by a new system, significantly less comprehensive. The change became a sign that the welfare state, in the way the Swedish people had gotten to know it, was undergoing a major reconstruction.

The U.S. Open title turned out to be Stefan Edberg's last Grand Slam title, and the last major victory for Swedish tennis during the Golden Era.

A SALT-AND-PEPPER GANG IN TOWN

"Aahh . . . these Swedes . . . they always beat me, I hate them."
—HENRI LECONTE

The Stockholm winter of 2014 is mild. Downtown the beggars remain outside the shops, paper cups in hand, even after darkness has fallen. Taxi cabs stop in front of the entrance to the Stockholm Waterfront Arena, a massive hotel and convention center in shiny steel. Men and women in suits and dresses arrive, nod happily, exchange greetings in the lobby. Mats Wilander and Stefan Edberg are in town to play in the ATP Champions Tour together with four other former top world players. A tennis celebration, even if it's make-believe.

In the real world, Swedish tennis fans have not had a reason to dress up and celebrate, not this winter, not for many years. The Davis Cup team labors in the lower divisions.

In the absence of this, Kings of Tennis turns into a stage lit by two types of spotlights. One glimmers in soft, golden colors and showcases a time that for each year that passes appears more mythical. The other throws a white light across the present and raises questions on what has gone wrong.

The crowd, of course, has come for the golden glimmer. A spotlight follows Mats Wilander as he walks out onto the court accompanied by Daft Punk's retromodern megahit, "Get Lucky." The crowd in the sold-out arena gives him a standing ovation. Mats waves, puts his tennis bag by his chair, tests the strings on his rackets, and takes his place by the net. The public announcer calls out his accomplishments through the speakers before turning to Wilander's opponent, Henri Leconte: "Yesterday you faced Stefan, today it's Mats. What do you have to say about these Swedes?" Leconte understands the role he's been given in this moment, that of the witness, the outside reporter. He sighs, grimaces, moans when he answers: "Aahh . . . these Swedes . . . they always beat me, I hate them."

The announcer confronts Mats with a claim delivered with laughter in his voice: "In the final in Paris in 1988, you won over Leconte, you were almost unbeatable that year." Now Wilander's hair is speckled salt-and-pepper gray, his flight has just landed. He smiles at the memory from 1988 but isn't interested in basking in the glory. Another match with the Frenchman, which he thinks better moves the perspective from past to present, appears in his memory, and he says: "The loss in the 1982 Stockholm Open final against Leconte was the most expected, because Leconte is so awesome indoors. And Henri isn't just good, he's funny, too."

The people in the crowd exchange glances; they're not exactly following this. It's as if people have been subject to the bright white light too long, they don't want to let the brilliance of the golden years be disturbed by nonsense. What does Leconte's humor have to do with this?

Wilander's legs twitch; it looks as if his body wants to start playing right away. In the outer edges of the spotlight, Leconte grabs a champagne bottle from an ice bucket and pretends to start drinking. He has a jerky way of moving, which reveals that Wilander's statement about his humor is correct. Some in the crowd chuckle. But most watch the prank without smiling, as if to mark that they haven't come to watch a funny Frenchman, but a tennis match a Swedish legend should win. The crowd's moroseness also emphasizes that people haven't picked up on what Wilander has just revealed about himself: he's here to have fun. What challenged Wilander in the past and was fun back then—solving the riddles of a tennis match—is no longer what drives him. Everything has its time. The goal here and now is to offer up, together with his opponent, spectacular points. To attempt difficult shots, laugh, have a connection with the crowd, and shoot the breeze.

Leconte has a round belly and doesn't exactly sprint for the balls. The Frenchman's physical appearance and Wilander's attitude indicate that what is about to happen at the Waterfront Arena isn't a competitive match in the true sense of the word. Even so, the Swedish crowd has transported itself to another era when play starts; it absorbs any sign that it is 1988. The easy shot that gives Wilander his first service break is met by ovations; a great passing shot hit under pressure while he is trailing receives relieved rather than overjoyed applause. A moment later, when Leconte misses a chance to break, two spectators, lively suit-clad men in their 60s, whisper to each other: "Why does he go for the net on a shot like that? Strategically a foolish move by Leconte."

The line judge then misses a shot from the Frenchman that obviously hits the line.

He yells: "But I paid the line judge 50 dollars to help me, and now she calls it like this."

Wilander gives Leconte the point in his famous sportsmanlike manner and yells: "I raised the bid to 60, but you can have it anyway."

"Raised the bid?!" cries Leconte. "That's unfair, I'm not that rich anymore."

A moment later, Wilander walks up to a man in the stands who's fiddling with his phone. He quietly leans in over the man's cell phone screen. Then, as he walks back toward the baseline, he shouts indignantly to Leconte: "Did you see that?" He's sitting there texting when I'm about to serve . . ."

Wilander wins the first set by pure inspiration and joy for the game. In the second, Leconte's classic technique and clean hits reap rewards, and he wins the set, 6–1. Then the play is paused by another exchange of words between the players. The crowd sighs, some people boo. Enough with the nonsense now. "Wilander shouldn't lose to Leconte," someone mutters.

With the score 1–1 in sets, the Senior tour rules state that the match will be decided in a 10-point tiebreaker. Wilander is tired. The atmosphere thickens on the court, the players no longer have the energy to talk. Now they play for real. The points get shorter, the pace quicker. At last, Wilander hits a ball out and Leconte wins it. The crowd is disappointed but claps politely. Wilander doesn't seem the least concerned. He smiles and waves and tells the announcer he's happy to have had the chance to participate in such a nice event.

The next evening, Wilander gets outplayed by Edberg, who hits numerous forehands that are outright winners, shots he barely could have hit back in the good old days. The umpire calls out the score with a dispassionate objectivity and seriousness that reflect Edberg's attitude on the court. The crowd can see with its own eyes that tennis in 2014 is two completely different games for the two former world number ones. Wilander, who for a long time built his success on a total focus on every stroke, can no longer play like that, and no longer wants to.

He says: "I want to have fun with my tennis, otherwise forget it. And if it's exhibition tennis, I think we should offer up some drama, even if it's make-believe drama. This way of playing for points straight up as if it's all about winning becomes too serious for me. It's possible that I'll return next year, but right now too many of us are taking this event way too seriously."

For Edberg, the opposite is true. The seriousness and the strive to win is what gives the game its meaning and joy. He rarely plays on the Senior tour for the simple reason that once he plays, he wants to be as well prepared as he can, for his own and for the fans' sake. It's as if with his conduct tonight he wants to say: "Is there a better way to express your passion for the game than to give it your very best effort? Is there a better way to show your opponent respect than to do everything you can to defeat him?"

"I enjoy playing in the Kings of Tennis very much," says Stefan. "The event is great and important for Swedish tennis. In addition, it provides a good opportunity for sponsors and business people to get together."

The next day, Stefan loses in the tournament's final to the eight-years-younger Swede Thomas Enqvist, whose baseline game has a faster pace. Enqvist is the bridge between then and now, between the soft, golden light and the sharp, white glare. Along with Magnus Larsson, Jonas Björkman, Magnus Norman, Thomas Johansson, Joachim "Pim-Pim" Johansson, and Robin Söderling, Thomas Enqvist carried on the legacy of Borg, Wilander, and Edberg into the '90s and '00s. Those two decades were filled with good results and occasions for celebration in Grand Slam tournaments:

Magnus Larsson: semifinal, the French Open 1994.

Jonas Björkman: semifinal, the U.S. Open 1997; semifinal, Wimbledon 2006.

Thomas Enqvist: final, the Australian Open 1999.

Magnus Norman: final, the French Open 2000; semifinal, the Australian Open 2000.

Thomas Johansson: win, the Australian Open 2002; semifinal, Wimbledon 2005.

Joachim "Pim-Pim" Johansson: semifinal, the U.S. Open 2004.

Robin Söderling: final, the French Open 2009 and 2010.

During those years, Sweden also won the Davis Cup three times: 1994, 1997, and 1998. That generation maintained Sweden's position as one of the tennis superpowers. None of the players were the best in the world, but all belonged to the absolute elite.

Thomas Enqvist has served as vice tournament director of the ATP Champions Tour event in Stockholm in recent years.

He says:

"You have to realize that there is an enormous difference between then and now, even if not that many years have passed. When I grew up, tennis was omnipresent. There was also a typically Swedish way of playing. We had invented the most effective way to play tennis, a Swedish style that was superior. You learned to play like that, from the baseline, solid ground strokes, no misses. . . . The generation of tennis players to which I belonged was perhaps overshadowed by Borg, Wilander, and Edberg. And at the same time, a player like Ulf Stenlund, 23rd in the world, didn't get any recognition at all in the '80s. Today, a player ranked around 20 would be a star in Sweden. What happened back then was so exceptional."

For those who stroll around at the Kings of Tennis event, it is easy to get the impression that the competition is as important to the sport as the Stockholm Open or the Swedish Open in Båstad. But rather, the Senior event fills the function of the Champion's Cup in Båstad in the '70s, when, in the years preceding Borg's breakthrough, it constantly coaxed Janne Lundqvist to make a comeback and measure his skills against renowned international players. As long as the annual event at the Waterfront counts Wilander and Edberg among its participants, the artificial life support can continue.

There is a sense that the tennis arenas once again have turned into reservations for the upper class. The Kings of Tennis echoes the era when Helen Wills Moody came to Stockholm and entertained a select few of society's most privileged, more than it does the folksy atmosphere around the Masters tournament in 1975.

The education options for Sweden's best tennis juniors have changed with the times, too. In the showcases at the Kings of Tennis, you can find brochures about a new tennis academy called *Good to Great*, led by Magnus Norman, Nicklas Kulti, and Mikael Tillström—three former elite players, of whom Magnus Norman reached the absolute top of the world. The name of the initiative is to signal, of course, that the three players know how to take the step from being a good tennis player to a world-class one. Their conclusion is that what is required is a type of elitist tennis academy that to date has not existed in Sweden. *Good to Great* is ambitious and goal-oriented, and a more qualified coach than Magnus Norman is hard to come by—he coached Robin Söderling to a place among the world's absolute best and has now accomplished the same with Stanislas Wawrinka from Switzerland. *Good to Great* is obviously an initiative of another kind from the broad effort that laid the foundation for the founders' own success when they began playing tennis in Mariestad, Jönköping, and Stockholm, respectively. Back then, Norman, Tillström, and Kulti were fostered in nonprofit clubs, supported by government and municipal grants. Foreign tennis experts used to come to Sweden in the '80s, scratch their heads, and wonder how the Swedish success stories were possible without tennis academies and centralized, early elite initiatives from the Swedish Tennis Association.

Nicklas Kulti explained to the weekly business magazine *Veckans Affärer*: "We think in more commercial terms and realize the importance of collaborating with business and industry."

There is no longer any connection between the former world-class players and the upcoming talents. The last shining star was Robin Söderling, a former world number four, who beat both Nadal and Federer at the French Open and had to retire in 2011 after suffering from mononucleosis. While young and ambitious Swedish players are longing for mentorship, the success of the past is an ever-present weight on their shoulders. Fredrik Rosengren, Davis Cup captain between 2012 and 2016, says that nothing makes him more bored than being asked to comment on the Swedish glory days: "This is a different era, and it is so unfair to the current players to compare their achievments to those of Borg, Wilander, and Edberg. Nothing they do seems good enough."

When Söderling made a brief comeback in 2017, his short doubles match with other retired players received more attention in national media than the national Davis Cup team, who at the same time fought for their honor in a qualification tie in Tunisia, Africa. There, the No. 569 Isak Arvidsson, age twenty-four, played the first five-setter of his career. After more than four hours of play, he sealed the match against Mohamed Aziz Dougaz, thereby avoiding relegation to the fouth division of the Davis Cup. "It's pure joy. It's overwhelming. I don't have words to describe my feelings," the jubilant Swede said in an article that appeared on the website of The Swedish national tennis federation.

The victory was celebrated with hugs and tears of joy, not broadcasted anywhere.

It was a victory that helped the Swedish to a modest climb in the ranking: up to 39, just behind Chinese Taipei, but ahead of Barbados.

In 1992, there was nothing to indicate that Stefan Edberg's U.S. Open title would be his last major win. The following year, he played in the final at the Australian Open, the quarterfinal at the French Open, and the semifinal at Wimbledon. In 1994, he reached the semifinal in Australia. Late into 1995, he held a place among the world's Top 10. But early in 1996, he announced that the year that had just begun would be his last on the tour. Stefan would hold a farewell speech to the crowd at every arena, the most emotional at the Kungliga Tennis Hall in Stockholm in the fall. And he was still good enough to play first singles when Sweden lost to France in the Davis Cup final that same year.

He says, "I had played nonstop my entire career, from 1984 to 1996. I might have gotten burned out by playing so much. If I'd taken a break, I might have been able to come back and play really good tennis again. But if you look at it historically, you'll see that the chances of winning a Grand Slam tournament after the age of thirty are a lot smaller. That influenced my decision. Strictly physically speaking, I had no problems. I almost played better a year or so after I had retired. I still lived in London for many years after my career had ended, and I trained with Tim Henman and Greg Rusedski when they were Top 10 in the world, and I almost never lost in practice. Never for many years. Never!"

When Stefan was thirty-five, the family returned to Sweden and settled outside of Växjö. Stefan tapered off his tennis playing and instead began to play squash. At forty, he represented Växjö Squash Club in the Swedish elite division.

He's still in the same town. Today he meets business partners as well as reporters at his office at the finance company Case Asset Management, located in the town center. The company engages in capital management, and Stefan was one of its founders back in 2004.

"If you've made a lot of money for yourself, after a while you'll also be interested in how to invest it," he says.

Stefan offers coffee and milk chocolate squares. This week, Annette is in London visiting their adult daughter, Emilie. Stefan's task at home is to drive Emilie's younger brother, Christopher, back and forth to tennis practice. That's what his everyday life looks like: family, the finance company, and sometimes work at the recently opened, environmentally friendly tennis facility on the other side of the lake, for which he was a driving force along with his tennis colleagues Carl-Axel Hageskog and Magnus Larsson.

The office is clean, tidy, and unpretentious, not totally unlike the principal owner himself. Stefan, like Borg and Wilander, comes from humble beginnings and took advantage of the fact that tennis in Sweden had been transformed from an upper society pastime to a sport for the people.

Now, he sees the pendulum swing back.

"It's tougher today," he says. "Financially especially, it costs a lot of money to be successful. The point system when I came up made it possible to climb in the rankings quicker. And you could make between $10,000 and $20,000 in the small tournaments. That's where it remains 25 years later. It was easy to get a sponsorship contract then, too; today only the very best get that. I've heard that if you are to make a real commitment as a fourteen- or fifteen-year-old, it'll cost between 500,000 and 1,000,000 kronor a year.

"In addition, it's much tougher to get courts and find a coach today. And if you want to train with the best, you won't find them here in Sweden. You'll have to travel, and that costs a lot of money. If you play soccer, you receive a salary from your club, a bus comes and takes you to your match, and you don't even have to play to get your salary. In tennis, you have to pay for everything yourself and perform week after week. Michael Ryderstedt was ranked around 300 in the world and didn't break even on his tennis. Compare that to number 300 in soccer. Where are you then? In the English Premier League perhaps, on a pretty good team, with a five-year contract. That's the reality today. Even with the right training and coach, you still have to resolve your finances. The Swedish Tennis Association has no money, the clubs have no money. Instead it's the private interests that have money."

Mats Wilander's life revolves around tennis even more than Stefan's, but in a different way. He lives with his family in a big house at the edge of the forest, a 15-minute drive from the small town of Sun Valley, Idaho. The major reason for settling down in this area is that one of his sons, Erik, suffers from a skin disorder called Epidermolysis Bullosa, which causes fragile skin that easily blisters. The Idaho climate makes Erik's symptoms slightly milder. Mats spends four to five months a year with his business partner, Cameron Lickle, also a good tennis player, in a giant RV. Under the name "Wilander on Wheels," Mats and Cameron travel around the North American continent and give tennis lessons to recreational players of all ages.

"The best thing about my career is that I didn't make enough money to quit working," he says. "Or rather . . . others who've made the same amount of money have managed it better, they didn't put 50 percent of the capital in a big house in Idaho. I won the French Open when I was seventeen, received a check, looked at it, and thought: *Okay, now I'll never have to worry about money again.* But that wasn't really true . . . I've always found finances totally dull, and I've never been particularly smart with my money.

In 2002, Mats accepted the job as Sweden's Davis Cup captain. For the Swedish Tennis Association, the decision to sign Wilander to a contract was a smart move to generate publicity around a sport fighting for media coverage. For Mats, the assignment was a way to get involved in the future of Swedish tennis, and also an opportunity to again camp out with Joakim Nyström, whom Mats selected as his assistant coach.

Nyström recalls a few nice years, although the results couldn't compare with those of the '80s and '90s.

"I was given the role of disciplinarian, since Mats is such an emotional person, totally unstructured," he says. "I was the one who set up practice times, thought about logistics, and submitted the team selections to the International Tennis Federation. The important thing for Mats is that it feels right. One time in 2005, when our match against India, in India, was fast approaching, he called and said: 'Nah, I'm quitting.' 'What? The match is two weeks away, you can't quit now!' 'Yes, it doesn't feel good to go there, I've lost my motivation.' I had to explain to him: 'You can't abandon the players now, we'll take this match and then you can quit after . . .' He changed his mind, of course. It was a great trip and we won the match."

Mats Wilander then stayed on as captain until 2009, when he was replaced by Thomas Enqvist.

Today, Mats works regularly as a tennis reporter and commentator for Eurosport and receives a lot of accolade for his analyses. But what he enjoys most is when he gets to step out on the court and hit some balls with amateur players.

"With Wilander on Wheels, we drive between 200 and 600 kilometers at a time. I rarely feel as much at home as when I travel in the RV and give lessons every day. Four students at a time, 24 students per day. To go out on the court and sweat and feel that the four students taking the lesson are fully present. They see us work hard, Cameron sweats like Andy Roddick, and I think it's so damn fun to just play and hit, just enjoy it. When evening comes, we have dinner, and by then I've learned all the 24 names. Then we throw our crap back in the RV, turn on Dylan and Ulf Lundell, and move on to our next stop. And I'm always in the same time zone as Sonya, and I can call her and ask how she's doing or just to say good night."

Now, with perspective, Mats believes there is an exaggerated focus among Swedish juniors to turn pro.

"The biggest mistake is that what seems to be forgotten is the process, the road to the top, and that's the fun part," he says. "But on the other hand, that's difficult to understand until you're actually successful. Then you realize it's not about winning, it's the road there that's fun. The Davis Cup was the most fun of all. After the fact, I don't remember if we won or lost. But we won most of the time, right?"

The Swedish tennis star that shone the very brightest is the one that nowadays is seen the very least. To find his foothold in life after the end of his career wasn't easy for Björn Borg. His entire adult life had been regulated and structured, tailored to maximize his performance on the tennis court. At the age of twenty-six, he found himself in a reality where neither Lennart Bergelin, nor his own finances, nor anything else set any boundaries.

Björn left Mariana after meeting the seventeen-year-old Jannike Björling, who was a participant in a wet t-shirt contest in which Björn was one of the judges. With Jannike, Björn had a son, Robin, in 1986, but the couple broke up two years later. In 1990, Jannike spoke out in the magazine *Z* about Björn's and her cocaine use. Björn sued the magazine for defamation and received damages, but he later admitted to having used the drug.

The articles about Björn were rarely positive during this time period. He entered into a stormy marriage with the Italian pop singer Loredana Berté that lasted a few years, he was pursued by the tax authorities, and he fought with his business partner, Lars Skarke, about the Björn Borg trademark and clothing company.

In the midst of all this chaos, he decided to make a comeback as a professional tennis player. Once again, Björn Borg's return to the tennis courts attracted a huge amount of attention. His first comeback, back in 1983, had been sincere. The curiosity about Borg had been genuine, his performance on the court good, if not sufficient. This time, Björn Borg was followed by the press and the public in the same way the bearded lady attracts attention at Coney Island. Björn Borg in 1991 was an anomaly and an anachronism. He arrived to the tournament in Monte Carlo with the same small wooden racket from Donnay that he'd used the last time around. Courtside stood Lennart Bergelin. He'd traveled to Monte Carlo at his own initiative. But there was no room for Bergelin in the coach's chair, nor for Percy Rosberg. Sitting there was the seventy-nine-year-old Irishman Ron Thatcher, who preferred to call himself Tia Honsai and was a self-appointed fitness guru and self-defense expert. Björn was soon to be thirty-five, hadn't played for eight seasons, and was powerless when Jordi Arrese, a competent clay court player from Spain, lunged at the balls with his large graphite racket. During 1992 and 1993, Björn played an additional ten matches, in the end with a modern racket, without winning one single match.

The failed businesses and his messy personal life colored the public's opinion of Björn Borg. Rather than being remembered as the greatest tennis player of all time, Björn was a common celebrity, a sort of jet-set figure who recorded a sloppy pop song with Dr. Alban and the soccer star Tomas Brolin.

The turnaround, or the redemption if you will, came at the Sports Gala in the Globen Arena in Stockholm in 2000, when Björn Borg was named Sweden's Sportsman of the Century. In an emotional acceptance speech, Björn Borg emphasized how he, during his travels in the '70s, always felt such great pride in representing the small country of Sweden. He especially thanked Lennart Bergelin and finished his speech by saying: "My life, as a person and as an athlete, is complete."

In 2002, Björn Borg got married again, to Patricia Östfeldt. They'd been introduced by Joakim Nyström and met when Björn participated in an exhibition tournament in Skellefteå, on the eastern coast of Sweden.

Östfeldt had gone there to watch the tennis and visit a friend. Björn soon settled in to a quiet and private life with his new family—Patricia and their son, Leo, born in 2003, and his two older stepchildren—in Värmdö, 20 minutes outside of central Stockholm. Occasionally, he'd stop in at the office of the Björn Borg clothing company to keep up to date with the latest development. Until recently, Björn still received a percentage from the underwear sold. And he saw Lennart Bergelin regularly. Bergelin, who passed away in 2008, used to go over to Borg's house to give him a massage, even in old age.

However, the quiet around Björn was broken in 2006, when he suddenly announced that he was going to sell his Wimbledon trophies and some rackets through an auction house in London. The collection was valued to over $450,000, per today's rate. The move set in motion another old rumor—that Björn's personal finances were in bad shape—and shook the tennis world. John McEnroe called Björn and asked if he was crazy. Andre Agassi got together with a group of his tennis peers to buy the trophies together, to ensure they didn't end up in the wrong hands. The hoopla prompted Björn, at the last minute and subject to penalties, to withdraw the sale.

Björn still receives so many requests and invitations that they would fill his entire calendar if he were to say yes to all. But he has no problem taking it easy, and he turns down almost everything. He's never participated in the Kings of Tennis.

Still, Björn has not abandoned tennis. On the contrary, a tennis facility is his absolute favorite place to hang out.

Janne Lundqvist's tennis hall in Kristineberg was built during tennis' greatest year; it was finished just after the 1976 Masters tournament. The building itself doesn't look like much. The rectangular wooden box sticks out more and more as gentrification creeps closer across this part of the Stockholm district known as Kungsholmen. A person who doesn't know what's inside would never think of paying a visit.

But open the door to the tennis hall, and it's like walking through the secret door to Narnia. Inside waits a world that only the initiated know. It's not just that the place is a living museum of the '70s—on one wall hangs Björn's old Donnay rackets, on another, pictures from his glory days, on a third a large panorama image in color from the televised doubles match in Båstad, by which Janne Lundqvist and Uffe Schmidt with their victory gave tennis interest in Sweden a solid push forward. It's also the good-natured atmosphere, the tempo that contrasts so sharply to Stockholm in the 2010s. The interior is dark with plenty of wood. There are two newly renovated locker rooms with saunas and showers, and a small cafeteria. A few times a week, Anders Lehman and Christer Lundberg, who own and manage the facility, receive assistance from the former Davis Cup player Rolf Norberg. They make butter and cheese sandwiches for those who are hungry and serve brewed coffee, all at magically low prices. When they have time, they walk down to the court and hit a few balls. Christer is often on the other side of the net when Björn Borg plays.

You'd think a tennis hall that has as one of its regulars one of the world's greatest athletes ever, and that every week welcomes 3,500 recreational players of all ages, would be invincible to outside threats. But the district's politicians want it gone, because they think the tennis hall disturbs the district's current exclusive character, and that the tennis hall blocks the view to the banks of Lake Mälaren, where an elegant marina and nice restaurants now make their home. In letters to the local newspaper *Mitt i Kungsholmen*, residents have for years demanded that the facility be torn down.

Not until an architect drew up a design proposal in which the tennis hall is hidden under a newly installed grassy hill did the residents calm down. The tennis hall invited the politicians to an open house. Björn Borg was there and spoke about the history of the hall. The opinion turned. A political majority was ready to announce the decision to save the hall, when the Liberal Party had an unexpected change of heart. Currently, Janne Lundqvist's tennis hall remains open, thanks to a temporary predemolition contract, but its future is unclear.

Björn Borg still arrives to his court time with time to spare. In that respect, a practice in Kristineberg when he's past sixty is no different from a Wimbledon final in 1980. Björn shows up 45 minutes before his practice start time. He goes down to the locker room, changes, tapes his fingers, focuses his mind, walks out onto the court. Christer follows. The two hit the ball back and forth a little while, and after a few minutes, they start keeping score. Björn sets a fast pace, he torments his younger opponent, drives him around the court.

"I had a lot of fun today," he says afterward. "Good pace, good workout. I really enjoy this place. It's like a cult, there's a great feeling and atmosphere here. And it's good to move around, good for your head, too. I don't go for runs in the forest anymore; this is where I complete my three hours per week of training."

The desire to play tennis is just as big as in the past, as big as it's ever been. Not even after he quit did Björn lose his drive to compete. It was because of that drive he made his surprising comeback in 1991. Many people today wonder why he'd subject himself to that comeback.

"The desire then was to play again, to compete again. But to go out and play in Monte Carlo's ATP tournament without having played and without preparation wasn't exactly a serious effort," he says. "That is, if you wanted to be serious. But just a year or so later, the Senior tour started. That suited me perfectly, that's where I found my thing. I went on to play senior tennis for all those years, with the old gang. All the old-timers got closer too, because the pressure wasn't as great. Of course, you want to step out onto the court and win and play well, but it wasn't a big deal to lose either, like before, when you're number one in the world. We had a great relationship, all the players. We had so much fun everywhere we went around the world."

As for his Swedish buddies from the glory days, Björn has essentially lost touch with all of them.

"I see Roffe [Norberg] here from time to time, but otherwise there's not much there," he says. "Kjelle [Johansson] and I've had a lot of fun, but we're not in touch now. I have that more with the foreign players. Vilas, McEnroe, Nastase, and I still get together occasionally. But I don't play on the Senior tour anymore. I like to play my hours here. McEnroe, he just keeps going, but he plays an easier style, his body is light. He's never injured."

One year at the Waterfront, the crowd spotted Björn Borg in the stands when Edberg played McEnroe. Everyone was affected by Björn's presence, that's how strong his aura still is. When McEnroe had chased after and lost several straight points, he limped over to Björn in the stands and asked for support and a hug. Björn laughed and gave his friend a long, warm embrace. McEnroe regained his strength and won a few points, which prompted Edberg to also run up to Björn and ask for a hug. It was a moment of reunion and love, a moment of happiness being back in the spotlight and

261

feeling the eyes of a crowd that won't let the players' receding hairlines or facial wrinkles diminish the love it has for its heroes.

Björn Borg, Mats Wilander, and Stefan Edberg. It doesn't matter how old they've become, they will always be the three players who personify the Swedish tennis miracle. They will meet people throughout their lives who remember where they were when Björn won the Davis Cup final in the Kungliga Tennis Hall, when Mats gave away match point to Clerc in Paris in 1982, or when Stefan fell backward at the net at Wimbledon in 1988.

Everything ties together. Top tennis has always been its own world, a proud world where, regardless of nationality, players are bearers of a culture, with personal relationships and contact between generations. Gustaf V played tennis with Gottfried von Cramm, who cared for and played with Percy Rosberg, who coached Björn Borg and Stefan Edberg—and then Edberg became Roger Federer's coach. There are only four handshakes between the Tennis Prince from the 1800s, "Mr. G.," and the tennis king of the '00s, Federer.

A week after Edberg had crushed Wilander in Stockholm, Mats interviewed Federer as part of Eurosport's broadcast from the big tennis tournament in Indian Wells. Mats told the Swiss that, before he asked any questions about what Stefan had meant to Federer's improved game as his new coach, Mats first wanted to know something else: "What is it that you have taught Stefan? What have you told him about his forehand? It's become a fatal weapon now. I have no chance anymore, that used to be his weak side."

Federer chuckled: "You're right. I didn't call up Stefan to ask him to be my new coach. Stefan called me because he wanted to start working on his forehand in his old age. He said he was willing to pay anything for my advice. I said: 'Sure.' So, we work on it daily, and he travels with me wherever I play and books additional lessons . . ."

Wilander shook his head with concern and started laughing.

ACHIEVEMENTS

BJÖRN BORG
Wimbledon: winner 1976, 1977, 1978, 1979, 1980; finalist 1981
The U.S. Open: finalist 1976, 1978, 1980, 1981
The French Open: winner 1974, 1975, 1978, 1979, 1980, 1981
The Australian Open: –
The Masters: winner 1980, 1981; finalist 1975, 1978
The WCT: winner 1976; finalist 1974, 1975, 1979
The Davis Cup: winner 1975 (singles record: 37 wins, 3 losses)
Weeks at world's number one (ATP): 109

MATS WILANDER
Wimbledon: –
The U.S. Open: winner 1988; finalist 1987
The French Open: winner 1982, 1985, 1988; finalist 1983, 1987
The Australian Open: winner 1983, 1984, 1988; finalist 1985
The Masters: finalist 1987
WCT: –
The Davis Cup: winner 1984, 1985, 1987; finalist 1983, 1988 (singles
    record: 36 wins, 16 losses)
Weeks at world's number one (ATP): 20

STEFAN EDBERG
Wimbledon: winner 1988, 1990; finalist 1989
The U.S. Open: winner 1991, 1992

BJÖRN BORG AND THE SUPER-SWEDES

The French Open: finalist 1989
The Australian Open: winner 1985, 1987; finalist 1990, 1992, 1993
The Masters: winner 1989
The WCT: finalist 1988
The Davis Cup: winner 1984, 1985, 1987, 1994; finalist 1986, 1988, 1989, 1996 (singles record: 35 wins, 15 losses)
Weeks at world's number one (ATP): 72

The lists of achievements include singles play and spots in finals in the Grand Slam tournaments, the WCT playoff, the Masters, and the Davis Cup. From 1973 to 1985, the Australian Open was considered a minor tournament; as an example, Björn Borg only participated in 1974. The WCT playoffs ceased in 1989, after a few years of declining status. Aside from his achievements in singles, Stefan Edberg also won three Grand Slam titles in doubles, Mats Wilander one. Stefan Edberg and John McEnroe are the only players who have been ranked first in both singles and doubles.

ATP RANKINGS 1973–1996

1973

1 Nastase, Ilie
2 Newcombe, John
3 Connors, Jimmy
4 Okker, Tom
5 Smith, Stan
6 Rosewall, Ken
7 Orantes, Manuel
8 Laver, Rod
9 Kodes, Jan
10 Ashe, Arthur

11 Borg, Björn

1974

1 Connors, Jimmy
2 Newcombe, John
3 Borg, Björn
4 Laver, Rod
5 Vilas, Guillermo
6 Okker, Tom
7 Ashe, Arthur
8 Rosewall, Ken
9 Smith, Stan
10 Nastase, Ilie

1975

1 Connors, Jimmy
2 Vilas, Guillermo
3 Borg, Björn
4 Ashe, Arthur
5 Orantes, Manuel
6 Rosewall, Ken
7 Nastase, Ilie
8 Alexander, John
9 Tanner, Roscoe
10 Laver, Rod

1976

1 Connors, Jimmy
2 Borg, Björn
3 Nastase, Ilie
4 Orantes, Manuel
5 Ramírez, Raúl
6 Vilas, Guillermo
7 Panatta, Adriano
8 Solomon, Harold
9 Dibbs, Eddie
10 Gottfried, Brian

BJÖRN BORG AND THE SUPER-SWEDES

1977

1 Connors, Jimmy
2 Vilas, Guillermo
3 Borg, Björn
4 Gerulaitis, Vitas
5 Gottfried, Brian
6 Dibbs, Eddie
7 Orantes, Manuel
8 Ramírez, Raúl
9 Nastase, Ilie
10 Stockton, Dick

1978

1 Connors, Jimmy
2 Borg, Björn
3 Vilas, Guillermo
4 McEnroe, John
5 Gerulaitis, Vitas
6 Dibbs, Eddie
7 Gottfried, Brian
8 Ramírez, Raúl
9 Solomon, Harold
10 Barazzutti, Corrado

1979

1 Borg, Björn
2 Connors, Jimmy
3 McEnroe, John
4 Gerulaitis, Vitas
5 Tanner, Roscoe
6 Vilas, Guillermo
7 Ashe, Arthur
8 Solomon, Harold
9 Higueras, José
10 Dibbs, Eddie

1980

1 Borg, Björn
2 McEnroe, John
3 Connors, Jimmy
4 Mayer, Gene
5 Vilas, Guillermo
6 Lendl, Ivan
7 Solomon, Harold
8 Clerc, José-Luis
9 Gerulaitis, Vitas
10 Teltscher, Eliot

1981

1 McEnroe, John
2 Lendl, Ivan
3 Connors, Jimmy
4 Borg, Björn
5 Clerc, José-Luis
6 Vilas, Guillermo
7 Mayer, Gene
8 Teltscher, Eliot
9 Gerulaitis, Vitas
10 McNamara, Peter

1982

1 McEnroe, John
2 Connors, Jimmy
3 Lendl, Ivan
4 Vilas, Guillermo
5 Gerulaitis, Vitas
6 Clerc, José-Luis
7 Wilander, Mats
8 Mayer, Gene
9 Noah, Yannick
10 McNamara, Peter

1983

1 McEnroe, John
2 Lendl, Ivan
3 Connors, Jimmy
4 Wilander, Mats
5 Noah, Yannick
6 Arias, Jimmy
7 Higueras, José
8 Clerc, José-Luis
9 Curren, Kevin
10 Mayer, Gene

19 Järryd, Anders
23 Sundström, Henrik

1984

1 McEnroe, John
2 Connors, Jimmy
3 Lendl, Ivan
4 Wilander, Mats
5 Gomez, Andres
6 Järryd, Anders
7 Sundström, Henrik
8 Cash, Pat
9 Teltscher, Eliot
10 Noah, Yannick

11 Nyström, Joakim
20 Edberg, Stefan

1985

1 Lendl, Ivan
2 McEnroe, John
3 Wilander, Mats
4 Connors, Jimmy
5 Edberg, Stefan
6 Becker, Boris

7 Noah, Yannick
8 Järryd, Anders
9 Mecir, Miloslav
10 Curren, Kevin

11 Nyström, Joakim
22 Sundström, Henrik
25 Gunnarsson, Jan

1986

1 Lendl, Ivan
2 Becker, Boris
3 Wilander, Mats
4 Noah, Yannick
5 Edberg, Stefan
6 Leconte, Henri
7 Nyström, Joakim
8 Connors, Jimmy
9 Mecir, Miloslav
10 Gomez, Andres

12 Pernfors, Mikael
13 Carlsson, Kent
19 Järryd, Anders
21 Svensson, Jonas

1987

1 Lendl, Ivan
2 Edberg, Stefan
3 Wilander, Mats
4 Connors, Jimmy
5 Becker, Boris
6 Mecir, Miloslav
7 Cash, Pat
8 Noah, Yannick
9 Mayotte, Tim
10 McEnroe, John

267

12 Carlsson, Kent
15 Järryd, Anders
16 Nyström, Joakim

1988

1 Wilander, Mats
2 Lendl, Ivan
3 Agassi, Andre
4 Becker, Boris
5 Edberg, Stefan
6 Carlsson, Kent
7 Connors, Jimmy
8 Hlasek, Jakob
9 Leconte, Henri
10 Mayotte, Tim

19 Pernfors, Mikael
22 Svensson, Jonas

1989

1 Lendl, Ivan
2 Becker, Boris
3 Edberg, Stefan
4 McEnroe, John
5 Chang, Michael
6 Gilbert, Brad
7 Agassi, Andre
8 Krickstein, Aaron
9 Mancini, Alberto
10 Berger, Jay

12 Wilander, Mats

1990

1 Edberg, Stefan
2 Becker, Boris
3 Lendl, Ivan

4 Agassi, Andre
5 Sampras, Pete
6 Gomez, Andres
7 Muster, Thomas
8 Sanchez, Emilio
9 Ivanisevic, Goran
10 Gilbert, Brad

11 Svensson, Jonas

1991

1 Edberg, Stefan
2 Courier, Jim
3 Becker, Boris
4 Stich, Michael
5 Lendl, Ivan
6 Sampras, Pete
7 Forget, Guy
8 Nováček, Karel
9 Korda, Petr
10 Agassi, Andre

12 Gustafsson, Magnus

1992

1 Courier, Jim
2 Edberg, Stefan
3 Sampras, Pete
4 Ivanisevic, Goran
5 Becker, Boris
6 Chang, Michael
7 Korda, Petr
8 Lendl, Ivan
9 Agassi, Andre
10 Krajicek, Richard

19 Holm, Henrik

1993

1 Sampras, Pete
2 Stich, Michael
3 Courier, Jim
4 Bruguera, Sergi
5 Edberg, Stefan
6 Medvedev, Andrei
7 Ivanisevic, Goran
8 Chang, Michael
9 Muster, Thomas
10 Pioline, Cédric

14 Gustafsson, Magnus

1994

1 Sampras, Pete
2 Agassi, Andre
3 Becker, Boris
4 Bruguera, Sergi
5 Ivanisevic, Goran
6 Chang, Michael
7 Edberg, Stefan
8 Berasategui, Alberto
9 Stich, Michael
10 Martin, Todd

19 Larsson, Magnus

1995

1 Sampras, Pete
2 Agassi, Andre
3 Muster, Thomas
4 Becker, Boris
5 Chang, Michael
6 Kafelnikov, Yevgeny
7 Enqvist, Thomas
8 Courier, Jim

9 Ferreira, Wayne
10 Ivanisevic, Goran

17 Larsson, Magnus
23 Edberg, Stefan

1996

1 Sampras, Pete
2 Chang, Michael
3 Kafelnikov, Yevgeny
4 Ivanisevic, Goran
5 Muster, Thomas
6 Becker, Boris
7 Krajicek, Richard
8 Agassi, Andre
9 Enqvist, Thomas
10 Ferreira, Wayne

14 Edberg, Stefan
17 Gustafsson, Magnus

In addition to the Top 10, the lists also include Swedish players in the Top 25.

BIBLIOGRAPHY

A New Gang in Town

Main sources: The authors' own interviews (2012–2014) with Björn Borg and Percy Rosberg; newspaper articles from *Aftonbladet, Dagens Nyheter, Expressen, Göteborgs-Posten,* and *Svenska Dagbladet* (November and December 1975).

Also: The authors' own interviews (2012–2014) with the banker Mats Törnwall and the tennis players Kjell Johansson, Rolf Norberg, and Anders Järryd; the article "The Bad Boy Who Went Good," *Sports Illustrated* (12/15/1975); Arthur Ashe's autobiography *Days of Grace* (1994); the biography *Nastase* by Rickard Evans (1978); the story "Are You Ready, Mr. Ashe?" in *Tennis* (10/20/2010); Steve Tignor's blog *Concrete Elbow* (2009); *Läroplan för Grundskolan* (1969); the books *Underbara dagar framför oss* by Henrik Berggren (2010) and *I takt med tiden* by Kjell Östberg (2008); and the essay *Idrottens framgångsspiral* by Johnny Wijk (2010).

From Royal Pastime to the People's Sport

Main sources: The authors' own interviews (2012–2014) with Björn Borg and Percy Rosberg; newspaper articles from *Dagens Nyheter* and *Svenska Dagbladet* (November 1932); written sources that describe the meeting between Lenglen and Wills on the Riviera in 1926, such as Wills Moody's autobiography *The Story of a Tennis Player* (1937); the article *Wills v Lenglen* in TIME magazine (03/01/1926); *Sports Illustrated* (10/16/1991 and 09/13/1992); the article "Two Women Bigger Than Babe Ruth" in the *New York Times* (06/12/1988); and the article "La Divine vs Poker Face" on the Blog tennis.com in April 2009. The main source for the report of the Wimbledon match between von Cramm and Budge 1937 is Marshall Jon Fisher's book *A Terrible Splendor: Three Extraordinary Men, a World Poised for War, and the Greatest Tennis Match Ever Played* (2009).

Also: The authors' own interviews (2012–2014) with Janne Lundqvist, Ulf Schmidt, Birger Folke, Kjell Johansson, Rolf Norberg, Ove Bengtson, Carl-Axel Hageskog, John-Anders Sjögren, and Birger Andersson; *Nationalencyklopedin;* the Blog *Bastadmalen.se.*

Around the Globe in Tennis Shorts

Main sources: The authors' own interviews (2012–2014) with Björn Borg, Percy Rosberg, Rolf Norberg, Ove Bengtson, Kjell Johansson, Mats Hasselqvist, and the attorney Lars Viklund, who protested against the Davis Cup match in May 1968.

Also: The documentary film *Den vita sporten* by Roy Andersson and Bo Widerberg (1968) and *Sagan om Björn Borg* by Folke Rydén (1998); *Båstadkravallerna*, radio documentary SR P3 (05/09/2009); articles in *Hallands Nyheter, Laholms tidning*, and *Nordvästra Skånes Tidningar* (May 1968); and the essay *Det folkliga genombrottet för tennis i TV-sofforna* by Johnny Wijk (2010).

Carrying Sweden on His Shoulders

Main sources: The authors' own interviews (2012–2014) with Björn Borg, Percy Rosberg, Kjell Johansson, and Ove Bengtson.

Also: *Barnjournalen* (January 1974) from Sveriges Television's Open Archive; "Two Greenies and A Whammy" in *Sports Illustrated* (02/04/1974); articles from *Expressen* and *Aftonbladet* (March-June 1974, October 1974, April 1975); and the book *Björn Borg: My Life and Game* by Björn Borg and Gene Scott (1980).

A One-Man Team in a Collective Time

Main sources: The authors' own interviews (2012–2014) with Björn Borg, Ove Bengtson, Rolf Norberg, Birger Andersson, Janne Lundqvist, Birger Folke, Ulf Schmidt, and Kjell Johansson; the article "Vägen till segern" by Jan Guillou in *Folket i Bild/Kulturfront* (No. 18, 1975).

Also: Newspaper articles from *Aftonbladet, Dagens Nyheter, Expressen,* and *Svenska Dagbladet* (September 1975). The quotations from Tommy Engstrand's interview with Olof Palme are obtained from the radio program *Sportåret 1975* (12/31/1975). The story about Björn Borg's visit to the disco in Munich was told by him in the radio program *Spelklart, Swedish Radio* (12/25/1975).

Desire, Wins, and Wimbledon

Main sources: The authors' own interviews (2012–2014) with Björn Borg and Kjell Johansson.

Also: The books *Laterna Magica* by Ingmar Bergman (1977) and *Dödsdansen (Dance of Death)* by August Strindberg (1897); the film *Annie Hall* by Woody Allen (1977); the book *Nastase* by Richard Evans (1978); newspaper articles from *Aftonbladet, Expressen, Dagens Nyheter,* and *Nordvästra Skånes Tidningar* (1976, 1977, 1978); "Wimbledon Was Never Better" in *Sports Illustrated* (07/15/1977); and "Raised by Women to Conquer" Men in *Sports Illustrated* (08/25/1978).

Fast Feet Versus Good Hands

Main sources: The authors' own interviews (2012–2014) with Björn Borg.

Also: The books *Borg vs McEnroe* by Malcolm Folley (2005), *High Strung* by Steve Tignor (2009), and *The Greatest Tennis Season Ever* by Matthew Cronin (2009); the films *Fire & Ice* (2009) and *Wimbledon Legends* (2001); and newspaper articles from *Aftonbladet, Dagens Nyheter,* and *Expressen* (1978–1981).

The Teens Who Copied Borg

Main sources: The authors' own interviews (2012–2014) with Mats Wilander, Joakim Nyström, Anders Järryd, Hans Simonsson, and John-Anders Sjögren; and newspaper articles from *Expressen* and *TT* (1981–1982).

Also: The authors' own interviews (2012–2014) with Stig Jansson, Onni Nordström, and Hans Olsson; the books *Slazenger's World of Tennis 1983: The Official Yearbook of the International Tennis Federation, Mats Wilander och spelet bakom rubrikerna* by Per Yng and Mats Wilander (1990), and *Open Tennis: The First Twenty Years* by Richard Evans (1988); newspaper articles from the *New York Times* (01/05/1981 and 07/12/1982), *Boca Raton News* (02/08/1985), *Dagens Industri* (12/14/1984), and *Hänt i Veckan* (1982); and video clips from Sveriges Television, ESPN, and NBC.

Good Guys Always Win

Main sources: The authors' own interviews (2012–2014) with Mats Wilander, Hans Olsson, John-Anders Sjögren, Anders Järryd, and Joakim Nyström.

Also: Articles from *Expressen, Dagens Nyheter, Göteborgs-Posten, TT,* and *The Guardian* (1983–1985); video clips from SVT, ESPN, and NBC; article from *Sports Illustrated* (June 1985) and the article "New Breed from the North" by Curry Kirkpatrick in *The Times* (June 1983); and the books *Open Tennis: The First Twenty Years* by Richard Evans (1988), *Game, Set and Deadline: A Tennis Odyssey* by Rex Bellamy (1986), and *Mats Wilander och spelet bakom rubrikerna* by Per Yng and Mats Wilander (1990).

A Lone Wolf with His Own Tactics

Main sources: The authors' own interviews (2012–2014) with Stefan Edberg, Mats Wilander, Tony Pickard, Hans Olsson, and Percy Rosberg.

Also: Articles in *Bravo* (March 1986), *Matchball* (March 1984), *La Stampa* (03/26/1986), and the *Chicago Tribune* (03/07/1987); *Tennis* magazine (years 1985 and 1986); the books *Fox Tales: My Conversation with Tony Pickard* by Arthur Brocklebank (2008), *Open Tennis: The First Twenty Years* by Richard Evans (1988), and *Mats Wilander och spelet bakom rubrikerna* by Per Yng and Mats Wilander (1990); *Made in Sweden* by Sveriges Television, 10/30/1986; SVT's broadcasts from The Stockholm Open 1986; and Ausopen.com.

When Småland Ruled the World

Main sources: The authors' own interviews (2012–2014) with Mats Wilander, Stefan Edberg, Tony Pickard, John-Anders Sjögren, and Joakim Nyström.

Also: The documentary *Stefan Edberg at Wimbledon* by The All England Lawn Tennis Club; video clip from Sveriges Television and ESPN; the books *The Player: The Autobiography* by Boris Becker (2005) and *Mats Wilander och spelet bakom rubrikerna* by Per Yng and Mats Wilander

(1990); "In the Comfort Zone" in *Sports Illustrated* (05/23/1988); and Wilanderonwheels.com and Wimbledon.com.

A Crack in the Facade
Main sources: The authors' own interviews (2012–2014) with Stefan Edberg, Mats Wilander, Hans Olsson, Joakim Nyström, Anders Järryd, John-Anders Sjögren, and Tony Pickard.
Also: Articles from *Expressen, Dagens Nyheter, Aftonbladet, The Associated Press, The Observer, The Independent, Tennis de France,* and *Svenska Dagbladet*; the books *Riv Pyramiderna!* by Jan Carlzon (1985) and *Hundra höjdare: Sveriges roligaste ögonblick* by Filip Hammar and Fredrik Wikingsson (2005); the essay *Idrottens framgångsspiral* by Johnny Wijk (2010); and Daviscup.com and Eurosport.com.

Artist in a Hairshirt
Main sources: The authors' own interviews (2012–2014) with Stefan Edberg, Percy Rosberg, Tony Pickard, and John-Anders Sjögren.
Also: "A Robot Joins the Human Race," the *Chicago Tribune* (09/14/1992); transcriptions from press conferences; usopen.org; and "A Stand-Up Guy" in *Sports Illustrated* (06/24/1991).

A Salt-and-Pepper Gang in Town
Main sources: The authors' own interviews (2012–2014) with Björn Borg, Mats Wilander, Stefan Edberg, Percy Rosberg, and Thomas Enqvist.
Also: The essay *Idrottens framgångsspiral* by Johnny Wijk (2010); Kingsoftennis.se and Atpchampionstour.com; Nicklas Kulti's comments in the magazine *Veckans Affärer* (02/08/2013); goodtogreatworld.com.

Mats Holm is a reporter at the acclaimed Swedish news magazine *FOKUS*, where he writes about politics, science, and sports. He is the author of six books.

Ulf Roosvald is the editor of the weekend magazine of the *Göteborgs-Posten* newspaper in Sweden. He has a background as a sportswriter and is the author of three books.